Lecture Notes in Computer Science   13723

Founding Editors

Gerhard Goos
Juris Hartmanis

Editorial Board Members

The series Lecture Notes in Computer Science (LNCS), including its subseries Lecture Notes in Artificial Intelligence (LNAI) and Lecture Notes in Bioinformatics (LNBI), has established itself as a medium for the publication of new developments in computer science and information technology research, teaching, and education.

LNCS enjoys close cooperation with the computer science R & D community, the series counts many renowned academics among its volume editors and paper authors, and collaborates with prestigious societies. Its mission is to serve this international community by providing an invaluable service, mainly focused on the publication of conference and workshop proceedings and postproceedings. LNCS commenced publication in 1973.

Bernhard Hämmerli · Udo Helmbrecht ·
Wolfgang Hommel · Leonhard Kunczik ·
Stefan Pickl
Editors

Critical Information Infrastructures Security

17th International Conference, CRITIS 2022
Munich, Germany, September 14–16, 2022
Revised Selected Papers

Springer

Editors
Bernhard Hämmerli
Lucerne University of Applied Sciences
Lucerne, Switzerland

Wolfgang Hommel
Universität der Bundeswehr München
Neubiberg, Germany

Stefan Pickl
Universität der Bundeswehr München
Neubiberg, Germany

Udo Helmbrecht
Universität der Bundeswehr München
Neubiberg, Germany

ENISA
Athens, Greece

Leonhard Kunczik
Universität der Bundeswehr München
Neubiberg, Germany

ISSN 0302-9743   ISSN 1611-3349 (electronic)
Lecture Notes in Computer Science
ISBN 978-3-031-35189-1   ISBN 978-3-031-35190-7 (eBook)
https://doi.org/10.1007/978-3-031-35190-7

Preface

Focus on Critical Infrastructures and Energy Security

This year's CRITIS conference 2022 (International Conference on Critical Information Infrastructures Security) was held at the Universität der Bundeswehr München (University of the Federal Armed Forces Munich). It was organized by the research group COMTESSA (Core Competence Center for Operations Research, Management-Intelligence-Tenacity-Experience, Safety & Security ALLIANCE) led by Prof. Dr. Stefan Pickl (Professorship for Operations Research) in cooperation with the research institute CODE (Cyber Defence and Smart Data) led by Prof. Dr. Wolfgang Hommel. Honorary Chair was Prof. Dr. Udo Helmbrecht.

Prof. Bernhard Hämmerli, Chairman of the CRITIS Steering Committee, welcomed more than 100 participants from science, industry, authorities as well as government, and especially operators of critical infrastructures.

The conference addressed the three scientific domains of information, infrastructures, and security in an interdisciplinary manner and specifically in the context of OR-based analyses and complex optimization methods. Within the framework of the conference, these central areas were examined from various sides, both scientifically and practically, under the aspect of criticality.

The presented proceedings volume documents these three interesting days, which took place 50 years after the Olympic attack in Munich in 1972.

Major General (ret.) Dr. Dieter Budde, who as a young officer was responsible for special protective measures at the site during the Olympic attack at the time, reflected in his speech on the importance and handling of critical infrastructures:

"After five days of ease, the world changed abruptly back then …"

Clemens Baumgärtner, Head of the Department of Labour and Economic Development of the City of Munich, also addressed this aspect at the City of Munich's reception in the city hall:

"The attack at that time led to a complete rethinking of security concepts … perhaps that's why Munich is now one of the safest cities in the world … conferences like this help to keep improving these concepts."

The publishers of this proceedings volume thanked the "Wiesnchef" (head of Oktoberfest) for this special reception and gave him the so-called CRITIS-COMTESSA stein, which was also created especially for the conference and is pictured below as a memento:

September 2022

Bernhard Hämmerli
Udo Helmbrecht
Wolfgang Hommel
Leonhard Kunczik
Stefan Pickl

Organization

General Chairs

Wolfgang Hommel   Universität der Bundeswehr München, Germany
Stefan Pickl   Universität der Bundeswehr München, Germany

Honorary Chair

Udo Helmbrecht   Universität der Bundeswehr München, Germany,
     and European Union Agency for
     Cybersecurity, Greece

Program Co-chairs

Maximilian Moll   Universität der Bundeswehr München, Germany
Saeid Nahavandi   Deakin University, Australia

Steering Committee

Chairs

Bernhard M. Hämmerli   Lucerne University of Applied Sciences, Acris
     GmbH, Switzerland
Javier Lopez   University of Malaga, Spain
Stephen D. Wolthusen   Royal Holloway, University of London, UK and
     NTNU, Norway

Members

Robin Bloomfield   City, University London, UK
Sandro Bologna   AIIC, Italy
Gregorio D'Agostino   ENEA, Italy
Grigore Havarneanu   International Union of Railways (UIC), France
Sokratis K. Katsikas   Norwegian University of Science and Technology,
     Norway

Eric Luiijf	Luiijf Consultancy, The Netherlands
Alain Mermoud	Cyber-Defence Campus, armasuisse S+T, Switzerland
Marios M. Polycarpou	University of Cyprus, Cyprus
Reinhard Posch	Technical University Graz, Austria
Erich Rome	Fraunhofer IAIS, Germany
Antonio Scala	IMT – CNR, Italy
Inga Šarūnienė	Lithuanian Energy Institute, Lithuania
Roberto Setola	Università Campus Bio-Medico di Roma, Italy
Nils Kalstad Svendsen	Gjovik University College, Norway
Marianthi Theocharidou	EC Joint Research Centre, Italy

Program Committee

Cristina Alcaraz	University of Malaga, Spain
Magnus Almgren	Chalmers University of Technology, Sweden
Fabrizio Baiardi	University of Pisa, Italy
Sandro Bologna	AIIC, Italy
Tom Chothia	University of Birmingham, UK
Gregorio D'Agostino	ENEA, Italy
Piet De Vaere	ETH Zürich, Switzerland
Steven Furnell	University of Nottingham, UK
Dimitris Gritzalis	Athens University of Economics & Business, Greece
Bernhard Hämmerli	ACRIS, Switzerland
Chris Hankin	Imperial College London, UK
Mikel Iturbe	Mondragon University, Spain
Sokratis Katsikas	Norwegian University of Science and Technology, Norway
Marieke Klaver	TNO, The Netherlands
Vytis Kopustinskas	European Commission, Joint Research Centre, Italy
Panayiotis Kotzanikolaou	University of Piraeus, Greece
Marina Krotofil	Maersk, Denmark
Linas Martišauskas	Lithuanian Energy Institute, Lithuania
Kieran McLaughlin	Queen's University Belfast, UK
Alain Mermoud	Cyber-Defence Campus, armasuisse S+T, Switzerland
Simin Nadjm-Tehrani	Linköping University, Sweden
Sebastian Obermeier	Hochschule Luzern, Switzerland
Diego Ortiz Yepes	Hochschule Luzern, Switzerland

Stefan Pickl	Universität der Bundeswehr München, Germany
Ludovic Pietre-Cambacedes	EDF, France
Peter Popov	City, University of London, UK
Awais Rashid	University of Bristol, UK
Anne Remke	WWU Münster, Germany
Inga Šarūnienė	Lithuanian Energy Institute, Lithuania
Andre Samberg	i4-Falme OU, Estonia
Henrik Sandberg	KTH Royal Institute of Technology, Sweden
Patrick Schaller	ETH Zurich, Switzerland
Roberto Setola	Università Campus Biomedico, Italy
Florian Skopik	AIT Austrian Institute of Technology, Austria
Vladimir Stankovic	City, University of London, UK
Nils Ole Tippenhauer	CISPA Helmholtz Center for Information, Germany
Alberto Tofani	ENEA, Italy
Florian Wamser	Hochschule Luzern, Switzerland
Jianying Zhou	Singapore University of Technology and Design, Singapore

Contents

Protection of Cyber-Physical Systems and Industrial Control Systems

Root Cause Analysis of Software Aging in Critical Information Infrastructure

Philip König[1]([✉]), Fabian Obermann[2], Kevin Mallinger[1,2],
and Alexander Schatten[1]

[1] SBA Research, Vienna, Austria
{pkoenig,kmallinger,aschatten}@sba-research.org
[2] Vienna University of Technology, Vienna, Austria
fabian.obermann@tuwien.ac.at

Abstract. This paper examines the role of Software Aging and Rejuvenation and their effect on Critical Information Infrastructure and thus Critical Infrastructure maintainability. Software systems tend to degrade over time by entering a failure-prone state and showing decreased performance. It is suggested that Critical Infrastructures are especially susceptible to the detrimental effects of Software Aging and that common Software Rejuvenation remedies are not suitable in this context. Instead of treating re-emerging symptoms, an alternative approach is presented that seeks to monitor, analyze and, identify potential root causes like underlying architectural problems of software used in Critical Infrastructure. Results of first applications are shown and intended next research and development steps discussed.

Keywords: Software Aging · Critical Information Infrastructure · Maintainabilty · Code Change Analysis

1 Introduction

Critical Infrastructures (CI) span a wide range of sectors, among others, power grids, communication, defense, or finance systems [12]. Critical means that in a case of their incapacitation, corruption, or interference of any sort, the following consequences could be catastrophic for economic and/or social welfare, and national security. In short, CI constitute the foundation on which modern living standards are built. Nowadays these infrastructures are increasingly dependent on information and communication technology [13]. These include among other things software and the hardware it is running on, which in this context are called Critical Information Infrastructure (CII) and thus become a crucial part of CI themselves [8,9]. This poses a problem as CIIs often show significant security weaknesses and operational problems. Competition between contractors or generally the pressure for a faster time to market interval and new functionality, leads them to offering ever faster development times for their product and to integrate new features on a regular basis [13]. The consequences include neglecting

B. Hämmerli et al. (Eds.): CRITIS 2022, LNCS 13723, pp. 3–8, 2023.
https://doi.org/10.1007/978-3-031-35190-7_1

long-term security, stability, maintainability or introduce architectural problems
which could compromise modularity of the code and thus impede its own replacement in the future should it become outdated. Such practices may be unnoticed
in the short run but can lead to critical points of failure in the future.

2 Software Aging and Rejuvenation

To monitor and deal with changes that software might undergo over time,
the field of *Software Aging and Rejuvenation* (SAR) emerged. This research
field proposes that software degrades over time or through processing demand
[2,4,14,15]. Avizienis et al. [1] identified causes, such as: memory bloat and leakage, unterminated threads, unreleased file locks, data corruption, storage space
fragmentation, and accumulation of rounding errors. These phenomena gradually proliferate unnoticed until a critical tipping point is reached, which then
leads to failures like increased response time or no service at all [7]. A dramatic
example of what can happen when this occurs in critical systems is the 1991
case of a Patriot air defense system malfunctioning and causing the death of 28
servicemen. [11] Patriot's function was to intercept incoming missiles through
calculating their flight path. The way in which it's software was written introduced a time lag depending on the running time of the system, which after
100 h of continuous operation built up to 0.3433 s. This resulted in shifting it's
scanning area by 687 m and thus missing an incoming missile. Many of such mal-
functions can be mitigated by doing a simple restart of the system, hence these
problems seldomly reach that tipping point in systems that are only operated
intermittently, like private PCs. CII that is implemented in systems that must
continuously be operable - like digital payment providers, emergency services,
or power grid management systems - cannot easily use simple restart mitigation
measures to enhance functionality [9,15].

This highlights a problem that Software Rejuvenation, the umbrella term
for methods dealing with such software aging related bugs, has. The common
methods to remediate the effects of Software Aging include stopping running
software, cleaning internal states, and restarting the system to restore it to a
known, less failure-prone state [2,5]. This is precisely what many CII systems
are, if at all, only able to do under great expenditures [15]. Further, even if such
treatments are successful and re-establish the original failure-free state, they are
generally not suited to prevent the resurgence of these failures in the future.

3 Goals

Avizienis et al. [1] stated that such failures stem from the software itself, more
precisely the way it is devised. Until rectified, they are permanently written
into the source code of a respective program. Therefore, it is impossible to fix
them by mentioned techniques of Software Rejuvenation, the purpose of which
is more akin to treating symptoms and not addressing the underlying problems that cause them. Lutz [10] came to a similar conclusion, emphasizing that

higher code complexity, and thus potential interdependence, in safety critical, embedded systems is a potential safety hazard and must be addressed early on in development. In that vein, Graves et al. [6] devised a fault prediction model on the assumption that code decay occurs when a system becomes so complex that each change to it introduced on average one fault and thus is deemed unstable. Inspired by this line of work, this paper postulates that common methods of Software Rejuvenation need to be supplemented by root cause analysis. To achieve this we derived three different indicators to help assess its maintenance quality: magnitude, quantity and clustering of code changes over time. Considering the example of well implemented modularity, in most cases there should be very little to no required manual changes in other, functionally unrelated, parts of the code when a certain module is modified. In contrast, when this is not done appropriately, modifications could for example manifest as a rat-tail of needed changes in modules that were not part of the original intended one.

Although, one must be cautious to not over-interpret clusters of change in modules in a singular commit. Only when coupled changes occur continuously over time, they become an indicator for further inspection. Such changes would be visible in the history of a given version control system and aggregate at the respective points in time. Complex dependencies of this nature could make future maintenance or replacement of modules very hard or even impossible and thus pose a risk factor if a vulnerability or error is detected in such a module. For this purpose, a proof-of-concept code change analysis methodology was developed, which is able to identify changes in the nature of the mentioned indicators.

4   Methods

Our methodology was conceptualized in a two-step pipeline. In the first step the target software is analyzed and multiple datasets for further processing are generated. In a second step a report from the used data is generated and visualized. A programs git history is used to create the datasets. The target application can be analyzed on three levels of detail: Files, Classes, and, Functions, which will be called scopes from here on. However, Class and Function support is at the moment only implemented for target applications written in Java and C#, in which Classes and File scopes are mostly identical. Changes are clustered by date to allow visualization of how often and intensely a scope changed and to allow the location of change hotspots. The magnitude of a change is calculated as percentual change of the lines modified/added/deleted in comparison of the total lines of the given scope before the change. The application also counts how often each scope was modified in combination with each other scope. The top results are tabled in the report, as these scopes highly depend on each other. For this specific use case, the GUI package of the *checkstyle* repository [3], an open-source java application, was used.

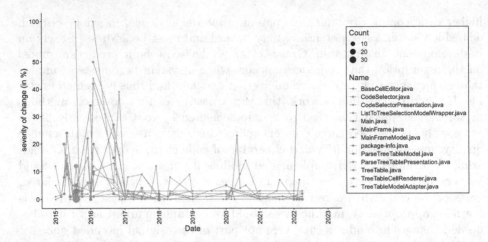

Fig. 1. Number of code changes and their magnitude over time. Quantity of changes represented by the diameter of the corresponding sphere, severity and thus magnitude by its height on y-axis. Code change cluster visualized through grouping of spheres.

5 Results

In Fig. 1 the x-Axis represents the lifetime of the repository in monthly granularity, while the y-Axis shows the magnitude of the change in the given month measured by percent. For multiple changes in one point of time the median was used. The diameter of the spheres corresponds to the number and thus quantity of changes in the given period and the color differentiates between individual files.

The life cycle of single files can be observed, as their corresponding first data point is their creation date and the last one the date of the last update. It can be seen that in recent years, activity increased with small intervals between the data points. Also, most of the code was written or refactored in 2015 and 2016. The granularity in this time period could be further improved by filtering out commits which changed almost every file, as they are most likely refactoring commits that did not alter noncommentary code. Regarding the dates with the most changes, a pattern becomes visible: they tend to cluster at the beginning of the year. The reason being that at the beginning of each year, the copyright headers in all files are adapted by changing the date to the new year. The only other commits that touched nearly every file were the mentioned huge Javadoc refactorings as can be seen in the periods from 2015 to 2016 and 2016 to 2017. Excluding the refactoring commits, the data still shows that commits generally are big, as most of them touch between 4 and 8 of a total of 14 files, potentially indicating that the components might be interdependent. In some cases, this is not necessarily a bad thing, as for example all TreeTable classes are usually modified together because their functionality was extended.

6   Discussion and Further Research

By using this method, it is possible to extract and visualize when, to what extent, and on which scope, code was changed. When displaying multiple items together over time, it can be observed if and when those were changed simultaneously like in the case of the TreeTable classes. This implicates that this approach is suited to monitor how a project or codebase changes over time and thus provide information about the interdependence of the individual scopes. Although the developed software is fully functional and can be used on real world applications like checkstyle, there are still some manual steps in the setup as well as in the evaluation process. To increase the quality of the output, better metrics for the magnitude of the change could be implemented by not only looking at the code at a line-by-line level, but also consider how much changed in a line. Also changes that consist of only whitespace characters could be ignored. A point that was not considered in this first implementation are comments. In the repositories we analyzed, a lot of changes often came from Javadocs or other general comments, which most likely should not be considered code change in this context. Although Graves et al. [6] mentioned that swapping out lines of code for noncommentary lines of code did not impair the performance of their fault prediction model, so there could be interesting information in doing multiple analyses, with and without noncommentary code and compare those. On top of that, deleted files are currently ignored by this methodology, but might provide valuable data if one wants to analyse how a program changed over time. Future research will also target the generation of an interactive html-based report. This will allow easier evaluation, enabling the generation of drill down charts, and jumping directly into the source code. Such data then could be linked to the history of bug reporting tools or failure data. Not only would a combined analysis of commit and failure history, directly linked to the source code, provide valuable insight in the emergence of failures, in a reverse manner it could also be analyzed which changes to the code were needed to eliminate it.

Conclusion

The continuous embedding of information technologies into critical infrastructures leads to increasingly unpredictable and complex systems. As these components are often developed without proper long-term maintenance or replacement strategies in mind, they introduce security vulnerabilities into all systems they are in contact with. These software systems degrade and age over time and established procedures to counter-act the most common detrimental effects are often not well suited for the kind of systems employed in CI. A supplemental methodology on the basis of three indicators of code change was presented that is not only able to monitor quantity and magnitude of changes in code over time but also track if certain items are periodically changed in tandem. Applied to large codebases or projects such coupled changes could indicate dependencies or modularity flaws and thus help identify potential risks that concern each associated system.

References

1. Avizienis, A., Laprie, J.-C., Randell, B., Landwehr, C.: Basic concepts and taxonomy of dependable and secure computing. IEEE Trans. Depend. Secure Comput.
   1(1), 11–33 (2004)
2. Castelli, V., et al.: Proactive management of software aging. IBM J. Res. Dev.
   45(2), 311–332 (2001)
3. Checkstyle git repository. https://github.com/checkstyle/checkstyle/tree/master/
   src/main/java/com/puppycrawl/tools/checkstyle/gui. Accessed 27 Apr 2022
4. Cotroneo, D., Natella, R., Pietrantuono, R.: Predicting aging-related bugs using
   software complexity metrics. Perform. Eval. **70**(3), 163–178 (2013)
5. Cotroneo, D., Natella, R., Pietrantuono, R., Russo, S.: A survey of software aging
   and rejuvenation studies. ACM J. Emerg. Technol. Comput. Syst. (JETC) **10**(1),
   1–34 (2014)
6. Graves, T.L., Karr, A.F., Marron, J.S., Siy, H.: Predicting fault incidence using
   software change history. IEEE Trans. Softw. Eng. **26**(7), 653–661 (2000)
7. Grottke, M., Matias, R., Trivedi, K.S.: The fundamentals of software aging. In:
   2008 IEEE International Conference on Software Reliability Engineering Workshops (ISSRE Wksp), pp. 1–6. IEEE (2008)
8. Kalashnikov, A., Sakrutina, E.: "Safety management system" and significant
   plants of critical information infrastructure. IFAC-PapersOnLine **52**(13), 1391–
   1396 (2019)
9. Lopez, J., Setola, R., Wolthusen, S.D.: Overview of critical information infrastructure protection. In: Lopez, J., Setola, R., Wolthusen, S.D. (eds.) Critical Infrastructure Protection 2011. LNCS, vol. 7130, pp. 1–14. Springer, Heidelberg (2012).
   https://doi.org/10.1007/978-3-642-28920-0_1
10. Lutz, R.R., Analyzing software requirements errors in safety-critical, embedded
    systems. In: 1993 Proceedings of the IEEE International Symposium on Require-
    ments Engineering, pp. 126–133. IEEE (1993)
11. Marshall, E.: Fatal error: how Patriot overlooked a Scud. Science **255**(5050), 1347–
    1347 (1992)
12. Moteff, J., Copeland, C., Fischer, J.: Critical infrastructures: what makes an infras-
    tructure critical? In: Library of Congress Washington DC Congressional Research
    Service (2003)
13. Nickolov, E.: Critical information infrastructure protection: analysis, evaluation
    and expectations. Inf. Secur. **17**, 105 (2006)
14. Parnas, D.L.: Software aging. In: Proceedings of 16th International Conference on
    Software Engineering, pp. 279–287. IEEE (1994)
15. Sabino, M.E., Merabti, M., Llewellyn-Jones, D., Bouhafs, F.: Detecting software
    aging in safety-critical infrastuctures. In: 2013 Science and Information Conference,
    pp. 78–85. IEEE (2013)

Threat-Driven Dynamic Security Policies for Cyber-Physical Infrastructures

Joseph Hallett[1]([⊠]), Simon N. Foley[2], David Manda[1], Joseph Gardiner[1], Dimitri Jonckers[3], Wouter Joosen[3], and Awais Rashid[1]

[1] University of Bristol, Bristol, UK
joseph.hallett@bristol.ac.uk
[2] Norwegian University of Science and Technology, Trondheim, Norway
[3] KU Leuven, Leuven, Belgium

Abstract. How does one defend Cyber-Physical Systems (CPSs) in the face of changing security threats without continuous manual intervention? These systems form a critical part of national infrastructure and exist within an ever changing dynamic threat environment. The static security policies programmed into systems cannot react quickly to changing threats. We describe how a MAPE-K-based threat-centered dynamic policy framework could reconfigure CPSs in the face of attack. The framework encodes threats, their mitigations, and a threat posture as a mechanism for deciding how best to react. We describe our framework, a prototype implementation and show how it be integrated within a testbed CPS demonstrator. Threat centered dynamic policies allow us to harden a system as the threat assessment evolves, reconfiguring a system and how on the basis of policy and perceived threat.

1 Introduction

The large Cyber-Physical Systems (CPSs) used in Supervisory Control And Data Acquisition (SCADA) systems, power grids, water treatment and high-value manufacturing, are increasingly connected to other enterprise systems. This enhances the visibility of the physical processes and allows for improved remote monitoring, optimization and gleaning greater business intelligence from the production processes. However, security wasn't a core design feature of the software, hardware and networking protocols in these systems. Their long lifespans, legacy devices and increased connectivity, therefore, expose them to a range of attacks. In the last few years we have seen high profile attacks against the Florida's water treatment plants, the Ukrainian Power Grid and a German Steel Mill [6,27,29], which alongside attacks like Stuxnet [12,25,26] have become international news.

Attacks, such as the Triton malware [20], show that the threats against such systems are continuously evolving and becoming more sophisticated. Securing such CPSs, therefore, presents a unique set of challenges. The devices employed in them are often resource-constrained in terms of available energy, processing power and bandwidth. Critically, they have strong real-time constraints: it is

B. Hämmerli et al. (Eds.): CRITIS 2022, LNCS 13723, pp. 9–26, 2023.
https://doi.org/10.1007/978-3-031-35190-7_2

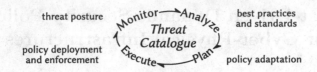

Fig. 1. MAPE-K loop for threat-driven dynamic policies.

not always feasible to deploy resource-intensive security policies—for example continuous active monitoring of a Programmable Logic Controller (PLC) in a SCADA system, heavyweight cryptographic functions or authentication services all risk overloading the PLC and compromising its core monitoring and control functions. Whilst a large CPS has at any time a number of security vulnerabilities or compromised elements, it is not desirable in most cases to suspend the system's operation to fix them. For example, shutting down or restarting a power grid is a non-trivial undertaking leading to societal disruption and business losses. CPSs need to operate in a risky environment, where it is infeasible to deploy traditional mitigations all of the time.

We propose moving from traditional static policy management to *dynamic threat-centered policies*. Instead of describing the policy in terms of *what the administrator wants the system to do*, we describe it in terms of *the threats to the system and the appropriate actions to mitigate them*. Suppose that an operator becomes aware that an attacker is attempting to remotely upload malicious firmware to CPSs within a city's electrical grid: the operator wishes to disallow remote updates whilst the attack is ongoing. When there are only a few such systems in a city, the feasibility of this manual change is okay—but the number of CPS is growing: there were almost 400 electricity power stations (each with similar control systems) in New York in 2018 alone [31], and these approaches are barely feasible on a city-wide, let alone regional or national scale.

Our approach provides a *threat-centered* view on policy administration based on a MAPE-K [23] loop (Fig. 1). Given a catalog of threat mitigations, when an attack occurs the approach uses the catalog to provide options for policy change—whether chosen by users in the policy administration loop, or through automation. Following the MAPE-K loop, we *Monitor* changes to the efficacy of the security policy, our threat posture and any changes in threat catalogs (*Knowledge*); *Analyze* based on best practices and standards as encoded in the policy catalog and decide whether we need to take action; *Plan* how to adapt the policy in order to mitigate the threats, and *Execute* by deploying the policy and enforcing its rules through an Event Condition Action (ECA)-based approach [28]. By managing policy knowledge in terms of threats [15,39], the threat-centered approach provides a framework in which security policies can be dynamically administered, rapidly and on-demand, in the face of unfolding attacks on a CPS.

Our contributions are as follows:

- A *threat-centered* policy framework for adapting CPS configuration on the basis of active threats, rather than a static administrator-driven policy.

– An implementation of our policy framework showing how policies can be enforced by reconfiguring a CPS testbed dynamically.

2   Threat-Centered Security Policies

2.1   Scenario

To describe our threat-centered policy framework, we first introduce a hypothetical water treatment plant to illustrate it, similar to other water treatment plants such as the one in *Oldsmar, Florida* that suffered a cyber attack in 2021 [6]. Water treatment plants take in waste water and sewage, and produce clean water. The job of the plant is to ensure that only clean water is output from the plant. If the plant fails at its task then the local area's water supply will be poisoned by sewage and chemicals. Alternatively, if the plant is shutdown then swathes of the population will be impacted by the disruption to the water supply.

The plant consists of a tank, with sensors, pumps and valves. Sensors monitor the bacterial level in the water treatment tank and filters. The pumps' rate is also controlled by a sensor and the PLC. All sensors send the raw data to a PLC which normalizes the data and stores it in a writable register. The value in the writable register is copied to the readable registers every hour. Whilst the values are written to the writable register frequently and instantaneously, the copying from the writable register to the readable register occurs only periodically as the control system is computationally limited. Faster refresh rates are possible, but have a computational and power cost, and so are generally avoided. Data from the PLC is available from an onsite Human-Machine Interface (HMI), and remotely via offsite analytics.

To attack the plant an attacker might aim to disrupt its functioning and, ideally, cause the water output to be poisoned or trigger a shutdown. Doing so would cause the plant operator to need to spend additional resources and money to protect and repair their plant. Alternatively, attacking a plant may disrupt the water supply to the local area. They might attempt this by tampering with the sensors to add more or less chlorine to the water, or by overloading the pumps and damaging the plant physically[1].

To defend against attack the plant has policies (that is, rules determining what should and is allowed to happen) in place which describe how the plant should operate and how it should react when certain threats occur. These policies can be related to functionality (e.g. the pump should run continuously), safety (e.g. if the pumps reach 80% of capacity then switch off to prevent damage), or security (e.g. only engineers can interact with the HMI)—the policies define how the plant works. They are typically enforced statically: the policies are hard coded into the devices and mechanisms within the plant. If one wanted

---

[1] One of the earliest known cyber attacks is on Maroochy Water Services in Australia which led to sewage spilling over a large area causing disruption and environmental damage.

to change the PLC's safety cut off, then the PLC would have to be physically reprogrammed[2]. Our goal in this paper is to introduce a policy framework that allows this reprogramming to be automated in predictable ways based on the currently identified threats.

2.2 Policy Framework

Our policy framework is based on modal logic [1], borrowing the syntax of Prolog to express rules and facts. Variables are denoted by symbols beginning with an upper-case letter, constants and predicates with a lower-case letter. A single underscore denotes a wildcard.

A policy is a collection of rules that defines whether it is permitted to engage an operation in a context. Principals assert rules, whereby $\phi(\mathtt{p}, \cdots)$ means that principal P asserts logic statement ϕ, defined in terms of system attributes, holds. A description of all of the predicates allowed in our framework is given in Table 1. For example, in our water treatment plant, the operator is always allowed to shutdown the plant. This could be expressed using the policy framework by the following assertion:

```
permit(operator, shut_down).
```

Sometimes, however, an action is unsafe to do. We declare these as *threats* to an action. For example, the operator can declare that it would be unsafe to open the valve releasing water from the plant back into the system if the filters show a high level of bacteria in their output.

```
threat(operator, open_valve, safety)
  ← says(plc, _, high_bacteria_in_filter).
```

Not all threats are as important all the time—we have a *threat posture* that states what threats need to be dealt with should they arise. Some threats are always critical, for example, an operator should always care about safety.

```
posture(operator, safety).
```

Othertimes an operator's posture may be dependant on other events: for example, an operator may only care about the threat of physical tampering with a device if there are signs that the site has had a break-in recently.

```
posture(operator, tampering)
  ← threat(operator, _, break_in).
```

If there are threats to actions a principal cares about, then actions should be taken to ensure appropriate countermeasures against the threats. These actions could involve doing nothing but acknowledging the threat: for example, an operator might acknowledge that there has been a break-in.

---

[2] More accurately a physical key would have to be turned to put the PLC into programming mode and allow any remote loading of logic into the PLC (e.g., in the Triton attack [22]).

```
mitigate(operator, _, break_in).
```

Alternatively the operator might want to take some corrective action, for example, in the case of high levels of bacteria in the filter, the operator may want to flush the system and add additional chlorine to the tank:

```
mitigate(operator, open_valve, safety,
   [flush_system, increase_chlorine]).
```

What happens then when a principal (such as the Operator) attempts to perform an action in general. We check the default rule: an action is only permitted if all threats currently present and in the principal's threat posture have been mitigated, alongside a basic access control check (responsible) to check that the principal is allowed to perform that action:

$$\frac{\texttt{responsible}\,(P,A) \quad \begin{pmatrix} \forall T \text{ s.t. } \texttt{posture}\,(P,T) \wedge \\ \texttt{threat}\,(P,A,T): \\ \exists\, \texttt{mitigate}\,(P,A,T,o) \end{pmatrix} \quad o \in O}{\texttt{permit}\,(P,A,O)}$$

Table 1. Predicates used to describe policies for CPSs. In both the mitigate and says, the obligations parameter O (marked with a star) is optional, and can be omitted if there are no additional actions that need to be performed.

Predicate	Description
posture (P,T)	P believes that they consider T to be a threat (that T is in their *threat posture*).
threat (P,A,T)	P believes that the presence of threat T would make the action objective A impossible without taking steps to mitigate the danger.
mitigate (P,A,T,O^*)	P believes that the danger presented by threat T to action objective A is mitigated by completing the obligations O (that is, P says if you do O then the threat T to the action A will go away).
says (P,P',F,O^*)	P believes that P' (a second principal) asserts that a fact F is true, if some additional obligations O are completed.
permit (P,A,O)	P believes that the action objective A is safe to do if the obligations O are completed.
responsible (P,A)	P is responsible for deciding if action objective A is allowed
test (E)	The last result of the efficacy test E was successful.

A policy catalogue is created by collecting these statements and handing them to a Policy Decision Point (PDP). The PDP is responsible for analyzing the policy and deciding if actions are permitted and orchestrating any configuration changes required, based on the evaluated threats. The policy author would not typically write rules for the permit predicate or the responsible predicate, rather they are predefined on the PDP.

2.3 Policy Management

The policy catalog may change over time, as a consequence of threat reports, and principals add and/or revoke policy assertions as new knowledge about threats and controls emerges. An operator's threat posture may also change. Furthermore, it may be determined that a control has failed and, therefore, its associated threat is no longer properly mitigated in the current policy. In these cases the operator may wish to adapt the system configuration by deploying alternative controls from the catalog in order to ensure mitigation of the risk posture. Alternatively, the operator may decide to accept the threat in some form by revising their threat posture or updating the knowledge in the catalog.

The configuration of the policy itself may also need to change in response to threats. We stated earlier that the monitoring of registers in the PLC was configurable. In risk and threat management frameworks [16,37,39] , the efficacy of a control (in mitigating a threat) is monitored via procedure tests and the failure of a procedure test indicates the presence of a potential threat. Procedure tests may execute to a schedule, be triggered by system or external events, or be continually running. For example, a failing test for water quality indicates that the purification control is not effective, and that an alternate should be selected.

The term `test(ids)` is the outcome of an Intrusion Detection System (IDS) test on the consistency between the replicated PLC registers. If this test fails then there is a threat to the consistency of the system. Intrusion detection systems can experience false positives (a well-known limitation of anomaly detection systems). In reaction to this the operator may chose to add rules to automatically update the polling frequency of the test (how frequently the result of `test(ids)` is updated) when the threat is detected.

```
threat(operator, consistency, bad_register)
  ← ¬ test(ids).
```

```
mitigate(operator, consistency, bad_register,
  [increase_ids_polling_frequency]).
```

By using obligations we can control settings outside of the logic of the framework—including how frequently the framework is updated and checked. This allows the framework to not only define *security policies* which establish how to react to newly identified threats, but also *monitoring policies* that define how to check for new threats that need a reaction. In general, a threat-centered policy comprises of assertions:

```
threat(Principal, Action, Threat).
```

```
mitigate(Principal, Action, Threat, Controls)
  ← test(T).
```

Failing procedure tests correspond to attack identification: the control is no longer effective at mitigating the identified threat.

2.4   Dynamic Policies

The policy catalog provides a *declarative* definition of security. It defines *what* an acceptable policy deployment is, but it does not define *how* to change (adapt) a policy. In principle, as a result of an attack, the catalog can be searched for an optimal replacement policy. However, in practice we may wish to provide an *operational* definition of *how* the policy should change. In this case ECA [28] style operational rules are used whereby procedure test failures match the event-conditions and the triggered consequence is an action to update the policy for the prescribed control. Typically, operational rules take the form:

```
mitigate(Principle, action, threat, Controls)
  ← ¬ test(something).
```

In this case we assume there is a mechanism outside of the policy that will update the desired controls on the basis of decisions made and policy queries. This could be supported through obligations or by a dynamic policy language in which changes can be explicitly encoded in the rules [5].

Actions are the operational means to affect the system's behavior based on its policies. Threat-centered policies are often highly domain-specific, incorporating knowledge about CPS operation and the underlying controlled process. Hence, many actions will impact this process; for example, by applying a specific strategy. The policies themselves can also be changed as a result of actions, in response to failed procedure test or updated risk postures (possibly based on operator input). The deployment and updating of a policy may in turn result in further actions to be carried out.

2.5   Example

With the policy framework outlined, we illustrate how it might be used in practice. An *Engineer* maintains a water treatment plant and uses the framework to manage threats to the system. The plant has an IDS that works by monitoring a register in a PLC, as well as a guard who walks past the plant daily to check for signs of a break-in. The Engineer is concerned about the monitoring failing (`bad_register`) and a break-in to the plant (`break_in`). The policy is shown below, but can be summarized as: if the IDS is triggered, and there is no current risk to the operations of the plant, then increase monitoring; the guard can identify if there has been a break-in; and if there is a break-in, then call a repairman for the fence to mitigate the threat and until the fence is repaired be aware that there may be an extra threat of sabotage or tampering.

```
mitigate(engineer, valve_open, bad_register,
  [increase_ids_polling_frequency])
  ← ¬ test(ids),
    ¬ threat(engineer, operations, _).

threat(engineer, integrity, break_in)
  ← threat(guard, integrity, break_in).
```

```
threat(engineer, valve_open, bad_register)
  ← ¬ test(ids).

mitigate(engineer, integrity, break_in, [call_repairman, add(
    threat(engineer, operations, sabotage))]).

posture(engineer, bad_register).

posture(engineer, break_in).
```

During operation of the treatment plant, the IDS identifies that the registers in the PLC appear to be faulty, and the result of the test is updated. The system monitors the changing threats and establishes that there is a new threat to the consistency of the system and the safe operation of the valve. Since there is no other threat to the operation of the plant the system adapts by increasing the monitoring frequency of the IDS. If the IDS returns to a good state, then the fault may have been a transient one. The treatment plant is allowed to return to normal behavior once the security threat has gone. Alternatively, the IDS returning to a good state could indicate that an attacker has breached the security system and is starting to cover their tracks. In this case the operator may choose to monitor additional sensors and actuators for signs of misbehavior until the threat has passed.

Updating the security policy is not just limited to low-level technical controls but can also combine facts taken from experts on site. The water treatment plant has a guard who regularly patrols the site. The Guard reports that a hole has been cut in the fence, and updates the policy with the additional threat; changing the threat posture as the policy is monitored and analyzed. To mitigate this threat the Engineer's policy calls the repairman. The repair will take time but will eventually be fixed. Until the repair is complete, the Engineer is wary that the plant may have been tampered with, and that there may be a security risk. The Engineer believes that there is a threat of *sabotage* to the plant. Now if there is a bad register this may be another glitch or it could be a sign that the plant is being tampered with, and the output of the plant poisoned. Since this could lead to the town being supplied with dangerous water, the Engineer can modify the policy to add an additional rule that mitigates these risks. If the IDS triggers when the plant has already established that there is a threat of sabotage then the secure thing to do may be to slow the flow of water through the plant, add additional filtration and chlorination schemes and, *if all else fails*, then consider shutting the plant as a last resort.

```
mitigate(engineer, valve_open, bad_register,
  [additional_chlorination, slow_flow])
  ← ¬ test(ids),
    threat(engineer, operations, sabotage).
```

Our policy is reconfigured on the basis of the changing threat posture and the catalog of threats. The framework allows us to describe CPS security policies on the basis of identified threats and react to them accordingly—whether by increasing refresh rates, shutting down plants and notifying towns, or any other mitigations or security controls the policy designers and engineers might wish to describe. We do not need to hard-code our security policies. We change them dynamically as threats are identified.

2.6   Implementation

Our implementation of the threat-centred policies framework consists of the decision protocol (a principal grants all actions they are responsible for if there is an acceptable mitigation in place for all the threats they identify) and knowledge base implemented in Prolog, alongside a server to enable remote querying and database acting as an archivist. To help integrate the policy framework with a real CPS, we also implemented a custom IDS—looking at Modbus[3] communication messsages (using Scapy[4]). We also implemented a bridge between our database and Kepware—a commercial data historian used in industrial automation and Internet of Things (IoT) systems—so that policies can incorporate data from existing analytics.

The implementation has been undertaken to enable us to explore and iterate on how policies could be written and to test the framework's expressivity. If threat-centered policies are to defend CPSs, then we must be able to express the threats to these systems. Due to our focus on exploring expressivity, the current implementation has several limitations: whilst it can analyze policies, decide whether actions are permitted, and list actions and policy changes that *should* be made, it has no means to enforce them. If a policy could permit an action through multiple policy rules, then we return the first we find rather than making a decision about which is the most appropriate (or easiest to enact). Future iterations of the implementation will address these limitations as we develop it further.

3   Evaluation on a CPS Testbed

To further explore what dynamic threat-centered policies can offer we integrated it with a CPS test bed to explore whether we express policies that can defend a CPS, and how our framework would react when an attack occurs. We integrated the prototype implementation into a national large-scale cyber-physical systems testbed [19]. The testbed includes a number of scaled physical processes: a water treatment plant, a factory and a building management system as well as PLCs, RTUs[5], HMIs[6], sensors and actuators as well as software platforms from a range

---

[3] Modbus is a standard PLC communication protocol.
[4] https://scapy.net/.
[5] Remote Terminal Unit: the interface between sensors and a SCADA system.
[6] Human Machine Interface: local controls for an engineer.

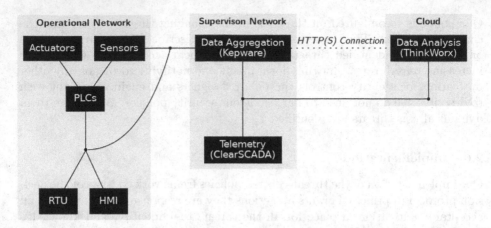

Fig. 2. Network of the CPS testbed.

of vendors that can be deployed in different architectural configurations for security analyses. As well as realistically modeling CPS architectures (and physical processes), the testbed also has a range attack chains that can be run against it when evaluating various security countermeasures.

For our evaluation, we utilize the attack chain from a national IoT demonstrator that we have previously developed [35]. The demonstrator involves a factory conveyor using commercial industrial IoT control systems, and which aims to be a realistic simulation of a production Industrial Control System (ICS). The deployed configuration includes an operational network consisting of the physical process (the factory conveyor), with PLCs, sensors, an RTU and an HMI. The operational network is connected to a local supervisory network, providing data aggregation and telemetry, which is itself connected to the cloud for data analysis (Fig. 2).

The attack proceeds as follows [35]:

1. The attacker compromises the Cloud-based data analytics platform via an unpatched exploit and a network takeover attack on the connection between the data aggregation and the data analysis.
2. The attacker compromises the supervision network via an engineer opening a malicious PDF (in this case, the help manual opened in response to an error displayed via the manipulated data analysis).
3. A command channel is set up through the connection between the aggregation and analysis software.
4. The attacker scans the Operational network looking for PLCs and recovers the logic from them.
5. The attacker exploits the RTU, blinding the control room from the unfolding attack.
6. The HMI and safety systems are blinded by manipulating the PLC's memory, and the PLC logic is overwritten.

7. The process is run outside of safe operational parameters, and the safety cut offs do not take effect. The process destroys itself.

Table 2. Threats presented in the attack on the demonstrator.

Threat From	Threat To	Detected By
Possible attack start	Continued operation	IDS detects NMAP scan
Possible attack start	Continued operation	IDS detects ET200S enumeration
Possible attack start	Continued operation	IDS detects S7-1200 enumeration
Lack of analysis	Continued operation	Interrupted connection to Thingworx
PLC logic exposed	Continued operation	IDS detects PLC logic dump
Running blind	Continued operation	IDS detects RTU is offline
Running blind	PLC updates	IDS detects RTU is offline
Malicious update	Continued operation	IDS detects an unauthorized PLC logic update

To decide how our framework might help defend the demonstrator, we first consider the possible threats to the system, and what they might threaten (Table 2). Each of these threats is then coded up using the framework, Prolog and through querying the IDS database and Kepware. For example, one route to detecting the attack starting is letting the IDS search for signs of an S7 enumeration (a common protocol for ICSs). To detect the scan we query the database (within a time window) for signs of an S7-1200 enumeration. Similar queries are built for NMAP scans (looking for SYN scans) and ET200S enumerations. If we detect the signs of a scan or enumeration, then we establish the presence of the threat. Whether we react to it or not is controlled by the threat posture, though that is also dynamically configurable. For instance, we only start to look for signs of a malicious update to a PLC if we are aware of an attack starting:

```
posture(op, malicious_write) ←threat(op, _, attack_start).
```

Rules were written for each of the threats we identified as part of the attack and each threat presented at the appropriate point as the attack progressed.

When implementing the policy, if a check required more data or a specific technique to establish a threat (for example the network monitoring above) then we implemented this as an external tool and allowed our policy to query (and reconfigure) these tools dynamically. The expressivity of our policy language comes from the ability to combine existing (as well as new) checks and tooling around establishing threats. We don't build any new checks and tools into our framework, rather we give the ability to organize and combine the results from existing tools into threat-centered policies. By identifying threats to a real system, encoding them using our framework, and then being able to use the encoded policy to detect when a real attack is underway suggests that our framework is expressive enough to capture and encode threats to real CPS systems. In other words, if one has a mechanism to establish when a threat is present, then one can use the framework to write a rule to react appropriately.

4   Related Work

4.1   Threats to CPSs

The risks involved with connecting networked computer systems to the internet are well established. When the computer systems form part of national infrastructure, however, the risks can be particularly dangerous. These systems and infrastructures exist in a vulnerable state in many sectors: Radmand et al. noted their prevalence in the oil and gas sector [34], and Giraldo et al. noted their prevalence in many others including smart grids, hospitals, manufacturing, transport and aircraft sectors [21]. Pal et al. suggest that collaboration between threat intelligence and threat response is vital for resilient security mechanisms but that these applying these principles to CPSs is often difficult.

As the attack on the water treatment plant in Florida [6] emphasizes, the threats to these systems are not necessarily very sophisticated. In that plant the attack consisted of a brief anomalous login with stolen credentials that was noted but not acted on early in the morning, followed by another login at lunch time that increased levels of lye in the water to dangerous levels. The change was noted by an operator and remote access was disabled, but we shouldn't only rely on vigilant operators to prevent attacks. An anomalous login should have placed the plant at a higher threat level when it first happened automatically. That the attack happened in the days preceeding a major sports event should have altered the plants risk posture. The plant did use pH level sensors that would have eventually noticed the increased levels of lye, but the polling rate and sensitivity of these sensors could have been adjusted automatically in response to the increased threats as we have proposed.

In 1999 Furnell and Warren suggested that networked infrastructure could be an attractive target for terrorists and hackers and that we need to take care to avoid a scenario like the *millennium bug*—where we have to take rapid remedial action to avoid significant disruption from something that could and should have been avoided [17]. A 2012 survey of 15 SCADA and critical infrastructure incidents showed, however, that infrastructure had been continuously attacked, mostly through malware, malicious (ex-) employees and compromised accounts [29].

DiMase et al. analyzed threats to CPS resilience [10]. They noted several persistent threats but did not look at the dynamic threats that came and went periodically. Cherdantseva et al. surveyed several different mechanisms for assessing risks in CPSs [8]. They noted several frameworks which could be used to establish risks to a system and others which could be used to establish threats, however they did not look at what to do when the threats have been established. Our threat-centered policies go further by considering not just how to establish threats but also how these threats change dynamically and what to do with that knowledge.

Gao et al.'s work on Security Information and Event Management (SIEM) based policy monitoring focuses on detecting various events and how they could be chained into taking actions based on policy [18]. They give the example of how if a recently fired employee (a threat) accesses the server room (a further threat), then this ought to trigger an alert. The approach treats specific threats with specific mitigations (send alert if fired employee accesses server) rather than the threat-first approach we propose (a fired employee creates a threat of retribution, an out-of-date login system gives a threat of mistaken authorization—mitigate both by updating accounts and logging all accesses).

Knowles et al. note that industrial approaches to risk assessment could be improved, and proposed a framework for performing assessments dynamically, and producing a *measure of confidence in security* [24]. As the systems have become more distributed new attacks have appeared. Petit and Shladover identified the potential for attacks on collaborative *self-driving* cars and that the systems could be seriously disrupted if given incorrect information [33].

4.2   Policy Frameworks

To specify our policies and threats we build on ideas from access control languages. Da Silva et al. described a role-based access control scheme that adapted to user's misusing their permissions dynamically [36], and Cheng et al. described an access control scheme that included a *risk level* as part of the policy [7]. By parameterizing the policy with risk Cheng et al. could allow users greater access if there were exceptional circumstances.

Our proposal for threat-centered dynamic policies is applicable to domains other than CPS; but, in this paper, we focus on the CPS domain because it is particularly suited to this threat-centered approach as these systems are harder to maintain and more dangerous when attacked than other types of systems.

Threat-centered dynamic policies can be described as a self-adaptive system based on threats. Other work in this area includes Pandey et al.'s work on developing hybrid planning for self-adaptive systems that allows it to choose between strategies for mitigating problems based on how urgently the problem needs to be resolved [32]. Adapting a system at run time, especially in adversarial environments, can lead to the system becoming inconsistent. To help detect if this happens Barbosa et al. created a tool to verify self-adaptive systems based on a probabilistic execution model [4], while [15] catalogs firewall rule configurations, according to the threats that they mitigate, using a searchable ontology that is used to generate suitable firewall deployments. Other techniques such as IDSs can also be used to help protect CPSs by looking for intrusion events [9]. The threat-centered policies we propose are more general and can handle a greater variety of threats than just intrusions.

4.3   Self-adaptive Systems

Whilst this work focuses on threat-centered policies it also builds upon earlier work developing self-adaptive systems for more general environments, as well as the more general application of MAPE-loops. Elkhodary and Whittle surveyed 4 self-adaptive application security approaches and developed a framework for evaluating them [11]. Tsuchida et al. used a MAPE-loop mechanism to alter an embedded system's behavior in response to its changing environment [38]. Whilst not specifically targeted at managing threats and security Tsuchida et al.'s work shows that MAPE loops can be applied effectively to reconfigure low-power devices such as embedded systems and CPSs. Arcaini et al. described a formal modeling techniques for verifying systems that use MAPE-K loops to ensure that the loops could not interfere with each other and were correct [3].

In summary, existing work has focused on how to adapt to problems as they appear. Our work takes a different approach: given a catalog of *potential* threats and possible future problems in a changing, and adversarial environment, how can we monitor, select and mitigate them automatically. By mitigating threats automatically we can avoid threats escalating, and security becoming fatally compromised. Additionally, further work is needed to empirically evaluate the benefits of a dynamic threat centered policy framework. Whilst many dynamic MAPE-based adaptive systems have been proposed for various domains; empirically demonstrating that they provide a measurable improvements is often overlooked [30]: the benefits of a threat centered policy must be proven beyond all doubt to see adoption.

5   Discussion

5.1   Threat Assessment and Policies

When exploring threat-centered policies on the demonstrator we closely tied our policy to a table of threats (Table 2). This helped tie the existing security risk assessments about the system to the policy adaptation necessary to defend the attacks as they unfold.

Most policy frameworks take a *goal-oriented* approach: an action is allowed if an explicit set of conditions is met. Policy frameworks infrequently include a notion of threats to a system [2,13,14], and it is unusual to express the policy wholly in terms of them (other applications have limited to networks and autonomous systems). This is somewhat surprising as when writing the policies it feels natural to organize a system's security policy around the threat assessment that inspired it. For CPSs in particular, where operators are resistant to dynamic configuration but comfortable with threat assessments, using threat-centered policies is a helpful stepping stone: providing mechanisms for organizing existing security controls around threats. After all we do threat modeling in terms of threats; by describing our adaptation policies in terms of threats too, we help ensure the link between them is clear, giving confidence to operators that the policy is correct and appropriate.

5.2   The Cost of Dynamism

Threat driven dynamic security policies allow us to configure CPSs to react to a changing threat landscape. The flexibility that is achieved through dynamic policies is not without cost, however. By allowing these systems to reconfigure themselves, even on the basis of a policy written by a specialist, there is a potential increase in attack surface. For example, if an attacker could see the policies that reconfigured a system then they may be able to see which checks and tests they need to trigger to put the system into a state that is beneficial for them. To illustrate this, consider again a PLC with an IDS that is dependent on register polling. The polling speed is configurable, but higher polling rates take resources from other functionality, effectively slowing the PLC's functionality for the benefit of better detecting another threat. If the attacker's goal is to make the PLC more expensive to run and they can exploit the policy to consistently force the PLC into the increased polling state then they can attack the system. Defending against these kinds of threats means still having humans *in-the-loop* to make changes, and update the policy so that automatic re-configurations reflect the current threat model.

In practice, it is no longer feasible to build static systems—and this will continue to be the case as we build more complex dynamic interconnected systems. Dynamic policies are an essential step towards better security. While the complexity of CPSs and the volume of deployed systems has gone up, we are still using static, hard-coded and even manual solutions to defend them. There is a growing awareness that existing systems are insufficiently secured. By carefully describing and testing threat-centered policies, we enable a path to more resilient systems that can react to dynamic threats. In even larger scale (massive) CPSs, such as smart city environments and automated transportation systems, the environment itself is highly dynamic—with devices connecting to each other as they traverse the CPS environment leading to dynamic service composition. In such massive scale CPS environments, static security policies can neither be feasibly constructed nor deployed as the environment is not under the control of a single stakeholder. Threat centered policies need further evaluation in these large scale environments to see if they can help bring dynamic adaptation between different systems and organizations.

6   Conclusion

Threat-centered dynamic policies let us describe policies from the perspective of threats and help cyber-physical infrastructures reconfigure themselves dynamically, on the basis of policy, to mitigate the attacks as they are identified. Existing techniques for securing CPS do not scale and cannot react to the changing threat landscape. Threat-centered dynamic policies give us a mechanism to reconfigure the monitoring rules automatically to ensure, for example, that we make appropriate tradeoffs for security only when needed; and that we only require human intervention if the policy fails, or if new threats are presented.

Dynamic threat-centered policies, are a stepping stone towards adaptive security in such environments in order to ensure that they remain resilient in the face of unfolding threats and continue safe operation even when parts of the infrastructure are compromised. Future work will explore how combinations of different policy mitigations can be selected to mitigate all threats, and integrate cost-functions with deploying them.

Acknowledgement. CHIST-ERA   project: DYPOSIT   (EPSRC   grants EP/N021657/1, EP/N021657/2).

References

1. Abadi, M.: Logic in access control. In: Proceedings of the 18th Annual IEEE Symposium on Logic in Computer Science, 2003. pp. 228–233. IEEE, IEEE, Ottawa, Canada (2003)
2. Ahmed, M.S., Al-Shaer, E., Taibah, M.M., Abedin, M., Khan, L.: Towards autonomic risk-aware security configuration. In: IEEE Network Operations and Management Symposium. pp. 722–725. IEEE, IEEE, Piscataway, NJ (2008)
3. Arcaini, P., Riccobenne, E., Scandurra, P.: Formal design and verification of self-adaptive systems with decentralized control. ACM Trans. Auton. Adapt. Syst. **11**(4), 25:1–25:35 (2017)
4. Barbosa, D.M., de Moura Lima, R.G., Maia, P.H.M., Junior, E.C.: Lotus@Runtime: a tool for runtime monitoring and verification of self-adaptive systems. In: IEEE/ACM 12th International Symposium on Software Engineering for Adaptive and Self-Managing Systems. pp. 24–30. IEEE, Buenos Aires, Argentina (2017)
5. Becker, M.Y., Fournet, C., Gordon, A.D.: SecPAL: Design and semantics of a decentralized authorization language. J. Comput. Secur. **18**(4), 619–665 (2010)
6. Cervini, J., Rubin, A., Watkins, L.: Don't drink the cyber: Extrapolating the possibilities of oldsmar's water treatment cyberattack. In: Proceedings of the 17th International Conference on Information Warfare and Security (2022)
7. Cheng, P.C., Rohatgi, P., Keser, C.: Fuzzy MLS: An experiment on quantified risk-adaptive access control. In: IEEE Symposium on Security and Privacy. pp. 222–230 (2007)
8. Cherdantseva, Y., et al.: A review of cyber security risk assessment methods for SCADA systems. Comput. secur. **56**, 1–27 (2016)
9. Chromik, J.J., Remke, A., Haverkort, B.R.: Bro in SCADA: dynamic intrusion detection policies based on a system model. In: 5th International Symposium for ICS & SCADA Cyber Security, ICS-CSR 2018. pp. 112–121. British Computer Society, Hamburg, Germany (2018)
10. DiMase, D., Collier, Z.A., Heffner, K., Linkov, I.: Systems engineering framework for cyber physical security and resilience. Environ. Syst. Decisions **35**(2), 291–300 (2015). https://doi.org/10.1007/s10669-015-9540-y
11. Elkhodary, A., Whittle, J.: A survey of approaches to adaptive application security. In: Software Engineering for Adaptive and Self-Managing Systems, 2007. ICSE Workshops SEAMS'07. International Workshop on. pp. 16–16. IEEE (2007)
12. Falliere, N., Murchu, L.O., Chien, E.: W32.Stuxnet dossier. Tech. rep., Symantec Security Response (2011)
13. Fitzgerald, W.M., Neville, U., Foley, S.N.: MASON: Mobile autonomic security for network access controls. J. Inf. Secur. Appl. **18**(1), 14–29 (2013)
14. Foley, S.N., Fitzgerald, W.M.: An Approach to Security Policy Configuration Using Semantic Threat Graphs. In: Gudes, E., Vaidya, J. (eds.) DBSec 2009. LNCS, vol. 5645, pp. 33–48. Springer, Heidelberg (2009). https://doi.org/10.1007/978-3-642-03007-9_3
15. Foley, S.N., Fitzgerald, W.M.: Management of Security Policy Configuration using a semantic threat graph approach. J. Comput. Secur. **3**(19), 567–605 (2011)

16. Foley, S.N., Moss, H.: A risk-metric framework for enterprise risk management. IBM J. Res. Dev. **54**(3), 3 (2010). https://doi.org/10.1147/JRD.2010.2043403
17. Furnell, S.M., Warren, M.J.: Computer hacking and cyber terrorism: the real threats in the new millennium? Comput. Secur. **18**(1), 28–34 (1999)
18. Gao, Y., Xie, X., Parekh, M., Bajramovic, E.: SIEM: policy-based monitoring of SCADA systems. In: Informatik 2016. pp. 559–570. Gesellschaft für Informatik eV, Bremen, Germany (2016)
19. Gardiner, J., Craggs, B., Green, B., Rashid, A.: Oops i did it again: Further adventures in the land of ics security testbeds. In: Proceedings of the ACM Workshop on Cyber-Physical Systems Security & Privacy. pp. 75–86. CPS-SPC'19, ACM, New York, NY, USA (2019). https://doi.org/10.1145/3338499.3357355
20. Gibbs, S.: Triton: hackers take out safety systems in 'watershed' attack on energy plant. The Guardian (December 2017), https://www.theguardian.com/technology/2017/dec/15/triton-hackers-malware-attack-safety-systems-energy-plant
21. Giraldo, J., Sarkar, E., Cardenas, A.A., Maniatakos, M., Kantarcioglu, M.: Security and privacy in cyber-physical systems: a survey of surveys. IEEE Des. Test **34**(4), 7–17 (2017)
22. Higgins, K.J.: Schneider Electric: TRITON/TRISIS attack used 0-day flaw in its safety controller system, and a RAT (2018)
23. Kephart, J.O., Chess, D.M.: The vision of autonomic computing. IEEE Comput. **36**, 41–50 (2003)
24. Knowles, W., Prince, D., Hutchinson, D., Ferdinand, J., Disso, P., Jones, K.: Towards real-time assessment of industrial control systems (ICSs): A framework for future research. In: Proceedings of the 1st International Symposium for ICS & SCADA Cyber Security Research. pp. 106–109. Leicester, UK (2013)
25. Kushner, D.: The real story of stuxnet. IEEE Spectrum **50**(3), 48–53 (2013)
26. Langner, R.: Stuxnet: dissecting a cyberwarfare weapon. IEEE Secur. Privacy **9**(3), 49–51 (2011)
27. Lee, R.M., Assante, M.J., Conway, T.: German steel mill cyber attack. SANS, Technical Report 2014 https://ics.sans.org/media/ICS-CPPE-case-Study-2-German-Steelworks_Facility.pdf (2014)
28. McCarthy, D., Umeshwar, D.: The architecture of an active database management system. ACM Sigmod Record **18**(2), 215–224 (1989)
29. Miller, B., Rowe, D.: A survey SCADA of and critical infrastructure incidents. In: Proceedings of the 1st Annual conference on Research in information technology. pp. 51–56. ACM (2012)
30. Montemaggio, A., Iannucci, S., Bhowmik, T., Hamilton, J.: Designing a methodological framework for the empirical evaluation of self-protecting systems. In: 2020 IEEE International Conference on Autonomic Computing and Self-Organizing Systems Companion (ACSOS-C). pp. 218–223. IEEE (2020)
31. New York Independent System Operator, Inc: 2018 load & capacity data "gold book". Tech. rep., ISO (2018)
32. Pandey, A., Ruchkin, I., Schmerl, B., Cámara, J.: Towards a formal framework for hybrid planning in self-adaptation. In: IEEE/ACM 12th International Symposium on Software Engineering for Adaptive and Self-Managing Systems. pp. 109–115. IEEE (2017)
33. Petit, J., Shladover, S.E.: Potential cyberattacks on automated vehicles. IEEE Trans. Intell. Trans. Syst. **16**(2), 546–556 (2015)

34. Radmand, P., Talevski, A., Petersen, S., Carlsen, S.: Taxonomy of wireless sensor network cyber security attacks in the oil and gas industries. In: 2010 24th IEEE International Conference on Advanced Information Networking and Applications. pp. 949–957. IEEE (2010)

35. Rashid, A., Gardiner, J., Green, B., Craggs, B.: Everything Is Awesome! or Is It? Cyber Security Risks in Critical Infrastructure. In: Nadjm-Tehrani, S. (ed.) CRITIS 2019. LNCS, vol. 11777, pp. 3–17. Springer, Cham (2020). https://doi.org/10.1007/978-3-030-37670-3_1

36. da Silva, C.E., da Silva, J.D.S., Paterson, C., Calinescu, R.: Self-adaptive role-based access control for business processes. In: IEEE/ACM 12th International Symposium on Software Engineering for Adaptive and Self-Managing Systems. pp. 193–203. Buenos Aires, Argentina (2017)

37. of Sponsoring Organizations of the Treadway Commission (COSO), C.: Enterprise Risk Management-Integrated Framework. Jersey City, NJ (2004)

38. Tsuchida, S., Nakagawa, H., Tramontana, E., Fornaia, A., Tsuchiya, T.: A framework for updating functionalities based on the MAPE loop mechanism. In: 42nd IEEE International Conference on Computer Software & Applications. pp. 38–47 (2018)

39. Waltermire, D., Quinn, S., Scarfone, K., Halbardier, A.: The Technical Specification for the Security Content Automation Protocol: SCAP Version 1.2. Recommendations of the National Institute of Standards and Technology, NIST-800-126 (2011)

High Data Throughput Exfiltration Through Video Cable Emanations

Llorenç Romá Álvarez[⊠], Daniel Moser, and Vincent Lenders

Armasuisse Science and Technology, Cyber-Defence Campus, Thun, Switzerland
{llorenc.roma,daniel.moser,vincent.lenders}@ar.admin.ch

Abstract. The present work investigates the feasibility to exfiltrate a large amount of data from a computer by leveraging the unintended electromagnetic emanations of an HDMI cable to reconstruct its content. The low signal strength and noise of the leaked signals make difficult to recover any useful information, particularly when the content information is text based, since it suffers from low readability. We consider a targeted attack in which malicious software executed inside the victim's machine encodes the desired information into QR codes, which are then modulated on the HDMI cable and in turn received and reconstructed by the attacker. The efficiency of this method is evaluated under practical conditions showing that the system is capable of achieving a data exfiltration rate up to 12.67 Kbps under optimal conditions or 2.08 Kbps at 50 m distance. To the best of our knowledge, these results outperform, in terms of distance range and exfiltration rate, previous work in the field of electromagnetic leakage from the literature.

Keywords: side channel · emanations · data exfiltration · hdmi · QR code · tempest

1 Introduction

The security issue resulting from the electromagnetic emanations of electronic devices was initially worked on by governments and military entities. The practice of eavesdropping and protecting from eavesdroppers and their study are encompassed in a framework known as TEMPEST, a term established by the National Security Agency (NSA) in the USA [8].

Our work has the objective of investigating the feasibility of exfiltrating large amounts of targeted data by leveraging video cable emanations. Our work focuses on HDMI, yet the results are generally relevant to any other types of video cable such as VGA [31]. The proposed exfiltration method allows an attacker to exfiltrate data without leaving any traces on the network, that is, avoiding detection by classical network-exfiltration countermeasures. We investigate QR codes to encode the data to be exfiltrated reliably and at high rates and we experimentally demonstrate data exfiltration throughputs several times higher than previously reported in the literature is possible.

B. Hämmerli et al. (Eds.): CRITIS 2022, LNCS 13723, pp. 27–48, 2023.
https://doi.org/10.1007/978-3-031-35190-7_3

Our main contributions are:

- A reliable technique of data exfiltration by combining the use of QR codes as encoding system with unintended HDMI cable emanations.
- Systematic evaluation of the impact of the distance and obstructions to the throughput.
- Experimental demonstration of data exfiltration rate up to 2.08 Kbps at 50 m distance, 5.12 Kbps at two floors away and a maximum rate above 12 Kbps under optimal conditions (antenna placed next to the target system).
- Open source software pipeline to reproduce the full attack (to be uploaded in a GitHub repository).

The rest of the paper is organised as follows: in Sect. 2 we present other works related to data exfiltration using side channels, in particular those exploiting video monitor emanations. In Sect. 3 we introduce the technical background of our work and describe how QR Code technology is used to exfiltrate data reliably in such attacks. In Sect. 4 we introduce the attacker model and describe the different stages of the attack. Section 5 outlines the details of the software pipeline implemented for the attack and Sect. 6 summarizes the results achieved after evaluating the attack in multiple scenarios. We performed experimental analysis covering different parameters that affect the transfer bitrate of the attack. In Sect. 7, we propose countermeasures and describe the drawbacks of our approach. Finally, in Sect. 8, we draw the conclusions derived from our work and future work to consider.

2   Related Work

Compromising electromagnetic emanations have been under research from the mid 1980's. Wim Van Eck published the very first analysis of video monitor emanations security risks in 1985 [32] where he described how to reconstruct the content from video monitor emanations without the need of professional and expensive equipment but with just a TV broadcast receiver. The threat was confirmed by implementing a practical attack in which he could reconstruct and monitor the content of a screen in a real world scenario. Years later, around the year 2000, Kuhn [25,28] analyzed the emanations coming from computer displays in depth and discussed the concept of a software based TEMPEST attack, showing that the electromagnetic emanations from LCD screens can be controlled to modulate data. The researchers also showed how recovering the content of the screen provided them a way to perform text-based exfiltration attacks at distances ranging from 3 to 10 m. Further, they proposed different techniques to improve the recovery of plain text from emanations via radio-character recognition. However, their proposal focus on recovery of text characters, which becomes more prone to error as the SNR decreases due to the similarity between different text characters (e.g., "i" and "l", or "v" and "u").

Other works exploiting video monitor emanations have been published since then. For instance, Guri et al. [14] presented a malware, namely *AirHopper*, which encodes text/binary data from a target into FM signals and uses a mobile phone as FM receiver. In order to achieve this, they modify the content of the monitor to control the emanated signals (FM signals) as discussed in different works and technical papers [12,25,28,32]. The maximum throughput they achieved was 480 bps at 1 m distance. Aside from electromagnetic emanations, other side-channels have been studied in the past. These air-gap covert channels are classified in seven main categories: electromagnetic, magnetic, electric, acoustic, thermal, optical and vibrational. In [20] the authors used cellular frequencies to exfiltrate data, achieving up to 1000 bps rate at 2.6 cm distance. Despite of this being the approach presenting the higher exfiltration rate it comes with a limitation regarding the distance. In [17–19,22] the authors used different covert channels providing exfiltration rates ranging from 1 bps to a maximum of 100 bps, and distances up to 1.5 m being the last one the slowest, exfiltrating 8 bits per hour using the CPU generated heat as a channel.

In this work, we investigate the data exfiltration rate from a video cable. Similar to the text-based exfiltration approach showed by Kuhn [25,28], we encode the information in the video signal. However, we combine it with QR codes in order to circumvent the limitations of text character recovery: since QR codes are highly resistant to errors, it results a much better coding scheme for environments where the SNR is reduced due to environmental noise, such as in the TEMPEST attack. Finally, we show how the system can effectively exfiltrate data from a computer from up to 50 m distance or alternatively, from different floors, achieving exfiltration rates and distances several times higher than other previous attacks. A comparison of our work and the previous related work using covert channels used for data exfiltration is shown in Table 1, where we can see the advancement of our approach in terms of exfiltration rate and distance.

3 Background

In this section, we first introduce the term TEMPEST and describe the HDMI data stream and nature of its leaked signals. Then, we detail the properties of QR codes and why we chose it as encoding scheme for data exfiltration.

3.1 TEMPEST

In 1972, the NSA conducted a classified study which was partially declassified later [8]. The document described how in one experiment conducted at Bell Labs, they were able to detect plain text from an emanated signal coming from a message encryption device. This device was used during the Second World War by the US army and that experiment highlighted the importance of having control over electromagnetic emanations. The term TEMPEST was then used to describe a set of standards, specifications and certifications [7,9] referring to the act of spying on information systems through leaking emanations, which includes unintentional electromagnetic signals, sounds and vibrations. TEMPEST also defines how devices can be protected against such attacks. Among these measures, the standards consider distance between equipment and walls, distance

Table 1. Comparison of current covert channels for air-gapped networks.

Attack (covert channel)	Type	Distance (m)	Rate (bit/s)
AirHopper [14] (FM signals)	EM	1-7	105-480
LCD Tempest [15] (AM signals)	EM		60-640
GSMem [20] (Cellular Frequencies)	EM	30 +	100-1000
AIR-FI [17] (WiFi signals)	EM	0-8	100
ODINI [22] (Faraday shield bypass)	Magnetic	0.05 - 0.1	1-40
PowerHammer [21] (power lines)	Electric		100-1000
Ultrasonic [23][24] (speaker)	Acoustic	19.7	20
BitWhisper [16] (CPU generated heat)	Thermal	0.4	8 bit/hour
BRIGHTNESS [19] (screen brightness level)	Optical	9	10
AiR VibeR [18] (computer fan vibrations)	Vibrational	1.4	0.5
Exfiltration with QR (QR code recovered img)	EM	1 - 50	2080-12670

between wires carrying classified and unclassified information, or masking information by introducing noise.

3.2   Video Signal

As described by Marinov [31] a video frame is built up from y_t lines formed by x_t pixels. The display refreshes a frame at f_v frames per second (fps). In addition to the visible pixels, there are also non-visible pixels (i.e., blanking pixels), which are used to synchronise the start and the end of a line or a frame. Each pixel is a combination of three colors (RGB). In the case of digital signals, the intensity of each RGB component is represented by a number n_b of bits ($n_b = 10$ bits for HDMI). Therefore, the bit duration is

$$t_b = \frac{1}{x_t \cdot y_t \cdot f_v \cdot n_b} \tag{1}$$

where x_t and y_t depends on the screen resolution and f_v is determined by the screen refresh rate. Then, pixel i is transmitted at $t_i = i \cdot t_b \cdot n_b$.

Consider a display transmitting a bit stream of values $c_k (k \in \mathbb{Z})$, where the k-th value represents the bit $(k \bmod n_b)$ of the binary number used to represent pixel intensity of pixel number $\lVert \frac{k}{n_b} \rVert$. The resulting video signal in the time domain is defined as [31]

$$\tilde{v}(t) = \sum_{k=-\infty}^{+\infty} c_k b(t - k t_b) \tag{2}$$

where $b(t)$ is the shape of a digital bit and $b(t) = 0$ for $|t| \gg \frac{t_b}{2}$.

This signal is going to be repeated at regular intervals at frequencies multiple of $\frac{1}{t_b} = x_t \cdot y_t \cdot f_v \cdot n_b$. In order to receive this video signal, the receiver needs to be able to pick up frequencies up to $f \geq \frac{1}{2t_b}$ to be above the Nyquist sampling rate. For example, using a laptop with $n_b = 7$ with resolution values of 800×600 @ 75 fps with $x_t = 1056$ px, $y_t = 628$ lines and $f_v = 75\,Hz$, we should expect the signal centered at multiples of $\frac{1}{t_b}$: 348.2 MHz.

3.3   QR Code

The QR code technology was created in 1994 as an alternative to the commonly used barcodes due to their limitations in terms of storage capacity. Initially the QR code was adopted by the car industry for efficient work management through a range of tasks. Subsequently, the use of this code was widely spread across multiple industries and nowadays almost every smartphone has a QR code reader. A QR code consists of a square-shaped figure built up from black and white squares, called modules. The main features of this technology are described below.

Encoding Modes. A QR code encodes a set of characters as a string of bits. The encoding can be optimized depending on the type of characters to encode by using one out of four encoding modes: numeric, alphanumeric, byte (including UTF-8) and Kanji (a set of Japanese characters that require three or four bytes to be encoded). The encoding mode will create the shortest possible string of bits for the input, so it will result in higher capacity. For instance, encoding a set of numeric characters in *numeric* mode will allow to encode more numeric characters than when they are encoded in byte mode.

Error Correction Level (ECL). QR codes are designed to be able to recover data if the code is dirty, damaged or partially obstructed. A sensible requirement stemming from their origin in industrial and production environments where codes could be easily degraded. Four error correction levels are available and the higher the level the higher correction capability. However, the increased tolerance to errors comes with a lower data capacity.

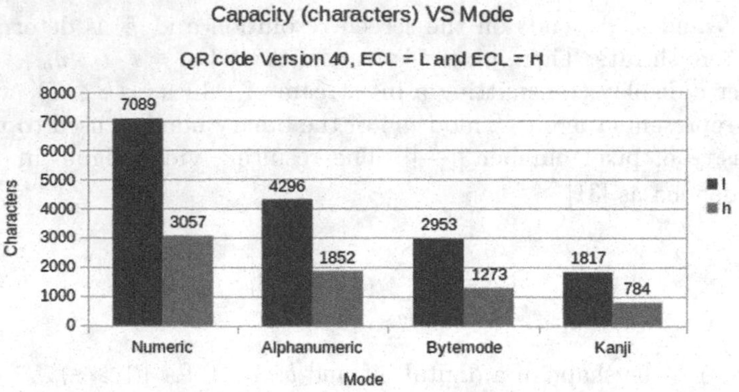

Capacity (characters) VS Mode

QR code Version 40, ECL = L and ECL = H

Fig. 1. Difference encoding capacity between QR codes with ECL set to L and H.

Data Capacity. How much data a QR code can store depends on three factors: the data to be encoded (encoding mode), the error correction level and the version of the QR code. The version of the QR code determines its dimensions in terms of modules - it is 21×21 for version 1 and 177×177 for version 40, the highest version number at the time of writing. Each version add 4 modules to each side of the QR code.

Figure 1 shows the maximum number of characters that a QR code of version 40 can store. It shows the capacity for the four encoding modes and the lowest (L) and highest (H) ECL. It can be seen that switching from the highest ECL to the lowest one is has a big impact in terms of the maximum number of characters that can be stored; it increases by more than 100%. See Appendix A for a list with the maxima for all possible combinations of encodings and ECL.

Motivation Behind the Use of QR Code for the Attack. QR codes have been invented and designed to encode arbitrary data into a visual representation that can be captured and decoded using electromagnetic (electro-optical) sensors, despite (a limited amount) of damage to the QR code (e.g., scratches) itself, low SNR on the optical channel (e.g., bad light conditions) and distorsions and faults (e.g., dead pixels) introduced by the sensor. However, the elements that optimize a QR code in terms of visual representation and transmission are also useful when reconstructing the visual representation from electromagnetic radiation of video cables. In particular, these are:

- Error correction capabilities account for errors at the module level; for example, a module that was black was reconstructed as being white.
- The well-defined structure of a QR code con be leveraged to reduce the difficulty of the recovery process. Its fixed size squares perfectly aligned on a grid make it easier to locate data units(square) and cope with distorsions to them. This in contrast to, for example, text-based approaches where the width of characters might vary and even small distorsions might make one character look like another (e.g., 'l' and 'i').

– Black/white have maximum hamming distance so, it is likely that despite errors, some distance remains and it is still possible to determine if a pixel should be black/white when reconstructing the QR codes.

Furthermore, with different encoding for different error correction levels, the QR code format enables an attacker to optimize throughput for different inputs and exfiltration scenarios; for example, with or without walls between the attacker and the video cable.

4   Attacker Model

Espionage by eavesdropping on the EM emissions of a video cable can in principle be carried out without manipulating the target system. The attacker must then simply hope that the user is watching something interesting and that this can then be reconstructed from the emissions. However, if specific data is to be exfiltrated and optimized with respect to the transmission method, this requires an active attacker. As a consequence, the attacker model includes at least the following capabilities and steps: (1) place malware on the target system (2) collect and exfiltrate data (3) receive and decode EM emanations from the victim's video cable. In the following, we discuss the steps in more detail. Figure 2 shows the setup after the attacker has successfully infected the system with their malware.

In a typical scenario, an attacker with access to internal data would exfiltrate to the Internet over the network. However, this would leave traces and make the exfiltration noticeable to the implemented security solutions, namely IDS (Intrusion Detection System), logs, firewalls etc. Since our attack does not exfiltrate the data over the network, it remains unnoticeable to such security measures. However, as discussed in Sect. 7, one of the limitations is that displaying QR Codes on the screen does leave traces on a different channel (e.g., to passers by).

4.1   Target Infection

There are many different vectors for infecting a target, starting with remotely exploitable vulnerabilities, compromised software updates, malicious employees or social engineering. Depending on whether and how a system is networked with other systems, more or fewer vectors come into play. Air-gapped systems probably present the most difficult hurdle here, but even this can be overcome in practice. Examples include Stuxnet [11,29] and Agent.btz [30]. Once the system is infected, the malware should be able to do its job; additional steps like local privilege escalation are often not required. After all, reading data and displaying images can be done by most users.

In the following subsections, we do not discuss step (1) any further. Our focus is on steps (2) and (3). For the reminder of this work, we assume that we were able to place our malware on the target system.

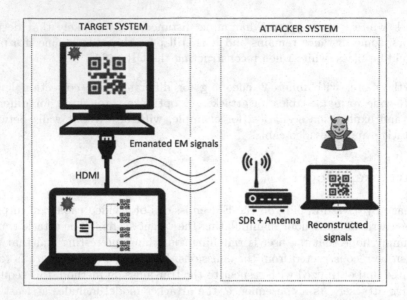

Fig. 2. Attacker model diagram.

The target computer, infected with malware, displays QR codes on the screen while the attacker receives the emanated signals with an SDR device to reconstruct the codes and extract information.

4.2   Data Collection and Exfiltration

Once the computer is infected, the malware collects sensitive data. It encodes the data into QR codes and finally displays the generated QR codes on the external connected screen. In such scenario, the screen's content is leaked through the HDMI emanated signals.

4.3   Signal Reception/Decoding

For reception, the attacker uses a computer with an SDR (see Sect. 5) and an antenna in order to detect, receive and process the signals to reconstruct the content from the emanated video signal. After signal acquisition, the attacker proceeds to the decoding of the recovered QR codes.

For this purpose, the attacker needs access to the target's surrounding where reception of the emanated signals is possible whilst not being discovered. This can be achieved in a multitude of ways. First it is important to note that the attacker does not have to be present during the attack but can place the receiver system at a suitable location and fetch it later to process the recorded signals. If the receiver can be hidden well enough, any rented-out or publicly accessible room that the target will use would do the job. If hiding it is difficult or the room will be checked for such devices before using it, the receiver could be placed in any room nearby, where the signal is still strong enough. The top candidates being the rooms above, below or next to the room in question.

5   Implementation

In this section, we describe the software pipeline we developed to experimentally investigate the exfiltration data rates in the proposed attacker model from previous sections.

5.1   File Encoding - QR Code Generation

The malware collects sensitive data and splits them in blocks of N characters where N is the capacity of the QR code version used. To identify recovered QR codes on the receiver side, a header is added on top of the encoded data. In our experiments we used the filename and the data block number encoded (see Fig. 3). Another identification method could be used (e.g., one byte per file and one byte per file data block).

Once QR codes are generated, they are displayed on the external screen to originate the emanations of the signal that will be recovered with the receiver system. It is convenient to display the codes in full-screen, thus, the modules are better differentiated on the receiver side and it is less prone to errors due to poor quality. Moreover, adding a black border helps to identify and delimit the area containing the QR code. An example of a generated QR code displayed on the monitor is shown in Fig. 4.

5.2   Signal Reception and Frame Reconstruction

To receive the emanated signals, we apply a band-pass filter centered at a multiple of the target's pixel frequency. The sampling rate was set at twice the target's pixel rate so each pixel is identified. We collected the RF signals with an SDR and they were send to a PC for demodulation and processing.

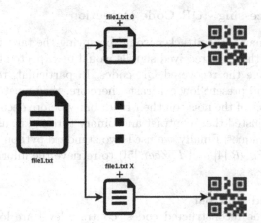

Fig. 3. QR code generation. A file is split in X blocks and encoded into several QR codes. A header with information about file name and the block of data is added to the content of each QR code.

Fig. 4. QR code generated on the target computer.

For frame reconstruction, we leverage the video signals properties as shown in Sect. 3. The decoding of the video signal relies on the values x_t, y_t and f_v of the screen. Different approaches to find these values are proposed by Marinov [26,31]. First, the signal generated might be considered periodic, and therefore, the received signal can be analysed to perceive patterns and obtain f_v. For instance, in [31] autocorrelation is used to discover repeating patterns of the received signal and to estimate f_v. Second, y_t is estimated from the repeating nature of frame blanking intervals (invisible pixels) from consecutive received samples. Last, there are a set of resolutions that are broadly used, for instance $2560 \times 1440@60\text{Hz}$ or $1920 \times 1080@60\text{Hz}$: an attacker could adjust the receiving parameters to match these resolutions.

Before displaying the reconstructed video frame, we applied digital frame averaging in order to reduce random noise and increase the signal SNR.

5.3   Image Processing - QR Code Detection

In a real-world scenario, the attacker would be spying the target computer from a certain distance, thus, the received signals would be expected to contain noise, which might damage the recovered QR codes. In particular, recovered images are in gray scale and present low contrast, therefore, they must be preprocessed to reduce the impact of the noise on their readability before decoding. To recover those codes, we adjusted their contrast and binary thresholds, as well as applied noise removal techniques. Finally, we used two standard python QR code decoding libraries (i.e., *PyQR* [4] and *PyZbar* [5]) to retrieve the information from the recovered QR codes.

– **Brightness and contrast**
   Since most of the reconstructed codes' contrast level are low, decoders are not able to distinguish well between black and white modules. For instance, the QR code in Fig. 5 (a) could not be decoded by any of the decoders.

- **Thresholding/ Binarization**

Sometimes, the code is not readable after increasing contrast and brightness. However, once the contrast is higher, black and white modules are easier to discriminate and, based on a threshold, we apply binarization to map gray values to black or white. Depending on the gray value, the resulting pixel is assigned as follows:

$$\begin{cases} 0 & \text{for x} < \text{threshold} \\ 255 & \text{otherwise} \end{cases}$$

where x represents the initial pixel's value in 8-bit format.

This part is error prone due to noise: some of the gray values which should be white are considered as black and the other way around, thus, if enough modules are wrongly interpreted, the code becomes unreadable. Figure 5 (b) is the result of thresholding Fig. 5 (a), initially not decoded. After applying thresholding, both decoders succeeded.

- **Noise removal - Erosion and Dilation**

All recovered images contain noise which we minimize by applying median filtering and linear gaussian filtering. These two techniques preserve the edges of the image, which in the case of the QR code modules is essential. Furthermore, there might still be some noise in the form of small lines all over the image as shown in Fig. 6. In order to reduce this type of noise, we apply dilation and erosion which reduce the small lines and dots.

(a) Recovered image without preprocessing. Not decodable

(b) Recovered image with increased contrast and thresholding applied. The decoded text is part of a book: "Preface to the Third Edition ..."

Fig. 5. Recovered QR codes before and after image processing.

Fig. 6. On the right image we applied dilation and erosion to reduce to noise. However, it is not decodable yet due to the small size of the modules which makes it impossible to differentiate.

5.4 QR Code Decoding and Data Recovery

Once QR code data is retrieved, we assembled the different blocks of data by analysing the header of decoded data as explained in Sect. 5.1. Figure 7 shows the steps on the receiver side, from signal reception to data recovery.

6 Evaluation

In this section, we evaluate the reliability and the data exfiltration rate of the attacker model in different scenarios.

6.1 Setup

The equipment used for the experiments and its specifications are described in the following subsections.

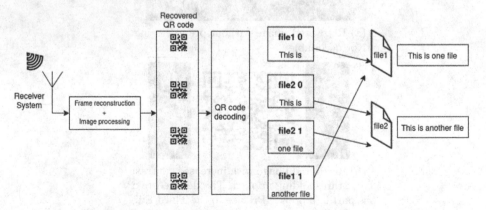

Fig. 7. Signal acquisition, frame reconstruction, QR code decoding and data collection process.

Target System. As the target system, we used an *HP Elitebook* running Ubuntu 20.0.4 with 16 GB of memory, an Intel Core i7-8550UCPU@1.8 GHz × 8 processor and Intel UHD Graphics 620 (KBL GT2) graphics. This system runs the malicious code described in Sect. 5. The computer is connected to an external video monitor: we tested an HP Z27n (27') model for the experiments and repeated them for different screens, including a modern super wide screen (*Samsung 49" QLED Gaming Monitor 5120 × 1440@60 Hz*). The decoding rates were similar for all of them.

Regarding the video cable, we tested different commercial 3 m long High Speed HDMI cables and repeated the experiments with a 15 m long cable. The cables did not have any special shielding.

Notice that we performed the experiments with a laptop connected to an external monitor only for convenience. That is, the results also apply to desktop PCs as the emanations come from the video cable and not the computer device [12,14,27,31].

Attacker System. To receive and process the leaked signals, we used a commercial off-the-shelf software-defined radio, namely the Ettus USRP B210 model [2]. We used a directional Yagi antenna (with frequency range of 698 - 3800 MHz MHz) since this type is well suited if we are targeting a specific computer. In our experiments we added a *Mini-Circuits* ZX60-3018G-S+ 13 dB amplifier [1] with an additional power supply of 12V and a filter to reduce the undesired signals [3]. Finally, we used another identical *HP Elitebook* to perform all the image processing and signal reconstruction tasks.

Receiving Parameters. In our setup, we recovered the images at 1210 MHz and sampling rate values between 15 MHz and 20 MHz.

6.2 Scenarios

We evaluated different scenarios. In each scenario, the antenna was placed in a different location. For each of the experiments, we evaluated the ability of the system to exfiltrate three text files encoded into 20 QR codes each, independently of the QR code version. That is, for an experiment to be successful, we should recover and decode 100% of the codes (60 in total). All QR codes were generated using *bytemode* (i.e., 8 bits each character).

Zero Distance. First, we evaluated a scenario in which the antenna was placed at less than 50 cm from the target system to avoid signal degradation due to distance. For this experiment, the Error Correction Level (ECL) is set to Low (L) and the time a QR code is displayed on the screen is 0.5 s. For the rest of the experiments, we consider the same ECL an display time if not specified otherwise.

The results for different QR code versions are shown in Fig. 8. The vertical axis represents the percentage of QR codes which are recovered out of the 60 total codes. For instance, 100% means that the whole set of 60 QR codes (20 per file) are recovered and decoded. In an environment with good conditions where

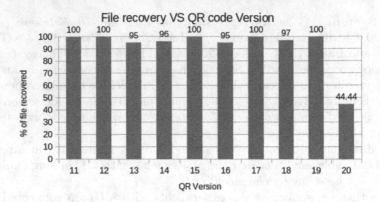

Fig. 8. File recovery percentage for different QR code versions. ECL is set to L and display time is 0.5 s.

the channel noise remains low, the file recovery rate is close to 100% up to QR code version 19. For higher versions, the modules of the QR codes are smaller. With small modules, subtle interference can cause adjacent modules to mix, introducing errors. Considering the capacities specified in Appendix A, using version 19 QR codes in bytemode (max of 792 characters), with the specified conditions (displaying time of 0.5 s and ECL set to L), we reach a maximum throughput of $\frac{6336 \, bits}{0.5 \, s} = 12672$ bps.

In the next evaluation, we examined the impact of reducing the time that a QR code is displayed on the exfiltration rate. The combination of a higher version code and lower display time will provide us a higher throughput. However, we will need to increase the sampling rate on the receiver and therefore, frames will start being dropped. Figure 9 shows the results. Using QR code version 11 and a display time of 0.25 s, we were able to recover the whole set of files. This results in a maximum throughput without errors of $\frac{2568 \, bits}{0.25 \, s} = 10272$ bps.

Finally, we evaluated how the value of the ECL impacts the recovery rate (shown in Fig. 10). In this experiment, we compared the file recovery percentage for different versions while using ECL set to L , Q or H. We placed the antenna at a longer distance in such a way that the noise introduced in the images is more noticeable and the effect of the ECL is observed. From version 9 on, we could not recover any block of data using level L whereas for levels Q and H it was still possible since they tolerate more degradation in the codes. We also evaluated lower versions not shown in the figure, as they all lead to a 100% recovery of the data. The main drawback is the high overhead introduced when increasing the ECL: for H level the capacity (352 characters) is about 40% lower compared to L level (848 characters).

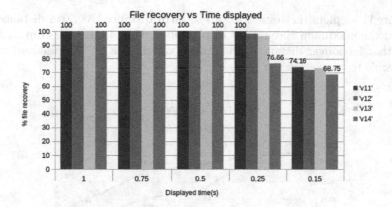

Fig. 9. File recovery percentage for versions 11 to 14 while modifying the display time of the QR codes. (Color figure online)

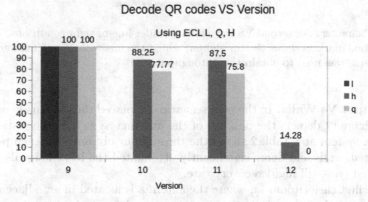

Fig. 10. File recovery percentage for versions 9 to 12 and ECL values L (blue), Q (yellow) and H (orange). For version 12, we can only recover some of the codes using high error correction level. (Color figure online)

Throughput vs Distance. We measured throughput obtained under line-of-sight conditions between the antenna and the target system over the distance. Despite being under line-of-sight conditions, the experiments were not performed in an interference-free environment but in a real office floor with other laptops and monitors used at the same time.

To get the maximum throughput, for each distance we combined the version and the displaying time values that allowed us to recover all the 60 QR codes.

Figure 11, depicts the results for up to 50 m distance. At 50 m distance, we obtained the maximum throughput displaying version 4 QR codes during 0.3 s. Notice that for longer distances, the image contained a lot of noise and it was not possible to recover all the files.

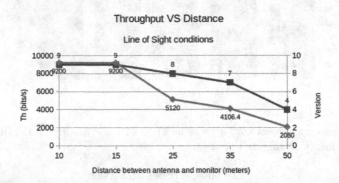

Fig. 11. Characters per second VS the distance under line-of-sight conditions. The line with diamond markers shows the throughput whilst the line with square markers shows which version was used to obtain this throughput.

Throughput Vs Walls. In the next scenario, we placed the antenna in adjacent rooms. Figure 12 depicts the position of the antenna as well as the distances to the target system and Table 2 shows the throughput obtained for each position. As expected, walls and doors significantly attenuated the leaked signals leading to a limited (yet still high) recovery rate.

In the first case (Room 1), where the antenna is located in an adjacent room with only one glass door in between, we managed to reach approximately the same throughput as in the line-of-sight experiment with no obstacles.

The second case (Room 2) considers the attacker to be located in an adjacent room, with two closed glass doors in between. With two doors and a longer distance (10 m) in between, the throughput dropped by 41.7% compared to the case with just one obstacle.

In the last case (Room 3), we placed the antenna in another room, at 15 m and again with two doors in between. The results show how the combination of the glass doors and the distance negatively impacts the recovery rate, which barely reached 22% compared to the results at the same distance in the line-of-sight scenario.

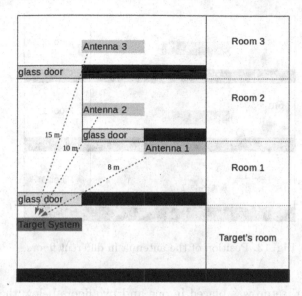

Fig. 12. Antenna and target position on the same floor.

Table 2. Maximum throughput in bits per second for different positions of the antenna on the same floor. Version and display time of the QR codes that provided the maximum throughput are shown for each position.

Room	Version	Time (s)	Distance (m)	Throughput (bits/s)
1	9	0.2	8	9200
2	6	0.2	10	5360
3	4	0.3	15	2080

Throughput vs Floors. If we consider a scenario in which an attacker has access to one floor in the same building of the target, we could assume that the victim would not notice the attacker's presence at all. For this experiment, we placed the attacker setup in different floors below the target system. Notice that the attacker should roughly know the target's position in order to point the antenna in such direction.

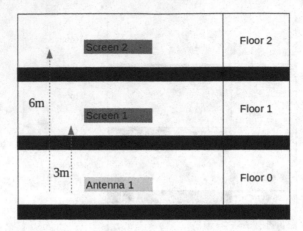

Fig. 13. Position of the antenna in different floors

The attacker' setup was placed in one and two floors below the target. The floors were built out of concrete. Table 3 shows the parameters that provided the highest throughput for each case. The throughput obtained in the latter case is around 44% less compared to the former.

Table 3. Highest QR code readable version and version and display time providing the highest throughput when positioning the antenna in different floors.

Floor	Version	Time (s)	Distance (m)	Th (bits/s)
1	9	0.2	≈ 3	9200
2	12	0.4	≈ 6	7336

7 Discussion

In this paper, we show how QR Codes can be used to increase the data exfiltration rate when exploiting electromagnetic signals from video cables compared to other related works. We demonstrate how this approach worked in different real scenario and saw that an attacker would be able to effectively exfiltrate high amounts of data in a limited time without need of high-cost equipment. The results in Sect. 6 show that the use of QR Codes provides a higher resistance to noise/signal degradation, allowing to achieve exfiltration rates much higher than in similar literature. We learned that lower versions of QR Code provide more reliability when the environmental noise is high, while higher versions of QR Codes may be used to increase exfiltration rate when the amount of noise is reduced.

However, these very good results also come with several limitations. First and foremost, displaying QR codes on a computer's screen won't go unnoticed by its user or any passers-by. While the malware could eventually detect the presence of a user (e.g., using sensors like camera, microphone/speaker, or monitoring keyboard/mouse activity) and not show the codes whenever one is present, this might be much harder or impossible to do for the case of random passers-by. Things are simpler when the attackers knows time slots where no one is around or when the malware displays QR codes in an way invisible to humans. The later could eventually be achieved with real-time watermarking [13] techniques or with dithering [26].

Another limitation of our approach is that the attacker has no way of controlling the malware after it has been deployed; there is no backchannel. The attacker has no way of telling the malware that decoding a certain QR code failed and to have it displayed again. Fortunately, for conservative settings (small QR code versions, where modules' size are bigger), this is very unlikely to happen as our experiments show. However, it cannot be ruled out completely and depending on the nature of the data to be exfiltrated, especially if loosing one QR code could void the whole exfiltration, measures to mitigate this should be considered. The first choice here would probably be adding inter QR code error correction as this consumes less of the exfiltration bandwidth than transmitting all QR codes twice (or more times). Another option would be the use of side-channels as backchannels. Depending on the available sensors on the target computer and the overall situation this might work but is rather iffy and not completely passive anymore.

Despite having achieved good results during the experiments, further research should be done to make the exfiltration more robust and reliable: as discussed, improving the image processing to decode very noisy QR Codes might provide a larger exfiltration rate. In addition, one of the main obstacles in our approach (and related work) is the user's presence: investigating how to hide the QR Codes from user's presence remains as a challenge.

7.1   Countermeasures

Designing an electronic device which does not emanate electromagnetic signals can be hard, however, there are measures that can minimize those emanations.

Different standards and specifications define the requirements that electronic systems should implement in order to protect against general TEMPEST attacks [7,9]. For instance, the *red* and *black* rule, or *zones* classification to define the perimeter to be controlled or prevent signal reception. However, we have shown that structural building elements such us concrete walls/floors, do not mitigate the exfiltration method described, if we can get close enough. Shielding the transmitter component appears to be a better countermeasure, however, the HDMI video chip also leaks signals and that might be more difficult to shield. Another defensive strategy involves monitoring the presence of passive eavesdroppers such as in [10]. However the current detection range of such system is far below the exfiltration range of the work presented in our paper.

Another alternative we propose is the use of High Bandwidth Digital Content Protection (HDCP), which is supported by almost every modern HDMI chip and encrypts the protected content at chip level before sending the signals through the HDMI cable. Thus, the signals received by the attacker would be encrypted and therefore, illegible. Currently, HDCP encrypts only Digital Protected content. The solution would consist of applying the encryption to all the content sent through the HDMI cable. We experimented by playing Netflix on the target system and the recovered content was completely scrambled.

Finally, the target system could apply a permanent invisible overlay that results in visible patterns on the receiver side, in such a way that the QR codes are obstructed with those patterns (i.e., a watermarking to block the QR codes).

8 Conclusions

In our work, we presented a method for exfiltrating data using a commercial off-the-shelf software defined radio without leaving network traces. The covert channel used is based on the electromagnetic waves leaked from a video cable connecting a computer to an external display. The software used for exfiltration leverages QR codes to encode the targeted data. We have provided the technical background about video signals and QR code technology, and justified the use of it as a low SNR resistant encoding scheme.

We have described the whole attack pipeline, from data encoding, to signal reception, noise reduction and data recovery. We have evaluated the method using extensive variations and encoding parameters. In our results, we demonstrated that the attacker model described is feasible even with an isolation of several concrete floors. We also showed that the screen and the video cable length do not have an impact in our proposed method. With the experiments, we showed an effective distance of 50 m without obstacles and also a scenario where the target was located at two levels above the receiving system. Compared to similar works, the presented method provides an exfiltration distance range and a throughput several times higher.

Finally, we discussed the limitations of our approach and proposed countermeasures to protect against such attack.

A QR Code Capacities

The following table shows the maximum capacity of different QR code versions using ECL levels L and H and for the different modes. We omitted the capacities for levels M and Q, and we just included a limited number of versions. For more details about the capacities of each version we suggest [6].

Table 4. Modules and capacities of different QR code versions for ECL L and H when using different modes.

Version	Modules	ECL	Numeric	Alphanumeric	Bytemode	Kanji
1	21 × 21	L	41	25	17	10
		H	17	10	7	4
2	25 × 25	L	77	47	32	20
		H	34	20	14	8
3	29 × 29	L	127	77	53	32
		H	58	35	24	15
4	33 × 33	L	187	114	78	48
		H	82	50	34	21
5	37 × 37	L	255	154	106	65
		H	106	64	44	27
40	177 × 177	L	7089	4296	2953	1817
		H	3057	1852	1273	784

References

1. Amplifier Datasheet. https://www.minicircuits.com/pdfs/ZX60-3018G+.pdf. Accessed 12 Aug 2020
2. Ettus USRP B210. https://www.ettus.com/all-products/ub210-kit/. Accessed 12 Aug 2020
3. Filter Datasheet. https://www.minicircuits.com/pdfs/ZX75BS-88108+.pdf. Accessed 14 Aug 2020
4. Python-qrcode. https://github.com/lincolnloop/python-qrcode. Accessed 12 Aug 2020
5. PyZbar. https://github.com/NaturalHistoryMuseum/pyzbar. Accessed 12 Aug 2020
6. QR Code Tutorial. https://www.thonky.com/qr-code-tutorial/. Accessed 12 Aug 2020
7. Agency, N.S.: National Security Agency Specification For Shielded Enclosures Specification NSA No. 94106 (1994)
8. Agency, U.N.S.: TEMPEST: A signal problem (1972)
9. Assurance, N.I.: Tempest equipment selection process (1981)
10. Chaman, A., Wang, J., Sun, J., Hassanieh, H., Roy Choudhury, R.: Ghostbuster: detecting the presence of hidden eavesdroppers. In: Proceedings of the 24th Annual International Conference on Mobile Computing and Networking, pp. 337–351. MobiCom 2018, Association for Computing Machinery, New York, NY, USA (2018). https://doi.org/10.1145/3241539.3241580
11. Clark, A., Zhu, Q., Poovendran, R., Başar, T.: An impact-aware defense against Stuxnet. In: 2013 American Control Conference, pp. 4140–4147 (2013)
12. Erik Thiele: Tempest For Eliza. http://www.erikyyy.de/tempest/ (2001). Accessed 12 Aug 2020 (2001)
13. Gugelmann, D., Sommer, D., Lenders, V., Happe, M., Vanbever, L.: Screen watermarking for data theft investigation and attribution, pp. 391–408 (2018). https://doi.org/10.23919/CYCON.2018.8405027

14. Guri, M., Kedma, G., Kachlon, A., Elovici, Y.: Airhopper: Bridging the air-gap between isolated networks and mobile phones using radio frequencies. In: 2014 9th International Conference on Malicious and Unwanted Software: The Americas (MALWARE), pp. 58–67 (2014)
15. Guri, M., Monitz, M.: LCD tempest air-gap attack reloaded. In: 2018 IEEE International Conference on the Science of Electrical Engineering in Israel (ICSEE), pp. 1–5 (2018). https://doi.org/10.1109/ICSEE.2018.8646277
16. Guri, M., Monitz, M., Mirski, Y., Elovici, Y.: BitWhisper: covert signaling channel between air-gapped computers using thermal manipulations. In: 2015 IEEE 28th Computer Security Foundations Symposium, pp. 276–289 (2015). https://doi.org/10.1109/CSF.2015.26
17. Guri, M.: AIR-FI: Generating covert WI-FI signals from air-gapped computers (2020)
18. Guri, M.: Air-viber: Exfiltrating data from air-gapped computers via covert surface vibrations (2020)
19. Guri, M., Bykhovsky, D., Elovici, Y.: Brightness: Leaking sensitive data from air-gapped workstations via screen brightness. 2019 12th CMI Conference on Cybersecurity and Privacy (CMI) (2019). https://doi.org/10.1109/cmi48017.2019.8962137
20. Guri, M., Kachlon, A., Hasson, O., Kedma, G., Mirsky, Y., Elovici, Y.: GSMem: data exfiltration from air-gapped computers over GSM frequencies. In: 24th USENIX Security Symposium (USENIX Security 15), pp. 849–864. USENIX Association, Washington, D.C. (2015). https://www.usenix.org/conference/usenixsecurity15/technical-sessions/presentation/guri
21. Guri, M., Zadov, B., Bykhovsky, D., Elovici, Y.: Powerhammer: Exfiltrating data from air-gapped computers through power lines (2018)
22. Guri, M., Zadov, B., Daidakulov, A., Elovici, Y.: ODINI: escaping sensitive data from faraday-caged, air-gapped computers via magnetic fields (2018)
23. Hanspach, M., Goetz, M.: On covert acoustical mesh networks in air (2014)
24. Hanspach, M., Goetz, M.: Recent developments in covert acoustical communications. In: Lecture Notes in Informatics (LNI), Proceedings - Series of the Gesellschaft fur Informatik (GI), pp. 243–254 (2014)
25. Kuhn, M.: Compromising emanations: eavesdropping risks of computer displays (2004)
26. Kuhn, M.G.: Compromising emanations: eavesdropping risks of computer displays, Ph. D. thesis, Technical Report Number 577. University of Cambridge (2003)
27. Kuhn, M.G.: Electromagnetic eavesdropping risks of flat-panel displays. In: Martin, D., Serjantov, A. (eds.) Privacy Enhancing Technologies, pp. 88–107. Springer, Berlin Heidelberg, Berlin, Heidelberg (2005). https://doi.org/10.1007/11423409_7
28. Kuhn, M.G., Anderson, R.J.: Soft tempest: hidden data transmission using electromagnetic emanations. In: Aucsmith, D. (ed.) Inf. Hiding, pp. 124–142. Springer, Berlin Heidelberg, Berlin, Heidelberg (1998). https://doi.org/10.1007/3-540-49380-8_10
29. Larimer, J.: An inside look at Stuxnet. IBM X-Force, pp. 1–37 (2010)
30. Lynn, F.: Defending a new domain: The pentagon's cyberstrategy. Foreign Affairs **2010**, 13 (2010)
31. Marinov, M.: Remote video eavesdropping using a software defined radio platform, Ph. D. thesis, MA thesis. University of Cambridge (2014)
32. van Eck, W.: Electromagnetic radiation from video display units: an eavesdropping risk? Comput. Secur. **4**(4), 269–286 (1985). https://doi.org/10.1016/0167-4048(85)90046-X. http://www.sciencedirect.com/science/article/pii/016740488590046X

Design and Justification of a Cybersecurity Assessment Framework for IoT-Based Environments

Luit Verschuur[(✉)]

LIACS, Leiden University, Leiden, The Netherlands
Luit_ver@live.nl

Abstract. Today, our world is more connected than ever. One of the main drivers of this connection is the uprise of the Internet of Things (IoT). Associated with this rise, there are numerous challenges. One of the main challenges for IoT is to keep the environments that include IoT devices secure. IoT devices are different from traditional computer devices. Therefore, they need special treatment and guidance to be kept secure. This research identifies the limitations of current assessment frameworks to cover IoT-specific challenges. It discusses the possible assessment methods to assess these challenges. In addition, the potential solutions to secure these environments are listed. Afterward, the processes and guidelines that can be implemented are identified. All to generalize these findings into an overall applicable cybersecurity assessment framework for IoT-based environments. These steps are validated by existing research, existing cybersecurity frameworks, and interviews with cybersecurity experts. Together, these sources provide valid ground to guide IoT-based environments to improve security with the assistance of an assessment framework. This IoT assessment framework is the first of its kind and therefore valuable for all IoT-based environments. However, it still needs to improve to reach its full potential.

Keywords: Internet of Things (IoT) · IoT-based environments · IoT specific challenges · security and protection · assessment methods · cybersecurity assessment framework

1 Motivation

Today, our world is more connected than ever. This connection is continuously spurred by technological advancements. One of the main advancements in recent years was the upcoming of the Internet of Things (IoT). IoT has been called the trend of the next internet by Gokhale et al. (2018), due to the expected large role it will play in our lives. IoT is defined as a global cyber-physical network of interconnected embedded objects. Besides the positive possibilities of IoT, there are also downsides to this trend. The implementation of IoT comes with major challenges and concerns. The major challenge that Alkhalil and Ramadan (2017) identified, is that IoT encounters high security risks.

B. Hämmerli et al. (Eds.): CRITIS 2022, LNCS 13723, pp. 49–55, 2023.
https://doi.org/10.1007/978-3-031-35190-7_4

In more detail, there are millions of IoT devices in use that do not meet the existing security standards. Therefore, there is a need to properly secure IoT-based environments. As IoT has specific characteristics, it has to deal with other types of challenges than.traditional computing devices. This implies that the current assessment frameworks do not apply to IoT-based environments. Therefore, the research objective is to develop an IoT-specific assessment framework to secure IoT-based environments. This is relevant as there is no existing assessment framework focusing purely on the security of IoT-based environments. The main research question that will provide this framework is:

How to assess challenges and differences in the security of IoT-based environments, compared to the security of traditional computing devices?

The main research question treated in this article is divided into 5 subquestions. These are the following:

- **SQ1:** *What are the limitations of the available cybersecurity assessment frameworks for IoT-based environments?*
- **SQ2:** *How can risks in IoT-based environments be assessed?*
- **SQ3:** *What are potential solutions to minimize the risks in IoT-based environments?*
- **SQ4:** *What overall process or guidelines can be implemented to improve the security of IoT-based environments?*
- **SQ5:** *How can the IoT-based environment security be generalized into an overall applicable assessment framework?*

Together, the answers to these questions will provide the assessment framework with a substantial theoretical base. The answers to the first three subquestions are based on previous research. This contribution summarizes the main results, present the framework, and at the end proposed a contribution of that innovative used path.

2 Cybersecurity Assessment Frameworks Limitations IoT

Currently, cybersecurity assessment frameworks fail on two different levels. The first level is the framework itself. On this level, Dardick (2010) states that frameworks often fail to be comprehensive in what components are included and assessed. In addition, Leszczyna (2021) issues that a lot of frameworks fail to be applicable. The second level focuses on the IoT-specific challenges that are neglected. Karie et al. (2021) identified five major challenges for current IoT security frameworks. These five challenges are: technical-, legal-, ethical-, operational-, and adaptive. These challenges need to be covered by a new IoT cybersecurity assessment framework. This is the motivation of the contribution that will be developed in the next paragraph.

2.1   Assessing the Risks in IoT

The limitations that are identified in the previous section, need to be assessed in detail. On the framework level, comprehensiveness can be measured by the extensiveness of the framework. This can be validated by covering all important components. In addition, Eldh et al. (2006) created a method to test the applicability of a framework. On the IoT challenges level, the assessment of these challenges is similar to the assessment of traditional computing devices. However, the challenges that need to be accounted for are different. These challenges need to be identified. Afterward, these can be assessed in the same way as the current best practice. Currently, the best known and most used cybersecurity assessment framework is from NIST created by Barrett et al. (2018). In the following paragraph we refer to IoT-specific challenges.

2.2   Proposed Solutions to Minimize the Risks in IoT

The IoT-specific challenges also need to be solved. In research, two levels of security solutions are proposed. The first level is environment-based, Patel et al. (2016) designed a secure implementation of the architecture of IoT-based environments. The second level is device-based, which means that solutions secure the design of IoT devices. These solutions differ for every device and solve specific security challenges. In addition, cybersecurity will always be based as good as the best and latest developments.

Four key research areas that keep improving the security level in environments are encryption, authentication, blockchain, and intrusion detection systems. Furthermore, all additional implemented solutions provide an extra security layer. Therefore, it is desirable to implement a variety of solutions concerning different challenges. The framework should include these different solutions that are summarized in the following section.

3   Framework Integration: Research by Design

The approach has the objective to propose a new concepted assessment framework; Therefore, the necessary method was *research by design*. This implies that all the design choices are validated. As the assessment framework is the first of its kind, an *explorative research design* is chosen to keep possible implementations broad. In addition, the availability of cybersecurity and IoT experts is limited. Therefore, a *qualitative research method* is chosen to retrieve the full potential of the information gained from every expert. The method that is chosen to retrieve the information from the experts is *interviews*.

These interviews were all conducted with PwC employees. In this approach, 10 different experts are interviewed, who vary in expertise, role, experience, education, and country. Due to the variation in the country, the choice was made to conduct the interviews in a digital environment.

The data retrieved from the interviews are analyzed with the *grounded theory*. This interview analysis method is most excepted because it provides the most guidance to validly interpret the findings. The eight steps of this method are identified by Online (2009).

1. Identify the substantive area, area of interest
2. Collect data about the substantive area
3. Open code the data when it is collected
4. Write memos throughout the entire process
5. Conduct selective coding and theoretical sampling
6. Sort the memos and find the codes that can organize the codes the best
7. Read the literature and integrate the theory with the codes
8. Write up the theory

Within this method, there is chosen for *open coding* by the researcher as there was no independent researcher available. In addition, to maximize the relevance of the retrieved data, *intermediate labeling* is applied.

4 Framework Design

To design the framework based on the different results and discuss these results, the eight steps of the grounded theory are followed: The first step is discussed in the literature review section. The second, third (*open coding*), and fourth (*intermediate labeling*) step are discussed in the methodology section. Together, these four steps have conducted 550 codes. In step five these codes are cleaned, similar codes are combined and double codes are eliminated. This step decreased the number of codes to 238. Afterward, step six sorted these memos to the subquestion they were relevant to, and organized them into categories and subcategories. After this step, every subquestion got a list of relevant categories, subcategories, and concepts to discuss and integrate with the earlier retrieved theory. In the following subsections, the most remarkable results are discussed:

The currently most relevant assessment frameworks are NIST by Barrett et al. (2018), CIA by Fenrich (2008), and IEC by IEC (2022). In addition, the most relevant work in IoT security is done by ENISA by Gines et al. (2017), IoTSF by WG1 (2021), and IEC 62443 by IEC (2020). Together, the scope included in this research is the scope that these frameworks cover collectively. Furthermore, the five main challenges by Karie et al. (2021) are highlighted.

The importance of comprehensiveness, the five main challenges, and the applicability are verified. The comprehensiveness and applicability should be considered in the evaluation of the assessment framework.

The five main challenges (technical, legal, ethical, operational, and adaptive) should be included in the assessment framework to generate structure. All categories can be assessed by six elements:

1. environment assessment
2. risk assessment
3. security standards
4. management assessment
5. regulatory monitoring
6. maturity management

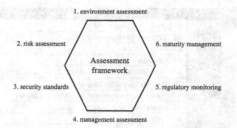

The range of solutions to improve the security of IoT-based environments is very broad. Most solutions that are retrieved from the literature and frameworks are verified by the interviewees. In addition, the solutions retrieved from the interviews are backed by research. Therefore, all the identified solutions could be included in the assessment framework.

The NIST cybersecurity framework by Barrett et al. (2018) will be used as the standard baseline. This baseline is complemented with the most important IoT solutions. These solutions can be found in the work of ENISA, IoTSF, and IEC 62443. In addition, solutions from research and retrieved data will be included to maximize the information in the assessment framework. In this framework, the six elements must be included.

The generated framework was able to include most of the desired characteristics of a new IoT assessment framework. However, the framework could not yet test the applicability of the assessment framework. In addition, the final assessment framework is not yet validated by experts. Furthermore, the regulatory challenge could not be solved. This framework does guide regulators to focus. However, is not able to solve the challenges. These limitations imply that the final assessment framework is not flawless yet. However, it does provide a lot of guidance for best practices in IoT-based environments. In addition, IoT security and its frameworks must be updated, as it is still a fast-changing field.

5   Optimization of the Framework

In this contribution, the theory is the final step of the optimization process of the assessment framework. The framework is based on the IoT challenges in NIST. In Fig. 1, the IoT challenges for the NIST framework categories are illustrated. In the core framework, also the solutions and best practices are provided to solve these challenges.

FUNCTION	CATEGORY	CHALLENGES
ID. IDENTIFY	AM. Asset Management	Technical, legal, ethical, operational, and adaptive
	BE. Business Environment	Technical and operational
	GV. Governance	Technical, legal, ethical, operational, and adaptive
	RA. Risk Assessment	Technical, legal, ethical, operational, and adaptive
	RM. Risk Management Strategy	Technical, legal, ethical, operational, and adaptive
	SC. Supply Chain Risk Management	Technical, legal, ethical, operational, and adaptive
PR. PREDICT	AC. Identity Management and Access Control	Technical, legal, ethical, operational, and adaptive
	AT. Awareness and Training	Technical, legal, ethical, operational, and adaptive
	DS. Data Security	Technical, legal, ethical, operational, and adaptive
	IP. Information Protection Processes and Procedures	Technical, legal, ethical, operational, and adaptive
	MA. Maintenance	Technical, legal, ethical, operational, and adaptive
	PT. Protective Technology	Technical, legal, ethical, and operational
DT. DETECT	AE. Anomalies and Events	Technical, operational, and adaptive
	CM. Security Continuous Monitoring	Technical, legal, ethical, and operational
	DP. Detection Processes	Technical
RS. RESPOND	RP. Response Planning	Technical, operational, and adaptive
	CO. Communications	Technical, operational, and adaptive
	AN. Analysis	Technical
	MI. Mitigation	Technical, operational, and adaptive
	IM. Improvements	Technical, operational, and adaptive
RC. RECOVER	RP. Recovery Planning	Technical
	IM. Improvements	Technical
	CO. Communications	Technical and legal

Fig. 1. IoT challenges related to the NIST categories

These solutions and best practices are based on literature. This literature can either have a challenge specific or have a more global focus.

6 Outlook

The generated assessment framework has a lot of advantages but also still faces limitations. However, the assessment framework is certainly adding value to the academic field of IoT security. Currently, the most important cybersecurity assessment frameworks fail to identify the five main IoT challenges (technical, legal, ethical, operational, and adaptive) by Karie et al. (2021).

In addition, the security standards have little focus on IoT-specific devices. The research and frameworks that do focus on IoT specifically are often only proposing single good practices but are not translated to assessment frameworks. This research translates good practices into an assessment framework for IoT-based environments and translates an IoT-specific assessment framework towards an IT, OT, and IoT converged cybersecurity assessment framework that can be applied to all environments that include embedded devices. Therefore, this contribution leads to new insights towards safer IoT-based environments.

Acknowledgements. The author acknowledges the generous support from the research internship agency PwC. In addition, the guidance offered by Nele Mentens and Stefan Pickl have made this research a success.

References

Alkhalil, A., Ramadan, R.A.: Io T data provenance implementation challenges. Procedia Comput. Sci. **109**, 1134–1139 (2017). 8th International Conference on Ambient Systems, Networks and Technologies, ANT-2017 and the 7th International Conference on Sustainable Energy Information Technology, SEIT 2017, 16–19 May 2017, Madeira, Portugal

Barrett, M.P., et al.: Framework for improving critical infrastructure cybersecurity version 1.1 (2018)

Dardick, G.S.: Cyber forensics assurance (2010)

Eldh, S., Hansson, H., Punnekkat, S., Pettersson, A., Sundmark, D.: A framework for comparing efficiency, effectiveness and applicability of software testing techniques. In: Testing: Academic and Industrial Conference-Practice And Research Techniques (TAIC PART'06), pp. 159–170. IEEE (2006)

Fenrich, K.: Securing your control system: the "CIA triad" is a widely used benchmark for evaluating information system security effectiveness. Power Eng. (Barrington, Ill.) **112**(2), 44 (2008)

Gines, A., Lorente, F., Perez, J., de la Torre, A., Babón, O.: Baseline security recommendations for Io T, November 2017

Gokhale, P., Bhat, O., Bhat, S.: Introduction to Io T. Int. Adv. Res. J. Sci. Eng. Technol. **5**(1), 41–44 (2018)

IEC: Quick start guide: an overview of ISA/IEC 62443 standards, ISA global cybersecurity alliance, June 2020

IEC: Information security, cybersecurity and privacy protection. Standard, International Organization for Standardization, Geneva, CH, February 2022

Karie, N.M., Sahri, N.M., Yang, W., Valli, C., Kebande, V.R.: A review of security standards and frameworks for Io T-based smart environments. IEEE Access **9**, 121975–121995 (2021)

Leszczyna, R.: Review of cybersecurity assessment methods: applicability perspective. Comput. Secur. **108**, 102376 (2021)

Online, G.T.: What is grounded theory? (2009). https://www.groundedtheoryonline.com/what-is-grounded-theory/. Accessed 16 Mar 2022

Patel, K.K., Patel, S.M., et al.: Internet of things Io T: definition, characteristics, architecture, enabling technologies, application & future challenges. Int. J. Eng. Sci. Comput. **6**(5) (2016)

WG1, I.S.: Io TSF Io T security assurance framework release 3.0 Nov 2021, November 2021

An Empirical Evaluation of CNC Machines in Industry 4.0 (Short Paper)

Marco Balduzzi[1(✉)], Francesco Sortino[2], Fabio Castello[2],
and Leandro Pierguidi[2]

[1] Trend Micro Inc., Sesto San Giovanni, Italy
marco_balduzzi@trendmicro.com
[2] Celada SpA., Cologno Monzese, Italy

Abstract. CNC machines are largely used in production plants and constitute a critical asset for organizations globally. The strong push dictated by the Industry 4.0 paradigm led to the introduction of technologies for the wide connectivity of industrial equipment. As a result, modern CNCs resemble more to fully fledged systems rather than mechanical machines, offering numerous networking services for smart connectivity. This work explores the risks associated with the strong technological development observed in the domain of CNC machines. We performed an empirical evaluation of four representative controller manufacturers, by analyzing the technologies introduced to satisfy the needs of the Industry 4.0 paradigm, and conducting a series of practical attacks against real-world CNC installations. Our findings revealed that malicious users could abuse of such technologies to conduct attacks like denial-of-service, damage, hijacking or data theft. We reported our findings to the affected controller vendors and proposed mitigation. This work wants to be an opportunity to raise awareness in a domain in which, unfortunately, security doesn't seem to be, yet, an important driver.

1 Introduction

The last decade has seen a surge in popularity in the adoption of network-enabled systems, including devices that historically were not offering such capabilities for several reasons. In the industrial world, for example, several kinds of such systems are largely used nowadays to support the manufacturing process in a smart, modern paradigm. The evolution observed on devices such as programmable logical controllers (PLCs), computer numerical controls (CNCs), industrial robots, automated guided vehicles (AGVs) applied to logistics etc., heads to models of interconnection, according to the general paradigm of the Industry 4.0, and is pushing manufacturing companies toward networked shop floors.

Although the need of connecting such modern machinery to wide networks, including the Internet, represents an important opportunity to create new business intelligence, for example to the collection and analysis of production data, it also opens the doors to potential threats impacting on security and privacy of organizations worldwide. This is further emphasized by reasons like: first, the heterogeneity of the technologies used in the industrial domain, with few standards available and far from being widely adopted yet; second, the lack of awareness in the domain, for example in adopting security best practices in the development or use of the machines; third, the lack of prior art showing in practice how such machines could be attacked; last, but not least, the strong push dictated by the market to rapidly reposition legacy machinery in form of modern, smart solutions.

Given these considerations, some previous research (even though very limited) looked into the risks connected with the introduction of the Industry 4.0. Quarta et al. [3] conducted a security analysis of an industrial robot. Maggi et al. [2] reported several practical issues related to smart manufacturing systems in general. Balduzzi et al. [1] looked at industrial gateways, i.e. gateways considered as IIoT equipment used in smart factories for enabling the communication between modern and legacy devices.

While these studied technologies are related to smart manufacturing, none of them deal with computer numerical controls. In this respect, we believe being the first to tackle this topic from a security standpoint. Modern CNCs consist of sophisticated machines that can be programmed with domain-specific languages and configured to operate autonomously in a fully-remote fashion, for example with networking frameworks and libraries made available by the vendors. The same machines can be extended in features by installing add-ons that act as software extensions, similarly to the mobile apps available on the app stores for download. These, and other domain-specific functionalities, make modern CNCs closer to fully fledged systems like an IT server rather than hardware-centric machines as it was to be. In fact, although under the hood they are still operating well-established automation routines, for example used to engrave raw material, they are ran by operating systems together with several layers of complicated software and technologies.

As security researchers, and given the complexity of this technological ecosystem, we believe there are wide possibilities for security abuses. For this reason, we conducted an assessment of the domain of CNC machines, by investigating CNCs offered by four representative vendors, in particular by focusing on the technological aspects needed to make such machines easy to be connected and operated remotely in a smart manufacturing environment.

The contributions of our work consist of: 1. We investigate the domain of CNC machines in term of security and privacy. To the best of our knowledge, we are the first to conduct a depth empirical analysis in this direction. 2. We identify four vendors as representative of this domain and conduct practical assessments on the technologies offered by their controllers. 3. We report security problems related to the abuse of such technologies that can result in attacks like denial-of-service, leak of sensitive information, hijack of the production, introduction of micro-defects, damage of machines and pieces, and safety. 4. We communicate our findings to the affected vendors in a responsible way, and do our best to raise awareness in this domain.

2   Evaluation

Our investigation began by identifying representative controller manufacturers, in particular manufacturers that: 1. are geographically distributed (i.e., with headquarters and subsidiaries spread across the world) and that resell on a global scale; 2. are on the market since decades already; 3. have a large estimated side, for example with a total a revenue topping a billion dollar; 4; use technologies widely adopted in the domain, and are present in different manufacturing sectors. In addition, we made sure that the manufacturers we identified offered controllers that we could use for our evaluation, i.e. either in form of simulators (i.e. a controller attached on simulated peripherals) or real machines.

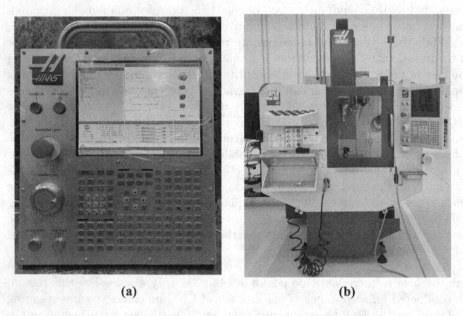

(a)   (b)

Fig. 1. (a) Example of simulator used for preliminary testing (b) Example of machine used for final testing

Table 1 provides a summary of the selected manufacturers together with the relative controllers we used in our research. For one vendor (Fanuc) we made use of two machines. Figure 1a provides an example of simulator we used in preliminary analysis of the controller, while Fig. 1b shows a machine employed for the final testing.

For all vendors, we conducted an equal evaluation of their machines – that we summarize in:

- We first identified the technologies adopted by the vendors to be "Industry 4.0 ready". This set of technologies consists of the interfaces (and related protocols) used to interconnect the machines so to serve in smart environments.

Table 1. Summary of the selected controller manufacturers and related CNC machines used in the research.

Vendor	Haas	Okuma	Heidenhain	Fanuc
Country	USA	Japan	Germany	Japan
Establishment	1983	1898	1889	1972
Estimated size	>$1B and 1,300 employees (2018)	$1.41B and 3,812 employees (2020)	$1.3B and 8,600 employees (2020)	$4.18B and 8,260 employees (2020)
Market	Controllers and machines	Controllers and machines	Controllers	Controllers and simple machines
Simulator	100.19.100.1123	OSP-P300S	TNC 640 v. 10.00.04	Not used
Controller	100.20.000.1110	P300MA-H	TNC 640	31iB5 iHMI and 32i-B
Machine	Super Mini Mill	GENOS M460V-5AX	HARTFORD 5A-65E	YASDA YMC 430+RT10 and STAR SR 32JII
Type	3-axis vertical machining center	5-axis vertical machining center	5-axis vertical machining center	5-axis vertical micro machining center and Swiss lathe

Table 2. Summary of the Industry 4.0 technologies adopted by the vendors.

Vendor	Default Technologies	Optional Technologies
Haas	MTConnect, Ethernet Q Commands	NaN
Okuma	NaN	THINC-API , MTConnect
Heidenhain	RPC and LSV2 (DNC)	OPC-UA
Fanuc	FOCAS	OPC-UA , MTConnect

These interfaces allow the machine to transmit outbound information to centralized systems such as production data for better management and cost reduction. They also enable remote management, for example for an operator to change the executed program or the configuration of the tooling in an easy way. A summary is provided in Table 2.

- We conducted a security assessment in a black-box fashion, which consisted of using automated vulnerability scanners like Nessus to identify potential known vulnerabilities or misconfigurations in the exposed services. Note that since the goal of our research is on domain specific technologies, we ignored all problems related to generic software like Windows services and moved forward looking for abuses in CNC interfaces.
- In this respect, we then went deep into the CNC-specific technologies previously identified, by analyzing the risks of abuses and conducting practical attacks on the controllers. For this, we developed attacking tools that leverage

the weaknesses we identified in the domain specific interfaces with the help of proprietary APIs we got access to.

– We collected evidence of our concerns and collaborated with the vendors suggesting mitigation. All evidence has been conducted on real world installations, but we also used the simulators for preliminary testing or when the machines were not available in the immediate.

We now give a short introduction on the domain specific technologies that we identified and discuss the related macro problems.

MTConnect is an effort to standardize the different protocols used in the industrial domain to collect machinery data like telemetry on production. The goal is indeed to provide guidelines for converting old and proprietary information to a common language. This will help organizations to handle machinery from different brands in an easier form. Along with our evaluation, we confirmed that 3 of the tested vendors support MTConnect, in particular Haas provides such feature on all default installations. In our analysis, we investigated the data that an attacker could reconstruct (or leak) from a machine exposing MTConnect over its network interface. A common scenario is, for example, the number of pieces that are produced, together with the associated program's name. In other cases, an attacker could infer the source code as well, making the attack very severe.

Proprietary protocols seem to be widely used in the CNC domain, in which manufacturers develop their own technologies for enabling their controllers to network. Some example of such protocols are Haas's Ethernet Q Commands, Heidenhain's RPC (also known as DNC/Option 18), or Fanuc's FOCAS. Unfortunately, our analysis reported major issues with these implementations: 1. authentication is rarely available, or not offered as default feature, which makes a malicious user able to log into the networking service and abuse it, 2. encryption is not adopted and data confidentiality is not guaranteed. Another important issue is the lack of authorization, making a malicious user able to tamper with privileged resources.

Okuma stands out from the market of the CNC controllers for one interesting feature: the modularity of the controller. In fact, while this vendor seems offering a controller with limited features, it instead provides a mechanism (called THINC-API) to highly customize a machine's functionalities. With this technology, any developer can implement a program that - once installed - runs in the context of the controller, in the form of add-on. From our analysis, it turned out that very simple security mechanisms that are nowadays very common on other platforms like mobile applications, for example resource control access, are not yet supported. As a result, if a miscreant manages to install a malicious application, she will be able to access all information stored internally in the controller, and - worse than that - to maliciously tamper with the behavior of the controller. The malicious application we developed for testing mimics a malware reaching out the attacker and waiting for commands to be prompted to the backdoored CNC.

Table 3. Summary of the attacks identified in our research.

Attack Class	Attack Name	Haas	Okuma	Heidenhain	Fanuc	Total
Compromise	RCE	y	y	y		3
Damage	Disable feed hold	y				1
	Disable single step	y		y		2
	Increase the tool life	y	y	y		3
	Increase the tool load	y	y		y	3
	Change of tool geometry	y	y	y	y	4
	Decrease the tool life	y	y	y		3
DoS	Decrease the tool load	y	y		y	3
	Change of tool geometry	y	y	y	y	4
	DoS via parametric program	y	y	y	y	4
	Trigger custom alarms	y		y		2
	Ransomware	y	y	y		3
Hijacking	Change of tool geometry	y	y	y	y	4
	Hijack of parametric program	y	y	y	y	4
	Program rewrite		y	y	y	3
Theft	Leakage of production information	y	y	y	y	4
	Leakage of program code		y	y	y	3
	Screenshot			y		1
	Total	15	14	15	10	

3 Findings

Overall, as depicted in Table 3, our evaluation identified 18 attacks (or attack variations[1]) that we grouped in 5 attack classes namely compromise, damage, denial-of-service, program hijacking, and theft.

Among the different controllers that we tested, we observed a consistency on the number of problems: Haas, Okuma and Heidenhain reported a similar amount of issues (15), with Fanuc confirming 10 attacks. This is a symptom that security doesn't seem to be yet a priority for controller manufacturers with our research showing that this domain lacks of awareness with respect to privacy and security. This, together with the possibility that CNC machines can be misconfigured or exposed to ·corporate networks (or to the Internet) creates serious and compelling problems.

When looking at the same table on a line basis, the scenario doesn't look better. Among all attacks, only two are confirmed to apply to a single vendor only

---

[1] Some attacks are reported multiple times because consisting of attack variations. For example, a malicious user can modify the geometry of a tool to achieve damage, hijacking, or denial-of-service - depending on the type of machine and manufacturing process.

Vice versa, the same user can conduct several attacks to achieve the same goal. For example, an attacker can take control of the production of an exposed CNC by hijacking a parametric program, by modifying the geometry of a tool to introduce a micro-defect, or by changing the executed program.

(i.e., disable feed hold and screenshot). Vice versa, 6 attacks are confirmed on all vendors. Features like the remote configuration of a tool's geometry, or the ability to influence the parameters of a program with values fetched remotely (via network) are needed when dealing with complex automation and unsupervised process. However, although these requirements are nowadays more common in manufacturing, vendors don't seem to take into account the unwanted consequences of these features, thus raising concerns about security.

In this work, we conducted an evaluation on the technologies introduced by representative controller manufacturers to adhere to the Industry 4.0 paradigm. We identified common problems across the different vendors, namely the possibility of abusing of such technologies to perform attacks like denial-of-service, damage, hijacking, and data theft.

We conducted real-world attacks against CNC machines and documented our findings in a full blown paper (currently under development) and with this one being a preliminary and shorter version. We reported our findings to the vendors, together with a discussion on the countermeasures that prevent our attacks to happen and will improve the current situation.

References

1. Balduzzi, M., Bongiorni, L., Flores, R., Lin, P., Perine, C., Vosseler, R.: Lost in translation: when industrial protocol translation goes wrong. Trend Micro (2020)
2. Maggi, F., et al.: Smart factory security: a case study on a modular smart manufacturing system. Procedia Comput. Sci. **180**, 666–675 (2021)
3. Quarta, D., Pogliani, M., Polino, M., Maggi, F., Zanchettin, A.M., Zanero, S.: An experimental security analysis of an industrial robot controller. In: 2017 IEEE Symposium on Security and Privacy (SP), pp. 268–286. IEEE (2017)

Dataset Report: LID-DS 2021

Martin Grimmer[✉], Tim Kaelble, Felix Nirsberger, Emmely Schulze,
Toni Rucks, Jörn Hoffmann, and Erhard Rahm

Leipzig University, Augustuspl. 10, 04109 Leipzig, Germany
{grimmer,kaelble,nirsberger,schulze,rucks,hoffmann,
rahm}@informatik.uni-leipzig.de

Abstract. To advance research on system call based HIDS, we present
LID-DS 2021, a recording framework, a dataset for comparative analysis,
and a library for evaluating HIDS algorithms.

1 Introduction

Unfortunately, attacks on IT systems are commonplace these days. To avoid
major damage, it is important to become aware of an ongoing attack as soon as
possible. Intrusion Detection Systems (IDSs) provide timely detection of attacks
on IT systems.

According to Debar et al. [4], IDSs are distinguished by the monitored platform and the attack detection method, among others. Network Intrusion Detection Systems (NIDS) use network interactions to monitor the behavior of possibly
multiple systems, while Host Based Intrusion Detection Systems (HIDSs) focus
on collecting data directly on the host. Though signature-based IDS can make
the detection for either NIDS or HIDS of known attacks transparent and comprehensible, they are incapable of detecting novel, previously unknown attacks.
Anomaly-based IDS open up the possibility of detecting these. Therefore new
methods for anomaly-based attack detection are being researched to keep up
with ever-changing developments by attackers. As more and more network communications take place in encrypted form, it is worth taking a closer look at
system call-based HIDS, as they can, among other things, directly monitor the
impact of those communications on the affected systems.

Modern datasets and comparable results are key factors for the progress of
HIDS research. Prior work has largely been based on inadequate datasets, which
have also been used in different (incomparable) ways. Some studies did not stick
to the partition of training, validation and test data given by the datasets. To
make it worse, some of them were not evaluated comparably to each other. For
example, by using different definitions of detection and false alarm rates. All
this leads to non-comparable results and hinders trustworthy scientific progress
in the field of anomaly-based HIDS.

1.1 Our Contribution

For these reasons, we present a new version of the **L**eipzig **I**ntrusion **D**etection
- **D**ata**S**et, the **LID-DS 2021** consisting of: an open source framework for

B. Hämmerli et al. (Eds.): CRITIS 2022, LNCS 13723, pp. 63–73, 2023.
https://doi.org/10.1007/978-3-031-35190-7_6

generating HIDS datasets, a modern and comprehensive system call dataset, including the implementation of all 15 of its scenarios and an open source library for evaluating and comparing HIDS algorithms on the given and other datasets. In doing so, we aim to contribute to the anomaly-based HIDS research not only a dataset but also guide other researchers to benefit from existing work and create comparable results in the future.

1.2   Paper Outline

The remainder of this paper is structured as follows: In Sect. 2, we address two questions: What makes a good HIDS dataset and what HIDS datasets are currently available? Then, we introduce the new LID-DS-2021 in Sect. 3. We will discuss bugs that we have fixed, how we generate better data in the new version and provide assistance in processing the data and in evaluating HIDS algorithms with the LID-DS-2021. In Sect. 4, we will compare the LID-DS-2021 with the other datasets presented in Sect. 2 and perform a simple baseline evaluation. In the final section, we summarize this paper and provide directions on which further research with the LID-DS can go.

2   Host Based Intrusion Detection Datasets

To answer the question "What makes a good HIDS dataset?" in this section, we will discuss what we believe to be important technical and then functional features. We will then present the HIDS datasets available so far and briefly refer to their content.

2.1   Preferred System Call HIDS Dataset Features

Technical Features
In our opinion, a HIDS dataset should meet the following technical characteristics to support the widest possible range of HIDS algorithms.

System Call Names: The basic information for system call based HIDS.

Arguments and Return Values: Different system calls have different parameters like quantity specifications such as the number of bytes to be written, identifiers such as file descriptors, strings for path specifications, flags, pointers to memory areas, read bytes, written bytes or error codes. As shown by Wagner and Paolo [15], so-called mimicry attacks can simulate the benignity of system call sequences but not of their arguments and return values. This is why these are not recognized by HIDSs which only analyze the sequences. Therefore this information should be taken into account by HIDS.

Thread Information and Process Ids: This information is important to avoid mixing data from different processes and threads running in parallel, as shown in the work of Pendleton et al. [13] and Grimmer et al. [6].

Timestamps: One should be able to reconstruct the exact sequence of system calls since most algorithms are based on this. In addition, timestamps of the system calls and their distances from each other can be useful features for anomaly detection. Timestamps can also be useful to model periodically occurring behavior. They should be as precise as possible.

User Ids: Invoking certain system calls is part of the normal behavior of a process and a corresponding user. The same system calls executed by the same process but another user may indicate an anomaly or an attack.

Data Buffers: This data may also contain important information. With them, it is even conceivable to learn models based on the unencrypted data transmitted e.g. via HTTPS. To what extent this is recommended and what significance it has for data security and privacy shall remain unanswered here. We are not aware of any previous use of the data buffers in a HIDS.

Network Data: Network data is an equally large and comprehensive data source from which much valuable information can be extracted. A HIDS dataset that also contains the host's network packets allows the development of hybrid IDS by combining system call and network data. In addition, a dataset containing both system calls and network packets allows the comparison of the performance of HIDS and NIDS approaches concerning a single host.

Resource Consumption: The resource consumption of a host can also be used to create a profile of the normal. A too-large or small consumption can indicate anomalies. Therefore, a dataset should also contain information about CPU, memory, network and storage usage.

Functional Features
In addition to the purely technical requirements, we believe the following more functional requirements for a HIDS dataset are just as important.

Real World Data: Ideally, a HIDS dataset contains real-world data. Any kind of simulated data is just simulated in the end. As the work of Arp et al. [1] states: This means that no matter how well prepared a laboratory-simulated dataset may be, it rarely can guarantee that the collected data sufficiently represents the true data distribution of the underlying security problem. But, real-world data also brings difficulties: What about the privacy of the data? Does it contain personal data? These are important points that must not go unnoticed.

Topicality: Software and operating systems change over time. That is why the dataset must represent up-to-date software and operating systems.

Complexity: The scenarios included in the dataset should vary in complexity to represent as many application areas as possible.

Labeled Attacks: The data for a HIDS dataset should be labeled as accurately as possible. Only then is it possible to automatically evaluate and confirm correct classifications, clustering, etc. Ideally, the labels are manually investigated to prevent label inaccuracy as described in [1]. Typically, HIDS datasets contain many recordings, each over a more or less short period of time. Accurate labels here also mean that within such a recording, a distinction is made between which part is normal and which is anomalous, i.e. contains an attack.

Availability: A dataset for development, evaluation, and research for HIDS is only useful if it is also available to as many researchers as possible. Therefore, there should be no barriers (e.g. a payment or login) to accessing the dataset.

Comprehensibility: To be able to explain possible observations in need of clarification in detail, it should be comprehensible how the data of a HIDS dataset was generated. Therefore, a HIDS dataset should publish its source code (as open source) with which it was created.

Expandability: Suppose a HIDS method requires more training, validation, or test data than provided in the dataset for a specific investigation. Ideally, it should be possible to extend a HIDS dataset with more examples of the existing scenarios or even add entirely new ones. In this way, potential gaps in the data can be filled in later.

Support in Processing the Data: To avoid errors or inaccuracies that would lead to incomparable results, a HIDS dataset should provide guidance on how to parse and load the data. Ideally, there are even ready-implemented data loaders that allow researchers to process the dataset without writing custom code to load the data.

2.2   HIDS Datasets

In the previous section, we discussed various technical and functional criteria for assessing HIDS datasets. Based on these criteria, we now want to assess existing system call based HIDS-datasets.

DARPA 1998 and DARPA 1999 Datasets: The DARPA Intrusion Detection Datasets from 1998 [10] and 1999 [11] consist among others of the Basic Security Module (BSM) part. It contains Solaris audit logs in the form of system call sequences, and provides arguments and return values, but no thread IDs. Also, no additional statistics about the system are included. With publication dates from 1998 and 1999, the datasets are also significantly too old to provide sufficient comparability with modern systems.

UNM Dataset: Another IDS dataset was released in 1999 by the University of New Mexico, called the UNM dataset. Just like the Darpa datasets, it is outdated. It has 9 scenarios, differentiated by normal and attack behavior. However, the records only consist of a sequence of process IDs and integer-coded system calls. Thus, neither arguments nor metadata are supplied. The UNM does deliver extensive descriptions of the scenarios but leaves the actual implementation of the recordings in closure and is therefore not expandable.

ADFA-LD: Even more, reduced in its data scope is the 2013 released ADFA-LD from the University of New South Wales (UNSW) in cooperation with the Australian Defense Force Academy (ADFA), which only consists of sequences of integer-coded system calls. Thus, system call parameters, processes and threads are fully ignored. Having only the system call identifiers it also lacks information about system statistics and the recorded software.

ADFA-WD: In 2014 Creech published the ADFA-WD [3], a Windows system call based HIDS dataset. It contains sequences of system calls and additional information such as Process names, PIDs and return values.

NGIDS-DS: Another UNSW cooperation with the ADFA had taken place in the year 2017. The NGIDS-DS contains thread information but lacks parameters and fine granular timestamps. Also, no information about the system resources is existent. Even though Haider et al. provided comprehensive specifications about the recording process of the dataset, the de facto implementation of the recording software is closed source.

AWSCTD: The Attack-Caused Windows OS System Calls Traces Dataset, is a Windows-based HIDS system call dataset published in 2018. Among other things, the paper of Čeponis and Goranin [2] mentioned the following goals of the dataset: Attacks should be publicly available to assure renewal and independent verification, should contain system call names, passed arguments, return values, changed files by attacks and the network traffic generated by attacks. However, the publicly available version[1] of the AWSCTD does not contain any of these data, but only simple system call integer sequences without any further parameters, return values or threads and so on.

LID-DS-2019: In 2019, the first version of the LID-DS [7,14] was released. Since we present a new dataset version in this paper, we name the old dataset LID-DS-2019 to distinguish it from LID-DS-2021, the new one. The publication of the LID-DS-2019 represented an attempt to overcome the problems of the previously described datasets. System calls were recorded with all their parameters, thread IDs, user IDs, payloads and fine granular timestamps. The dataset consists of several up-to-date attack scenarios that were comprehensively recorded and contrasted with benign data to deliver a reliable base for the evaluation of modern anomaly detection systems. Unfortunately, the implementation of the included scenarios had not been published.

3   The New LID-DS

Since we released the original LID-DS, we have been able to do a lot of interesting research with the data it contains. We have received feedback from other users of the dataset and have been able to learn from papers that use it as their data. However, in the process, we noticed a few inaccuracies, errors, and hurdles in the LID-DS-2019. In this section, we will list these and address how we fixed them in the new version of the framework, dataset and library.

---

[1] https://github.com/DjPasco/AWSCTD - date accessed: October 17, 2022.

3.1 Bugs

Attack Timing: Due to the method used to determine the attack timing, some of them were incorrect. In detail, this was because in LID-DS-2019 the time at which an attack was started on the attacker's system was used as the attack time of the label. Since some attacks in the dataset require a specific startup time, the corresponding effects on the victim can only be found later. In addition, in some rare cases, there are traces where an attack is expected according to the data record, but none occurs. The reason for this is that the attack, due to the large startup time, apparently did not start until after the end of the recording. To fix this problem, in an automatic post-processing step, we searched for the attacker's network packets in the pcap data, matched them with the victim's receiving system calls, and thus found the true start time of the attack on the victim's system.

Databuffer Encoding: The data buffers in LID-DS-2019 contained the first 80 bytes of all data buffers passed to system calls. This made it possible to analyze e.g. parts of SQL statements or other data. However, these data buffers could also contain non-printable byte values. All these values were encoded as "." (dot) in the records in LID-DS-2019. That's why in the new version the data buffers are encoded as base64 strings. In this way, we prevent potentially important information from being lost. Nevertheless, we maintain a human-readable encoding for the rest of the data.

3.2 Better Data

Distribution of User Actions: In the LID-DS-2019, almost all user behaviors had the same temporal distribution. This was modeled after the paper by Deng. [5] We changed this in the new version. Now user behavior is sampled from real-world web-server log files. Thus the scenarios are still not real-world data, but at least their access timestamps are generated from real-world data.

System Resources: Since the LID-DS-2019 did not contain information about consumed system resources, we have fixed this in the new version. We use Docker's built-in method to query (victim) container resource usage statistics to get them once per second. So for all its records, the LID-DS-2021 contains the following values once per second: CPU usage, memory usage, network received, network send, storage read and storage written.

Network Data: A HIDS that not only considers the behavior of the system to be monitored but also the communication of the system, can achieve better results. Therefore, in addition to the system calls and system resources, we also recorded the network communication to and from the victim in pcap format using tcpdump. This even allows HIDS and NIDS to be compared on the dataset in terms of their detection and error rates.

IP Range: In LID-DS-2019, the attacker and all normal users had the same IP because they were running as scripts on the recording host. As a result, all network communication took place only between the host that performed the recording and the victim. While this is not necessarily unrealistic, it is also not a standard use case. With LID-DS-2021, however, all users and the attacker are each running from their own Docker containers with their own IP addresses. As a result, there are no longer only connections to one other host in the data.

Multi Step Attacks: All scenarios of LID-DS-2019 have a perfect attacker, i.e. one who directly attacks the vulnerability without analyzing the system beforehand. In reality, this is usually not the case. Therefore, for the new version, we have also designed scenarios that include not only the attack itself, but also the steps of preparation and several exploited vulnerabilities.[2] For example, we describe scenario CVE-2017-12635_6[3] which implements vulnerabilities CVE-2017-12635 and CVE-2017-12636 in CouchDB up to version 1.7.0. In this scenario, the attacker performs several steps in succession that a real attacker could also perform. First, he performs a port scan using Nmap. Then, in an optional second step, he performs a brute-force attack using hydra in combination with the rockyou password list to log in to the database. In the next step, using CVE-2017-12635, a privilege escalation technique, the attacker changes the database user's privilege to give them administrator rights. Finally, a remote code execution occurs using CVE-2017-12636 to open a reverse shell. It is worth mentioning that each of these steps is labeled in the LID-DS-2021.

Source Code: With the original LID-DS, we released the recording framework as open source. This allowed new scenarios to be added to the dataset. However, it was not possible to create more recordings of existing scenarios with this, as the source code of the scenarios was not included. Therefore, in addition to the source code of the new framework, we also released the source codes of all 15 scenarios of the new dataset as open source. This makes it possible to create new scenarios, extend existing ones, and also perform in-depth analyses where the calling code from the attacker, normal user or victim is necessary.

3.3   LID-DS Library

Establishing the comparability of different research results is not an easy task. On the one hand, there are papers like [12] that do not adhere to the division of the data into training, validation and testing as specified in the datasets.

---

[2] A list of the LID-DS-2021 scenarios including their description, classification by simple/multi-step, and their source code can be found at https://github.com/LID-DS/LID-DS/wiki/Scenarios.

[3] Common Vulnerabilities and Exposures (CVE): a reference-method for publicly known information-security vulnerabilities and exposures. See: https://cve.mitre.org/.

On the other hand, not all studies use the same methodology to determine the performance metrics such as detection rate, false positives and so on. It happens that some works evaluate their algorithms for entire records as the work of Wunderlich et al. [16], although both normal and abnormal ranges can exist within a record as shown in the paper from Grimmer et al. [6]. As a consequence, results are not comparable even if they would use the same dataset. We have addressed this issue with the LID-DS-2021.

First, along with the dataset, we released a Python library that contains a data loader that can be used by researchers to load data from different HIDS datasets and encourages them to stick to the dataset division of training, validation and testing. At the moment, the following datasets are supported: ADFA-LD, LID-DS-2019, and LID-DS-2021 and it provides an easy-to-understand interface with functions like `training_data()`, `validation_data()` or `test_data()`. Second, in addition to the data loader, using a system of so-called building blocks, existing features and algorithms can be freely combined to build complex HIDS algorithms, as indicated in Fig. 1. A building block represents one step in a machine learning pipeline like extracting a feature from a system call, calculating an embedding, n-gram or an anomaly score using an autoencoder. On top, new features and algorithms can be added simply by implementing the existing interfaces. Thirdly, the full process starting with loading, feature extraction, anomaly detection to evaluation can be performed automatically using our library.[4] The method used in the paper by Grimmer et al. [6] for system call accurate evaluation is applied here.

4   Evaluation

We conduct an initial, simple evaluation of the LID-DS-2021 by comparing the dataset in tabular form with the other datasets presented in this paper. Then we will give information about its size and performance regarding a baseline algorithm.

As can be easily seen from Table 1, the LID-DS-2021 beats all other HIDS datasets in terms of the requirements we worked out before. The number of system calls and the average baseline performance over all scenarios using the STIDE algorithm [9] implemented with our library can be seen in Fig. 2. As the lower F-score, lower detection rate, and higher number of false alarms show, the 2021 version is slightly more difficult to solve with the base algorithm than the 2019 version. A code snippet for this baseline evaluation can be seen in Listing 1.1. The large amount of system call data including the mentioned system call attributes, network data and resource consumptions should allow many different types of HIDS to be developed and evaluated. From simple sequence-based

---

[4] Example code: https://github.com/LID-DS/LID-DS/wiki/ids_example.

Table 1. Datasets evaluated with respect to the presented criteria. Ratings: 0 = feature not included, 0.5 = feature partially included, 1 = feature included.

	DARPA	UNM	ADFA-LD	ADFA-WD	NGIDS-DS	AWSCTD	LID-DS-2019	LID-DS-2021
technical features								
system calls	1	0.5	0.5	1	1	0.5	1	1
arguments	1	0	0	0.5	0	0	1	1
thread info	0.5	0.5	0	0.5	0.5	0	1	1
timestamps	0.5	0	0	1	0.5	0	1	1
user ids	1	0	0	0	0	0	1	1
data buffers	0	0	0	0	0	0	0.5	1
network data	1	0	0	0	1	0	0	1
resource consumption	0	0	0	0	0	0	0	1
functional features								
real-world data	0	0	0	0	0	0	0	0
topicality	0	0	0	0	1	1	1	1
complexity	0	0	1	1	1	1	1	1
labeled attacks	0.5	0.5	0.5	0.5	1	0.5	1	1
availability	0	1	1	1	1	1	1	1
comprehensibility	0	0	0	0	0	0	1	1
expandability	0	0	0	0	0	0	0.5	1
support in processing	0	0	0	0	0	0	0	1
sum	5.5	2.5	3	5.5	7	4	11	15

algorithms over sophisticated ML methods to provenance-based graph solutions like Unicorn [8]. The LID-DS-2021 enables this and perhaps completely novel methods that take into account all the information contained in the dataset.

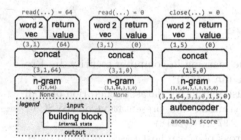

LID-DS-2019		LID-DS-2021	
Scenario	# Syscalls in million	Scenario	# Syscalls in million
CVE-2012-2122	5.7	CVE-2012-2122	20.7
CVE-2014-0160	4.0	CVE-2014-0160	1.9
CVE-2017-7529	1.8	CVE-2017-7529	1.3
		CVE-2017-12635_6	1311.7
CVE-2018-3760	19.2	CVE-2018-3760	115.1
CVE-2019-5418	18.0	CVE-2019-5418	400.9
		CVE-2020-9484	223.6
		CVE-2020-13942	849.1
		CVE-2020-23839	33.9
Bruteforce	5.7	Bruteforce	9.5
EPS_CWE-434	126.2	EPS_CWE-434	296.3
		Juice-Shop	484.9
PHP_CWE-434	22.2	PHP_CWE-434	97.5
SQL_Injection	23.6	SQL_Injection	96.2
ZipSlip	252.1	ZipSlip	111.1
F-score	0.63	F-score	0.57
detection rate	0.65	detection rate	0.59
avg. false alarms	19.80	avg. false alarms	24.47

Fig. 1. Example usage of Building Blocks (BBs): Input (from left to right) is a stream of system calls (read, read, close) including their return values. Here, the BBs are combined to create n-grams with $n = 3$ of embedded system calls and their return values, which are then input to an autoencoder for anomaly detection.

Fig. 2. Number of system calls in scenarios of the LID-DS and average results of the baseline algorithm STIDE over all scenarios, with $n = 7$ and $w = 100$.

```
1    # map each system call to an integer
2    int_embedding = IntEmbedding()
3    # build ngrams from these integers
4    ngram = Ngram([int_embedding], False, ngram_length=7)
5    # calculate the STIDE algorithm using these ngrams
6    stide = Stide(ngram)
7    # build a sum over a stream window of length 100
8    stream_sum = StreamSum(stide, window_length=100)
9    # use our IDS class for automatic evaluation
10   ids = IDS(... , resulting_building_block=stream_sum, ...)
11
```

Listing 1.1. Baseline HIDS Algorithm (STIDE) using LID-DS library

5   Summary

In this paper, we presented the LID-DS-2021. A recording framework, a dataset and a library for system-call-based HIDS. We have shown which alternatives are currently available and that these are not sufficient or have errors. We described how we fixed the bugs of the LID-DS in the new version and briefly touched on the new possibilities of the associated library. As a result, the LID-DS-2021 again takes research for system call-based HIDS a step further. The data, source code, examples and documentation of the LID-DS are available via GitHub[5].

Acknowledgement. This work was supported by the German Federal Ministry of Education and Research(BMBF, 01IS18026B) by funding the competence center for Big Data and AI "ScaDS.AI" Dresden/Leipzig.

References

1. Arp, D., et al.: Dos and don'ts of machine learning in computer security. In: Proceedings of the USENIX Security Symposium (2022)
2. Čeponis, D., Goranin, N.: Towards a robust method of dataset generation of malicious activity for anomaly-based HIDS training and presentation of AWSCTD dataset. Baltic J. Modern Comput. **6**(3), 217–234 (2018)
3. Creech, G.: Developing a high-accuracy cross platform host-based intrusion detection system capable of reliably detecting zero-day attacks, Ph. D. thesis, UNSW Sydney (2014)
4. Debar, H., Dacier, M., Wespi, A.: Towards a taxonomy of intrusion-detection systems. Comput. Netw. **31**(8), 805–822 (1999)
5. Deng, S.: Empirical model of www document arrivals at access link. In: Proceedings of ICC/SUPERCOMM1996-International Conference on Communications, vol. 3, pp. 1797–1802. IEEE (1996)
6. Grimmer, M., Kaelble, T., Rahm, E.: Improving host-based intrusion detection using thread information. In: Meng, W., Katsikas, S.K. (eds.) EISA 2021. CCIS, vol. 1403, pp. 159–177. Springer, Cham (2022). https://doi.org/10.1007/978-3-030-93956-4_10

---

[5] https://github.com/LID-DS/LID-DS.

7. Grimmer, M., Röhling, M.M., Kreusel, D., Ganz, S.: A modern and sophisticated host based intrusion detection data set. IT-Sicherheit als Voraussetzung für eine erfolgreiche Digitalisierung, pp. 135–145 (2019)
8. Han, X., Pasquier, T., Bates, A., Mickens, J., Seltzer, M.: Unicorn: runtime provenance-based detector for advanced persistent threats. arXiv preprint arXiv:2001.01525 (2020)
9. Hofmeyr, S.A., Forrest, S., Somayaji, A.: Intrusion detection using sequences of system calls. J. Comput. Secur. **6**(3), 151–180 (1998)
10. MIT Lincoln Laboratory: 1998 darpa intrusion detection evaluation data set. https://www.ll.mit.edu/r-d/datasets/1998-darpa-intrusion-detection-evaluation-dataset (1998). Accessed 10 Mar 2022
11. MIT Lincoln Laboratory: 1999 darpa intrusion detection evaluation data set. https://www.ll.mit.edu/r-d/datasets/1999-darpa-intrusion-detection-evaluation-dataset (1998). Accessed 10 Mar 2022
12. Park, D., Kim, S., Kwon, H., Shin, D., Shin, D.: Host-based intrusion detection model using Siamese network. IEEE Access **9**, 76614–76623 (2021)
13. Pendleton, M., Xu, S.: A dataset generator for next generation system call host intrusion detection systems. In: MILCOM 2017–2017 IEEE Military Communications Conference (MILCOM), pp. 231–236. IEEE (2017)
14. Röhling, M.M., Grimmer, M., Kreubel, D., Hoffmann, J., Franczyk, B.: Standardized container virtualization approach for collecting host intrusion detection data. In: 2019 Federated Conference on Computer Science and Information Systems (FedCSIS), pp. 459–463. IEEE (2019)
15. Wagner, D., Soto, P.: Mimicry attacks on host-based intrusion detection systems. In: Proceedings of the 9th ACM Conference on Computer and Communications Security, pp. 255–264 (2002)
16. Wunderlich, S., Ring, M., Landes, D., Hotho, A.: Comparison of system call representations for intrusion detection. In: Martínez Álvarez, F., Troncoso Lora, A., Sáez Muñoz, J.A., Quintián, H., Corchado, E. (eds.) CISIS/ICEUTE -2019. AISC, vol. 951, pp. 14–24. Springer, Cham (2020). https://doi.org/10.1007/978-3-030-20005-3_2

Analytics, Strategic Management

Strategic Anticipation in Crisis Management Through the Lens of Societal Values
The SANCTUM Project

Agnès Voisard[1], Christian Després[2(✉)], and Jean-Louis Olié[3]

[1] Freie Universität Berlin, Fraunhofer FOKUS, Berlin, Germany
agnes.voisard@fu-berlin.de
[2] Ministry for an Ecological Transition, Paris, France
christian.despres@developpement-durable.gouv.fr
[3] Paris, France

Abstract. The SANCTUM project - Crisis Anticipation by Uchronic Modeling Process - was defined in order to support decision makers who lack the required tools to make a rational decision. A "rational decision", as used here, is one that is free of subjective considerations of all kinds (be it cultural, based on cognitive biases or other influences) likely to skew the analytical process and sap decision. SANCTUM provides over time the tools required to strengthen the predictive capabilities of crisis centers via a specific methodology and the modeling of predictable situations, referred to as "uchronia" (Neologism based on the prefix "u"-, already used by "utopia" and the Greek word "chronos". For this term, we attribute the meaning of alternative history based on a total rationality.) (i.e., alternate scenarios). It is not oriented toward tactical decisions entailing the operational implementation of crisis management measures but rather towards providing a common and previously agreed upon strategic framework for tactical decision making. The SANCTUM approach has been tested during the first waves of COVID 19. This paper presents the main concepts of our project.

Keywords: Crisis anticipation · governance · cascading effects · scenarios · decision-making

1 Introduction

Traditional crisis management methods usually consider the crisis management system to be implicit, where the crisis framework is assumed to be the usual (or everyday) environment, with the priority given to the search for the appropriate measures to contain and then make the crisis recede as soon as possible.

This is the "Common Operational Picture" describing the situation at a specific moment in time t, which, as (Wybo and Latiers, 2006 [14]) point out, is difficult to construct, even in a crisis management center.

Beyond the different perceptions of the players concerned by the crisis (i.e., decision-makers, victims, rescue personnel, public opinion), intervention speed is almost systematically viewed as the qualitative crisis management factor.

© The Author(s), under exclusive license to Springer Nature Switzerland AG 2023
B. Hämmerli et al. (Eds.): CRITIS 2022, LNCS 13723, pp. 77–92, 2023.
https://doi.org/10.1007/978-3-031-35190-7_7

However, with hindsight, while intervention speed is fully vindicated in terms of tactics, the move to the strategic level may require a substantial contextualizing effort. This is why SANCTUM - Crisis Anticipation by Uchronic Modeling Process - endeavors to introduce a preliminary phase in crisis analysis, which consists of making explicit the fundamentals of the human environment called into question by the crisis. This clarification – in the case of a major crisis – must go beyond the analysis of the crisis's functional consequences on economic and social life, which is usually confined to ensuring business continuity, even under deteriorated conditions, and must not avoid ethical issues.

This clarification is required because any major disaster in one location may have domino effects in many other locations, as described in Voisard and Petrie, 2019 [12]. Each of these follow-on emergencies will be responded to by local authorities. This occurs, for example, during inter-sectoral or systemic crises, with domino effects affecting separately or simultaneously various matters of concern to society (e.g., health, energy, transportation, housing, economy, education, or public order). In France, these responses will be conducted at the territorial level such as the Operational Centers of French prefectures or local administrations. In France, the Inter-ministerial Crisis Center - in French: Cellule Internationale de Crise (CIC) - is responsible for coordinating this level of crisis management.

But how are limited national resources to be allocated? How are the territorial resources to be coordinated? It is not enough to try to pre-plan all of these possibilities, and it is not feasible to preempt local decisions about emergency tactics. Rather SANCTUM provides a common framework for working through a disaster, before and during.

The added value of SANCTUM comes to bear in times of complex crises during which severe challenges - national crises - necessarily require prioritization because of domino effects of the initial crisis and the need for coordination of responses by distributed authorities. SANCTUM addresses prioritization by providing a rational framework on which all parties can agree prior to a disaster, so as to minimize fighting for resources. A major contribution of the SANCTUM framework is to abstract what emergency responses are trying to do in all cases, and to realize that prioritization of responses must be based on cultural values. How are these values to be adjudicated during the emergency?

The SANCTUM framework provides a common process for questioning the overall meaning that the concerned human society intends to give to its existence and future and by what means of intervention and representation it can express this meaning. This allows the crisis responders to set the priorities necessitated by the scarcity of resources specific to any crisis situation and to implement the decision-making processes (Cf. (Anderson, 2010 [1]). SANCTUM also proposes an adjudication process that does not depend upon local political decisions but rather shared cultural values decided at the tactical case level by designated people in various roles. Politicians will still ultimately be in charge but their options will be well informed and transparent and the consequences of their decisions will be known by all affected parties.

Finally, the SANCTUM abstract framework of general crisis management is so well-defined as to be almost mathematical. This has two advantages. One is that ambiguity will be minimized among the participants, facilitating common understanding and cooperation. The other is that this framework can more easily be translated into various kinds of computer systems that can automate at least some of the planning and reinforce human decision-making.

This approach, which constitutes the SANCTUM project's basic substance, offers a highly instructive analysis grid of measures taken throughout the Covid-19 crisis.

Part of this work has been published as reports of the project (Després, 2019 [3]; Fertier et al., 2019 [4]; November and Gueben-Veniere, 2019 [7]; Olié J.-L., 2019 [9]; Voisard and Petrie, 2019 [12]) or at international conferences (November et al., 2020 [7]; Petrie and Voisard, 2019 [13]), however, an overall description of the novelty of the approach has not been published so far.

This paper is organized as follows. Section 2 provides the fundamentals of the system that we propose. Section 3 defines our notion of "goal" and crisis as well as "oracles" to control the overall process. Moreover, the SANCTUM mechanism is described. Section 4 presents the concepts of progress loops and uchronias (alternative scenarios). Finally, Sect. 5 draws our conclusion.

2 The Fundamentals of the Proposed Method

The organization or agency impacted by the crisis will naturally seek to place itself in a defensive situation. It will thus adopt a defensive posture in order to mitigate the observed vulnerabilities. This posture necessarily includes constraints that are themselves sources of new vulnerabilities. In other words, the management of a crisis - initially exogenous - engenders another crisis, but this time endogenous.

Recent events provide us an example of this type of situation. Leaders responded to the pandemic (exogenous) by mandating strict lockdown measures (endogenous), which generated a diversity of concerns the dimensions of which are hard to gauge. Lacking comprehensive control of the crisis's effects and the counter-effects of the response measures, crisis management can turn out to be, at minimum, inefficient and, at worst, it may aggravate the problem.

The response proposed by SANCTUM consists of defining an automated crisis management system, which seeks to describe as completely as possible the fundamentals of the defending organization, which are presented thereafter.

2.1 Defending Organizations

We consider the following defending organizations:

- the **system** is the human, physical, legal, and technological framework in which crisis unfolds. It brings together the defending organization and its organization;
- the **values** are definitions, essentially moral, which create public popular support at the time of the crisis (Schwartz, Shalom H., 2006 [10]) bear in mind that said values, by nature highly stable, are nonetheless designed by the automated crisis management system as likely to evolve; they will thus be configurable in our modelling;
- the **governance** is made up of the bodies (institutions) that ensure the system's continuity in accordance with its values (Galam, S., 2012 [5]);

- the **supporting assets** are the material or intangible means that enable the system to continue functioning on an ongoing basis (e.g., economic and social infrastructures) or which support governance (e.g., public services);
- the **players** are the specific or specialized human resources who develop or operate the assets; they intervene, either on the governance level or with their own strategy, which may not entail cooperation;
- the **stakes** are the vital functions which are essential to ensure the system's sustainability. The fulfilment of these functions established the conditions for the constitution of the assets and the organization of the players (e.g., housing, heating, healthcare, education). The term "impact(s)" means the total or partial loss of mentioned vital functions (or stakes) following an event in which support assets are damaged.

In the final analysis, the SANCTUM automated crisis management system brings forward a coherent interlocking of its constituents, highlighting the key notion of stake. The calling into question of the stakes is what triggers a crisis. It is not the attack on the supporting assets, the value of which fluctuating over time (for instance, in 1940, the Maginot line was a major asset, but the issue was national defense).

2.2 The Concept of Goal and a Practical Definition of the Crisis Concept

So far, we used the term "crisis" without defining it, since, in our crisis management system, this concept's definition is not established early in the decision process – as a sort of intrinsic dysfunction that only gets worse causing organizations to become overwhelmed – but later as a systemic deduction stemming from the analysis of the impacted organization (Lagadec, P., 2008 [6]).

We have made a static description of our automated crisis management system. In reality, the system that it supports is in perpetual motion to ensure, among other things, its continuity. This self-sustaining dynamic enables it to attain the **goals** necessary for its development, because, as we have seen, we exclude that the defending organization remain in a vegetative or go into a regressive state.

These goals must concretely reflect the search for maximum value satisfaction. They constitute the roadmap for governance. Once the crisis breaks out, they become the stakes to be safeguarded. The stakes themselves are a function of the supporting assets and conditioned by the interaction of the players. The goals to be determined are thus a function of the time concerned (health, education and material well-being), but their intrinsic consistence must be considered constant (Massimi and Tononi, G., 2018 [11]).

The following is a case in point. If the goal is the quality of human development, one stake is education whilst the supporting assets are the locations where education takes place, and the players are those who promote or hinder education. The crisis, in the context proposed by SANCTUM, may then be seen as a disturbing phenomenon of the crisis management system that could call into question its goals.

The advantage of this definition, compared to the traditional, more qualitative ones referring more to the impairment of an equilibrium[1], is that it is somewhat measurable

---

[1] "Situation in which a system suffers disruptions that cannot be accounted for by the usual mechanism or regulatory processes", common definition.

(the state of crisis could be the gap between the situation and the goal) therefore suitable for modelling.

2.3 Practical Examples of the Anticipation Process

Table 1 shows two simplified examples of SANCTUM's anticipation process: one entailing probabilistic risk and the other, a terrorist threat.

Table 1. Two examples of the anticipation process

	Seismic risk	Terrorist threat
System in defense mode	A territorial district with its population	A country coming out of a civil war tries to begin reconstruction in the face of persistent political instability
Values and governance	A democratically elected government mandated to implement an economic, social and environment program	Power is held by the liberation army, which, above all, seeks to restore internal security
Goal	Among program points: improve quantity and quality of drinking water and sanitation	Put an end to terrorist acts carried out by small groups opposed to the restoration of order in the country
Danger	Part of the population lives in the seismic zone	Persistent insecurity hinders the government's effort to attract investors
Definition of the state of crisis	Significant deterioration in the quality and quantity of drinking water and sanitation	Deterioration in popular and investor sentiment regarding security
Stakes	Supply of drinking water Wastewater treatment	Lacking investment, the population's living condition remain poor, and authorities lose support
Players	Local population using water Population living near wastewater discharge sites	Investors and public service providers
Supporting Assets	Drinking water treatment plant Wastewater reprocessing plant	Public utility companies

3 Control Process of the Automated Crisis Management System

The automated crisis management system's development must be carried out in a controlled way to ensure its convergence towards uchronia, which will become the object of a decision proposal. We must exclude the fact that there is no solution found because decision-makers cannot avoid making a decision. In this section, we present the notion of oracles as well as the five stages of the SANCTUM approach, i.e., the kernel of our methodology.

3.1 Oracles

What we refer to as the Oracles intervene on the automated crisis management system's dynamic. We distinguish between four different types of oracles:

- the **Wise men**, who control the values-linked choices. These choices require compromises (e.g., risk acceptability thresholds). They can amend the governance rule to be established, if need be;
- the **Judges**, who apply the rules validated by the sages to estimate the impact and exposure levels and issue verdicts at this level;
- the **Analysts**, who determine, in the most quantitative way possible, the issues, the vulnerability of assets, the search for actions and inventory of available resources;
- the **Spin doctors** (communicators and influencers), who define the influence measures to be performed in the defending organization or vis-à-vis players;

The oracles, by virtue of their expertise, focus on carrying out corrective measures in their respective fields of competence in accordance with the automated crisis management system's values and the rules set forth by the Judges.

3.2 Stages in the SANCTUM Process

Let us imagine ourselves in the anticipatory operating conditions of a crisis situation.

The **first step** consists of identifying our automated crisis management system, notably, how the crisis is deemed to call into question the goals of the defending organization, undermine its values and handicap its governance.

The **second step**, which is meant to be more concrete, consists of identifying the stakes the impairment or destruction of which is likely to call into question the automated crisis management system's goals. The results will allow us to deduce the list of supporting assets and players concerned by said stakes.

During the **third step**, SANCTUM gives way to classic risk analysis.

As seen in Fig. 1, the high-stakes assets may be undermined by the vagaries of (1) probabilistic occurrence (hazards) and/or (2) determinist threats (malevolent).

In the first case (hazards), the asset's exposure level L is:

$$L = \text{Probability} * \text{Destructive force}$$

In the second case (malevolent threat), it is:

$$L = \text{Feasibility} * \text{Attractiveness}$$

RISKS GENERATION

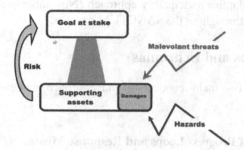

Fig. 1. Risk generation

In both cases, the impact I is the measure of harm, i.e., the damage to one or more of the system's vital functions or stakes: loss of human life, production loss or decrease in activity, and so on.

Conventionally, risk R is expressed as follows:

$$R = L \times I$$

We can thus build a risk diagram on which we can locate each supporting asset according to its L and I coordinates. It is displayed on Fig. 2.

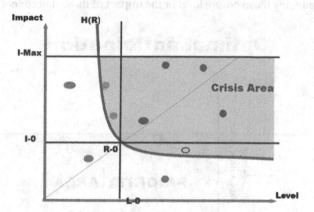

Fig. 2. Risk diagram

The locus of the constant product of L × I is a hyperbola whose positioning on the plane depends on the value R-0 set to R. This determination is fundamental because, by delineating the "crisis area" on the bi-dimensional risk space, it attributes a level of severity to the crisis. The oracles attribute this value of R-0 and factor in the defending organization's admissible level of suffering, its societal effects, the scientific and technological response capacities, etc.

We should keep in mind that, at this stage, this risk analysis is based on information "with a finite useful lifespan", which is equivalent to the time during which the data is deemed "stable" (Wybo, 2013 [15]). The crisis management time is a structuring item of the dynamic and adaptive anticipatory approach (November et al. [7]), which must be taken into account throughout the SANCTUM process.

4 Progress Loops and Uchronias

This section presents two major concepts of our approach, namely concept loops and uchronias.

4.1 The Concepts of Progress Loops and Response Measures

SANCTUM's "progress loop" is set to undergo digital modelling. It takes as a starting point the risk mapping the creation of which was described in Sect. 3. This mapping may be viewed as the conceptual projection of the crisis situation. In what follows, we assume that the supporting assets and players have their own temporal dynamics, the determinants of which can be known and modelled.

This modelling may initially be basic (e.g., linear changes as a function of time) or more complex (e.g., group or individual modelling of behavior to any laws of evolution). This complexity can today and, a fortiori, in the future, be taken on thanks to progress in the field of AI and possible learning from Big Data (Bénaben et al., 2008 [2]).

The next step in the SANCTUM process (Step 4) thus consists of performing risk reduction work by extracting a certain number of major supporting assets in the area at-risk and by reducing the exposure level or the impact of those that cannot be extracted.

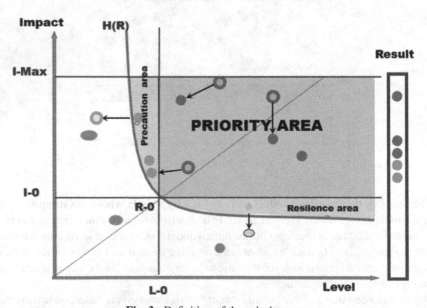

Fig. 3. Definition of the priority area

Figure 3 shows the area we should concentrate on, the priority area. It leads to the notions of mitigations and opportunities. These two types of measures consist of protecting the stakes:

- by reducing the risks via measures on the level of the impact and exposure level of supporting assets or players;
- by proposing new solutions when the risk-reduction measures are not successful in preventing risk materialization.

Mitigations consist of triggering a change in the system so as to reduce the level of risk, but by only intervening on factors currently known by the system. We may speak of endogenous evolution.

Opportunities assume the intervention of an outside factor, the effects of which are likely to reduce the risk level. It may be predictable, but this evolution is initially weighted by a low probability or unanticipated risk level. It may seek to adjust to the consequences of the destruction suffered to make acceptable another form of system organization.

The difference in nature between these two types of measures may be illustrated by the management of a power output crisis during exceptionally cold weather. Mitigations may be measures to protect generators so as to minimize production loss. On the other hand, higher-than-expected temperatures could constitute an opportunity to restructure the power transmission organization and eliminate weaknesses stemming from certain facilities.

4.2 Concept of Uchronia

The "progress loop" is a recursive phenomenon where the system re-assesses the overall situation and tests the crisis exit at the end of each loop.

The crisis exit is fundamentally decided by governance, but the latter intervenes in the final stages. The Sages, intervening in the early stages, assess quantitatively the convergence toward the desired goals.

Convergence is measured by comparing the changes in the indicators stemming from the adjustments (mitigations and opportunities) to the projected changes and by performing a projection of said changes over time. The system also draws from the measures taken to strengthen its self-learning and maximize the configuration of the progress loop, if the latter needs to be relaunched.

The oracles carry out these functions on the operational level:

- the Wise men, who assess the extent of the damage suffered and the gap to be closed in order to meet the goals and the time needed to return to "peace mode";
- the Analysts, who use the data produced and set forth the efforts to be asked of the players or the assets.

If the model converges, it will be able to produce crisis exit scenarios. To "scenario", we prefer the term "uchronia", deemed to be devoid of any subjective bias.

If the model does not converge, the Wise men must recalibrate the crisis, who establish a new value R-0. The progress loop is then relaunched, with fewer resolutory constraints, which assumes a heavier weight of the automated crisis management system (level of suffering or economic or social costs on the rise).

The progress loop ends up converging and the model provides us three scenarios:

- the worst case,
- the likely case,
- the optimal case.

Figure 4 shows the hyperbole of risk threshold together with the three types of scenarios mentioned above.

The worst-case scenario may be defined as the accumulation of the impacts, if all the risks in the priority zone and those selected in the priority area materialize.

The likely scenario may be defined as the accumulation of the impacts, if all the risks in the priority area and those selected in the resilience zone materialize.

The optimal scenario may be defined as the list of residual impacts, if all the risks remaining in the priority area and those remaining and selected in the resilience margin zone materialize.

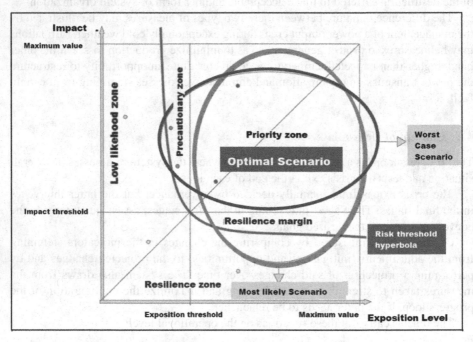

Fig. 4. Risk mapping and representation of alternate scenarios

4.3   Summary: The Five Steps of the SANCTUM Approach

Below are the five steps of our approach before taking a decision.

Preliminary Step
Definition of the role, responsibilities, and relationships of the anticipation cell's participants.

Note that the mobilization of common intelligence requires maximum fluidity in exchanges. The participants must perfectly understand their place in the system and identify the roles of the other participants. Relationship quality and efficiency are key to the success of the cell's work.

Step 1: Stakes and the Crisis Management System
Sharing of thoughts among participants about the situation.
> Identification of the stakes.
> Qualification of the crisis management system (i.e., values, governance, goal at stake).

Step 2: Analysis of Stakes
Further analysis of the stakes (e.g., public order, health, education, energy, transportation, or economic performance).
> Identification of the assets and players concerned by these stakes.

Step 3: Risk Analysis
Conventional analysis of risks to which the assets at-stake are exposed;
> Risk = level of (asset's) exposure * impact sustained
> Note that the exposure level depends on the risk type (deterministic or probabilistic).
> Preparation of crises map showing the "crisis area".

Step 4: Treatment of the Crisis Area
Preparation of measures allowing for the reduction of the crisis area by using the assets:

- by mitigation (internal actions in the system in crisis);
- by taking advantage of opportunities (external actions).

The implementation of mentioned measures and the projection of their effects enabling the emergence of evolving "alternate scenarios" (objectified scenarios).

Step 5: Description of the Evolving Alternate Scenarios
Understanding of the anticipated with the following three alternate scenarios:

- the worst case (maximum impact);
- the likely case (maximum exposure level);
- the optimal case (maximization of the mitigation measures and opportunities).

Conclusion: Decision-Taking
The authority makes crisis-management decisions based on the description of alternate scenarios.

5 Conclusion

In this paper, we described the main concepts on which SANCTUM relies: the defending organizations, the notion of goal, oracles, as well as the stages in the SANCTUM overall process.

Even though it has been tested in real situations, SANCTUM remains a conceptual project for the time being, but one that lays the groundwork for a new crisis management approach, the need for which has become particularly apparent in the course of the Covid-19 pandemic. Its purpose is to show that, in spite of the complexity of organizations, all the functions of an automated crisis management system can be analyzed as a flow of iterative processes controlled through a "progress loop", which benefits from a self-learning system using artificial intelligence-specific resources to assess and improve performances.

SANCTUM's innovation consists in proposing a comprehensive breakdown of the automated crisis management system in which the crisis unfolds by considering from the outset, for example, that the values of the society affected by it are configurable and that the decision-making processes can be rendered perfectly objective by bypassing humans in favor of the Oracles.

This resolutely rational approach does not dehumanize the crisis management because, by endeavoring to remove the human from the cogs of crisis management – where s/he can be as disruptive as s/he is productive – it leaves the human the key role of final decision-makers, but with the essential predictive tools, alternate scenarios – uchronias - at their disposal.

The SANCTUM approach has been tested during the first waves of the COVID-19 crisis, as shown in the appendix.

Acknowledgements. The authors wish to thank the French ministry for an ecological transition and the French High Council for Strategical Building and Research (CSFRS).

Appendix: SANCTUM and the Covid-19 Pandemic in France

The purpose of this appendix is to provide a general illustration of SANCTUM's analytical system, previously described from a theoretical standpoint, in light of an overall review of the management of the Covid-19 crisis in France.

Notwithstanding the impressive number of its victims, this pandemic, which has affected the quasi-totality of humanity in 2020 and 2021, amounts to an exceptional benchmarking tool for testing the SANCTUM system's consistency and potential added value.

Conversely, the absence of a coherent model to describe the situation can largely explain the various controversies that have arisen during the management of this pandemic, including the restrictions and, especially, the lockdown justifications.

The comments we have collected from crisis managers in "classic" mode[2] can illustrate this situation. In response to our questions about the determinants of the Covid-19

---

[2] As opposed to SANCTUM mode.

crisis, they first cite the problems with the hospital response, in particular, the lack of material and human resources in intensive care.

From the perspective of SANCTUM's analytical model, this vision is narrow in that it had the effect of circumscribing the analysis to the healthcare sector and, thus, limiting the scope of decision-making. One of the visible effects was the alteration of the country's governance. The traditional institutions – which, it is worth recalling, are the legal institutions – found themselves vying with an institution, the Scientific Council.

Governance

Without going farther into the matter, much less engaging in a political discussion, the introduction of a derogatory governance mode in the midst of the crisis raises an issue. This question is characteristic of SANCTUM's analytical contribution: are we sure of the governance model we have designated to navigate the crisis? Let's consider what actually happened.

The government's traditional crisis management bodies assumed control of the Covid crisis in early March: initially, by an Interministerial task force within the "leading" ministry" i.e., that in charge of health matters, which evolved, in accordance with the government's directives, into the Interministerial Crisis Unit within the Ministry of Interior.

The jurisdiction of government bodies was thus respected. In fact, a parallel governance was set up with the emergence of an "Interministerial crisis unit bis" headed by the prime minister. In parallel, "Scientific Council" rose in importance, which, given the importance of its decisions, became a sort of core government health advisory.

The purpose of the SANCTUM model is, of course, not to call into question this special organization, but it must be cognizant of its real powers and acknowledge that the relevant institutions no longer exercised effective governance of the crisis. The integration of this change in the decision-making process is essential for the management of the crisis.

Values

SANCTUM considers that, like in the case of governance, the automated crisis management system's values can evolve. In this regard, the French president's now famous quote "whatever the cost" is far from being trivial. On first reading, one has the impression that he views the value system as intangible. After a second look, it seems like an unrealistic assertion; it introduces the "wolf", which is the cost of the measures to be taken, into the sheepfold of values.

This context presents the following question for SANCTUM: what are the actual values of the automated crisis management system applicable to the pandemic?

The "whatever the cost" may be considered as the constant line of conduct of governance in just about all crises (excluding wars, which fall outside the scope of our analysis). There have been a number of situations where considerable human and technical means (sometimes seemingly disproportionate) have been deployed to save a handful of individuals whose lives were not necessarily at risk!

With the implied "hope of lives saved"/"risk of lives put at risk" ratio always being above 1 ab initio, the question of values did not seem to exist.

The pandemic has reshuffled the cards on the quantitative level. This is nothing new, since the treatment of epidemics has throughout history given rise to measures that, from a distance, seem cruel. But crises of such magnitude have slipped from memory. Even memories of the Spanish flu epidemic of 1918–1920 were largely eclipsed by the trauma of the first world war.

The harsh lockdown measures inflicted on France from 17 March 2020 gradually brought to the surface this forgotten question of the variability of values. The confrontation sharpened as the days passed between the values relating to health security, basic freedoms, essential economic and social functions and the exigencies of cultural and spiritual life.

SANCTUM, which already identified a health governance, can predict a priority given to health values.

Goal

Bear in mind that an automated crisis management system like SANCTUM's sets itself an overall goal over time; it is the calling of this goal into question that characterizes the state of crisis. The pandemic has assuredly shaken up matters. The question raised by SANCTUM is to identify the nature of said challenges by structuring them so as to distinguish those which can be offset by a palliative and those which may lead to a redefinition of goals.

This leads us to revisit the classic dichotomy between the existential and the essential. By sticking to the economic and social aspects, specifically the work world, the pandemic has called into question the notion that work must be performed at a set location at a set time period. Telework, long dismissed by employers – public administrations not being less resistant than the private sector – became acceptable, recommended and then, obligatory[3] !

But, whilst telework offers an existential response to the pandemic's economic and social impact, SANCTUM suggests that reflection be extended at the existential level. In a context characterized by material abundance, overconsumption of resources, etc., can productive work and its added value remain goals likely to influence those of health security?

The question of "goals' is of an eminently political and philosophical nature. SANCTUM's job is not to intercede in this type of choice, but simply to make explicit its components and to bring them to governance, which may revise them as a function of the values such as they were defined, above, in the automated crisis management system.

Stakes, Assets, and Players

Crisis managers typically begin their analysis at this stage, attributing only relative importance to previous stages whilst the SANCTUM model said the earlier stages as essential.

Keep in mind that the "stakes" are the vital functions indispensable to the system's sustainability. In the case of Covid, the traditional analysis will quickly put forth the volume of the health and hospital responses as one of the predominant stakes. The

---

[3] A bit like Christianity before Constantine. History contains other examples of this sort of counterintuitive development!

supporting assets are the intensive care capacity and the availability of competent staff. The capacity of said facilities is increased somewhat and the country is locked down in order to prevent the development of an imbalance in the supply and demand of said assets.

At the beginning of the crisis, the principle of this reaction, dictated by the emergency, seems to make sense. However, the other stakes must be quickly considered. But how do we prioritize them all? SANCTUM's response is to review the data of the automated crisis management system that may be called into question: governance, values, goals. A quantitative approach can be performed, like that relating to the value of human life, making it possible to determine an equilibrium point from which the effects of the lockdown measures become more predatory than lifesaving.

Decision Support
The management of the pandemic crisis, based on SANCTUM's model, would have been highlighted by the following points:

- the exigency to make governance explicit;
- periodic reviews of the value system;
- revision of the exigencies and the guidelines of the automated crisis management system;
- A greater weighting for non-health states.

As for a decision, this would have led to an early easing of the March-April 2020 lockdown measures with a more nuanced approach, involving, for example, keeping schools open.

These thoughts were developed at the height of the lockdown in early April 2020. We note that the proposed approach closely resembles that which the government adopted during the pandemic's second wave from October 2020.

References

1. Anderson, B.: Pre-emption, precaution, preparedness: anticipatory action and future geographies. Prog. Hum. Geogr. **34**(6), 777–798 (2010)
2. Bénaben, F., Chihab, H., Lauras, M., Couget P., Chapurlat, V.: A metamodel and its ontology to guide crisis characterization and its collaborative management. In: Proceedings of the 5th International Conference on Information Systems for Crisis Response and Management (ISCRAM) (2008)
3. Després, C.: SANCTUM, a step forward in helping to make strategic decisions, Preventative, no. 166 (2019)
4. Fertier, A., Benaben, F., Dolidon, H.: SANCTUM – concept. SANCTUM report, Conseil Supérieur de la Formation et de la Recherche Stratégique (CSFRS) and Ministry of the Ecological Transition (MTE), Paris, France (2019)
5. Galam, S.: Sociophysics: A Physicist's Modelling of Psycho-political Phenomena. Springer, p. 439 (2012). https://doi.org/10.1007/978-1-4614-2032-3
6. Lagadec, P.: The big decision: capitulation or invention, in the face of extreme events. Technical report of the French Ecole polytechnique, Paris, France (2008)
7. November, V., Gueben-Veniere, S.: SANCTUM – State of the art and investigations. SANCTUM report, Conseil Supérieur de la Formation et de la Recherche Stratégique (CSFRS) and the Ministry of the Ecological Transition (MTE), Paris, France (2019)

8. November, V., Azémar, A., Lecacheux, S., Winter, T.: The anticipation/decision pair grappling with the exceptional, the unforeseen and uncertainty, EchoGéo (2020)
9. Olié J.-L.: SANCTUM – General methodology, SANCTUM report, Conseil Supérieur de la Formation et de la Recherche Stratégique (CSFRS) and French Ministry of the Ecological Transition (MTE), Paris, France (2019)
10. Schwartz, S.H.: The core values of the person: theory, measures and applications. Revue française de sociologie **4**(47) (2006)
11. Massimi, M., Tononi, G.: Sizing up Consciousness: Towards an Objective Measure of the Capacity for Experience. Oxfors Scholarship Online (2018)
12. Voisard, A., Petrie, C.: SANCTUM – Proof of concept. SANCTUM report, Conseil Supérieur de la Formation et de la Recherche Stratégique (CSFRS) and Ministry of the Ecological Transition (MTE), Paris, France (2019)
13. Petrie, C., Voisard, A.: AI Planning Applied to GIS-based Disaster Response. In: International ACM SIGworkshop on "Emergency management" (EM-GIS) (2019)
14. Wybo, J.- L., Latiers, M.: Exploring complex emergency situations' dynamic: theoretical, epistemological and methodological proposals. Int. J. Emergency Manage. **3**(1), 40–51 (2006)
15. Wybo, J.-L.: Percolation, temporal coherence of information, and crisis prevention. Safety Sci. **57**, 60–68 (2013)

An Assessment Model for Prioritizing CVEs in Critical Infrastructures in the Context of Time and Fault Criticality

Erfan Koza[✉] [ID]

Clavis Institute for Information Security, University of Niederrhein,
Mönchengladbach, Germany
erfan.koza@hs-niederrhein.de

Abstract. Assessing vulnerabilities in operational technology (OT) and industrial control systems in a multifaceted manner is challenging, particularly in the context of critical infrastructures. In practice, different standards support vulnerability management and incident response management. Here, it is not enough to understand only the theoretical concepts; the operational efficient models, and tools, which are ultimately responsible for the implementation of the standards, play an essential role. This paper presents a coherence model and its Incident Response Evaluation Tool (IRET) developed and evaluated for OT networks. It is used for time-efficient decision-making for successful defense against cyber-attacks and reduces the acquisition, analysis, and decision effort of Common Vulnerabilities and Exposures (CVEs) by 72% on average, from regularly 19 min to 5 min, and allows to evaluate CVEs in according to objective facts through its mathematical coherence model of vulnerabilities and the modified Observe-Orient-Decide-Act loop as main framework. It also demonstrates the possibility of integrating the coherence model into the context of vulnerability management to evaluate CVEs by reliable determinants in IRET, thus increasing efficiency and simultaneously increasing coverage in complex OT environments.

Keywords: Vulnerability Management · Incident Evaluation · Coherence Model · Critical Infrastructure · Common Vulnerabilities and Exposures

1 Introduction

A multitude of information technology systems responsible for monitoring and controlling industrial processes and facilities interact with each other in a global network with 24/7 availability (always on status) and are embedded in a bi- or multi-directional communication network. Such systems are used for a single reason: to ensure economic prosperity, which can be reconciled through process optimization, efficiency improvement and decreasing production and personnel costs

© The Author(s), under exclusive license to Springer Nature Switzerland AG 2023
B. Hämmerli et al. (Eds.): CRITIS 2022, LNCS 13723, pp. 93–118, 2023.
https://doi.org/10.1007/978-3-031-35190-7_8

[1]. Here, the function of a system or application, which should lead to an increase in efficiency, is placed in the foreground. However, this usually ignores the following security considerations: Is the software securely coded? Have developers considered methodological approaches for developing secure systems (e.g., security by design)? Have the systems been successfully tested in terms of their functional security? This is because security processes of this type, lead to increasing development times and costs and make products more expensive. If we now look at the mechanisms in the free market economy, we could summarize the following postulation: If there is no demand for "secure IT," there will also be no supply for "secure IT." Actually, a truism. The consequences are reflected in the fragility and vulnerability of these systems. In the meantime, several software and hardware products are in commercial circulation, which are also used by operators of critical infrastructures (CRITIS), especially within the technical basic infrastructures (e.g., energy, water, information, and communication technology (ICT) sector). As a rule, implemented industrial generation and supply systems consist of heterogeneous components and are widely distributed over large spatial distances. Thus, a long physical distance must be bridged between the individual centralized and decentralized technical instances for monitoring and control. However, the interaction between these decentralized and central components must be designed to ensure uninterrupted and cost- efficient supply of electricity, gas, and water. The orchestration and interaction of the (electro-) technical components requires reciprocal, valid, and secure data acquisition of system states as well as a fine-tuned information technology concept. This concept mainly includes the physical and logical fusion of electrical and IT system components, which are combined in the central distributed control system (DCS) with Supervisory Control and Data Acquisition (SCADA) systems and in the decentralized network interconnection points, transformers and substations, and waterworks via programmable logic controller (PLC), sensors, and actuators. These systems can be consolidated in their overall view under the term Industrial Control System (ICS) or Cyber Physical Systems (CPS), whose instrumentation is used for data acquisition, data analysis, and for the execution of intelligent algorithms and commands for the purpose of control and is summarized in the further course under the term Operation Technology (OT). Such systems consist of scalable system units ranging from a few modular control components to larger, more complex, and distributed control instances with a multitude of bi- and multi-directional data connections via central system nodes and decentralized peripheral stations. By using CPS and ICS, many electrical and physical parameters can be digitized and forwarded via data link interfaces to the central process and control system for the purpose of analysis and monitoring (comparison of actual process variables with the desired target-process variables) and calculation and control (derivation of options for action or switching commands).

The implemented DCS and SCADA systems in power generation (both conventional power plants and virulent power plants), power grid distribution, and in water collection, water treatment, and wastewater disposal offer a variety of system-relevant functions [21]. These functions include higher-level control and monitoring of all decentralized plants as well as plant components, which are located, for example, in individual transformers and substations or waterworks. A breach of the information security objectives (e.g., availability, integrity, and confidentiality) of such systems can lead to an interruption in the security of supply in the sense of the provision of public services, and ensure that, for example, the energy, water, or stationary supply of the population is no longer guaranteed. In addition to economic and monetary damage, such attacks can lead to reputational damage and, much worse, danger to life and limb. Damage can also have cross-sector effects on downstream processes or industries, triggering so-called domino or cascading effects [2]. Based on our original premise, CRITIS use a variety of software and hardware products, whose security levels can often be described as inadequate owing to coding errors, insecure interfaces, logical vulnerabilities, and security holes. This makes Vulnerability Management (VM) and Incident Response Management (IRM) key topics in defending OT systems. In VM and IRM, targeted principles and requirements are developed to detect potential vulnerabilities and the resulting threats before they are exploited [3,4]. The hypothesis underlying this work is that security practices and standards that currently exist in VM and IRM are merely descriptive. In other words, they describe what needs to be done. However, they do not address how the "what" must be implemented [5–7]. Before such vulnerabilities can be addressed, they must be detected and identified. This detection can be performed internally (within the boundaries of an organization) using intrusion detection prevention systems or security information event management systems. For the global detection of such vulnerabilities, the so-called Common Vulnerability Scoring System (CVSS) method has been established, which identifies vulnerabilities worldwide under the term Common Vulnerabilities and Exposures (CVE) and quantifies them with a global rating on a scale system between 0–10. However, what must also be considered here is the fact that the global CVE assessment is only an orientation, which still requires an organization-specific assessment and prioritization with reference to its own specific OT network landscape. Consequently, there are a few fundamental truths when it comes to vulnerability remediation. First, there are too many vulnerabilities to address immediately. Previous work has shown that organizations typically address 5–20% of known vulnerabilities within a month. Second, only a small number (2–7%) of published vulnerabilities have been exploited. This creates the need for good prioritization methods, as organizations cannot and do not need to fix everything immediately [8]. The goal of this work is to conceptualize and operationalize a coherence model to assess and prioritize CVEs based on the modified Observe-Orient-Decide-Act (OODA) loop. The model integrates determinants into a software-based tool called Incident Response Management Tool (IRET). To this end, IRET integrates a mathematical computational model to rapidly assess and prioritize CVEs based on facts (i.e., based on objective evaluation criteria). Its practical implementation was tested for one year at an internationally operating CRITIS in the energy sector with coal production, power generation in conventional (gas) power plants, operators of wind farms and photovoltaic plants and power supply in public high and medium-voltage grids.

2 Related Work

The research focus here is primarily on global vulnerability collection, consolidation, and assessment CVSS and the Exploit Prediction Scoring System (EPSS)) in [9–12]. EPSS combines vulnerability information (CVEs) with evidence of actual exploitation. Gathering this information can improve vulnerability prioritization by assessing the likelihood of a vulnerability being exploited. The model provides a value between 0 and 1 (0% and 100%). The higher the value, the more likely the vulnerability to be exploited [8]. Other approaches, such as game theory in the context of VM and IRM, which focus primarily on the human factor to make its decision-making more effective, can be found in [13,14]. There are also ontological and game-based approaches that analyze the relationships between vulnerabilities and draw on a wide range of knowledge to support attacks [15]–[16]. [17] describes an ontological holistic concept involving various community-driven standards CVSS, Common Attack Pattern Enumeration and Classification (CAPEC), CVE, Common Weakness Enumeration (CWE), Common Platform Enumeration (CPE). Therefore, there are dedicated standards (e.g. ISO/IEC 27001, 27002, 27035, NIST Cybersecurity Frameworks, NIST Special Publication SP 800-35 and NIST Special Publication SP 800-61) that define organizational structures that are used for the detection, treatment, and confirmation of weak points. One of the few ways to evaluate CVE damage is through web-based application services such as calculators, which are made available to analysts via the NIST NVD website, for example. Here, analysts are given the opportunity to individually select and evaluate the temporal and environmental metrics of CVE. The applied calculators change the CVE value based on the selected levels to evaluate the CVEs individually.

However, the selection process is purely intuitive and subjective. Individual evaluation levels are defined globally and are not usually easily related to the local view of a network. Thus, there is a risk that an arbitrary and subjective evaluation is carried out here, which sometimes leads to falsification of the result. This leads to an increase in inefficiency, as a CVE may be selected for further treatment, which is defined as a "false positive (FP)" and thus should never have been selected [18]. If another analyst performs this evaluation, the results of the CVE evaluation may be different because there is no uniform and objective evaluation pattern with the corresponding rules and relationships. In addition, CVEs are evaluated according to their degree of vulnerability, so that the most important determinant "probability of occurrence" is not included in this evaluation. In [19], an interactive system is described that visualizes cybersecurity threats. Thus, this reporting and alerting can occur in an organization. However, this system only serves as a support tool for more transparent and better detection of CVEs. Therefore, it does not explicitly serve as a decision support tool, but rather interactively facilitates the user to overview relevant issues (filtering and ordering).

Methodology

The following research guidelines can be defined, which can be integrated into design-oriented research:

Research guideline 1 (**R1 2**): How can reliable decision criteria (quantifiable and instantiable) be defined as a coherence model to determine the effectiveness and efficiency of the upcoming CVEs according to time criticality, failure consequence criticality and effort criticality?

Research guideline 2 (**RG 2**): Can the insights from the OODA loop be transformed as a dynamic framework into IRET, so that the decision-makers get an adequate tool to register, analyze, evaluate, and document the CVEs?

The operational execution of the individual research guidelines is based on the design science research cycle model and v-model, which is used for clarifying research questions in engineering to ensure scientific viability through relevance and rigor. First, a rough outline is used to determine which detailed objectives (derived from **RG 1** and **RG 2** as well as from the industrial needs identified in workshops with cyber security analysts) are to be defined. The coherence model and IRET should be understood in its entirety as an operational and efficient tool that simplifies the work of cyber engineers and network analysts and enhances security. The field of observation can be visualized and defined within a simple modeling between the recording of a CVE (CVE entrance) and the closing of a CVE (documentation). This is exactly where the coherence model and its operationalization IRET, are to be used. Based on the requirements and goals from the first step (goals 1 to 5) (Fig. 1), the analysis of the determinants, which are to be embedded in the coherence model, is carried out in the second step. For this purpose, the determinants are identified and set in direct or indirect dependence to specify the possible correlations and causalities between the individual determinants. The basic idea is to identify system- and network-oriented determinants, which allow an evaluation based on facts.

This should make it possible to conduct the evaluation process objectively and independently of (subjective) decision-makers and analysts. Thus, the possibility can be generated to evaluate CVEs after objective characteristics (system-dependent and network-dependent characteristics) and to make the results at any time reproducible and in the sense of verifiable and traceable validity. A fundamental objective is the instantiability of the coherence model. The coherence model must be considered as a meta-model for determining CVE evaluation criteria, which can be operationalized and used independently of the field of application. Derived from the coherence model, the computational model is developed in a further step, with whose assistance the coherence model can be transferred into a quantification model. The computational model primarily defines the way in which the individual determinants can be quantified and evaluated. Second, it provides a classification scheme for how a CVE can be classified as an incident and treated with an appropriate treatment strategy. In the third step (RG 2), the methodological approach of the OODA loop is modified by transforming the properties of the OODA loop and applying them to IRET requirements.

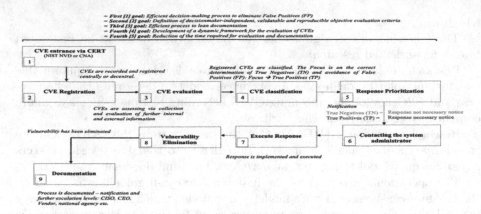

Fig. 1. Research field and the corresponding detailed goals.

3   Research Results

3.1   Coherence Model and Its First Meta-Level (Intrinsic CVE Factors)

The coherence model represents the adaptive meta model and can be applied as a template to any CVE categorization and prioritization concepts. For this purpose, the methodology of risk assessment is now transferred to a CVE. Hereby replace a CVE as an equivalent variable the risk factor. To enable the complexity and flexibility (i.e., adaptability and scalability) of the coherence model, it was built in two meta-level (Fig. 2). The first meta-level comprises the "intrinsic CVE factor" *(intrinsic CVE factor (C) = ($b_{intensive}$ + $b_{extensive}$) = ((b_1 + b_2) + (b_3 + b_4))* and reflects the internal system properties and information. The second meta- level (F) goes back to the "extrinsic CVE factors," which are to be located outside of the system and can thus be determined by external influences. The idea is to develop a model that can combine the global assessment of a CVE with the internal and external information of a network landscape to generate an individual assessment. The intrinsic CVE factor forms the first area of consideration for assessing the extent of damage of a CVE and comprises determinants (specified by the sub-determinants) in its entirety. A distinction is made between the $b_{intensive}$ and $b_{extensive}$ determinants. While intensive determinants evaluate the depth of damage of a CVE, extensive determinants evaluate the extent of damage of a CVE. Both areas of the intrinsic CVE factor are based on internal and objective system properties and architecture, so that these are best suited as objective criteria for evaluating a CVE. Moreover, a mutual relationship exists between the intensive and extensive (coherence) intrinsic CVE factors. It is important to consider two domains (intensive and extensive), which can be divided into several differentiated sub-determinants. However, these can be defined differently, depending on organization, system architecture and network settings. This is where the first advantage of the coherence model lies. It represents a generally valid model that can be individually transported to the individual structure of a network landscape. In the coherence model, the intensive domain is characterized by its sub-determinants with the acronym (e_1.... $e_{(n+1)}$) and the extensive domain by its sub-determinants with the acronym (f_1.... $f_{(n+1)}$). Thus, both domains can be specified and determined by a variety of sub-determinants. Here, the value of the $b_{intensive}$ ranges can be determined by adding its sub-determinants ($e_1+...+ e_{(n+1)}$). This procedure is also used in the same analogy for the determination of the value of $b_{extensive}$ ranges ($f_1 +...+ f_{(n+1)}$). This mathematical approach to the coherence model is called computational model, which will be specified later with a concrete example. Thus, the extent of damage of a CVE can be determined by adding the individual and objective sub-determinants *(extent of damage = intrinsic CVE factor (C) = ($b_{intensive} + b_{extensive}$)* $= ((b_1 + b_2) + (b_3 + b_4)) = ((e_1 +...+ e_{(n+1)} + 0) + (f_1....f_{(n+1)} + 0)).$

$$Risk = R = f\ (Frequency,\ Consequence) \rightarrow R = F \times C.$$
$$R = CVE\ \text{(Risk is replaced by a CVE)}$$
$$F = Extrinsic\ CVE\ factor\ \text{(Attack Prediction or likelihood)}$$
$$C = Intrinsic\ CVE\ factor\ \text{(Extent of damage)}$$

$$\rightarrow R = CVE = f\ (F = Extrinsic\ CVE\ factor,\ C = Intrinsic\ CVE\ factor)$$

$$\rightarrow CVE = (Extrinsic\ CVE\ factor) \times (Intrinsic\ CVE\ factor)$$

$$\rightarrow CVE = (E\text{-}Class) \times (I\text{-}Class)$$

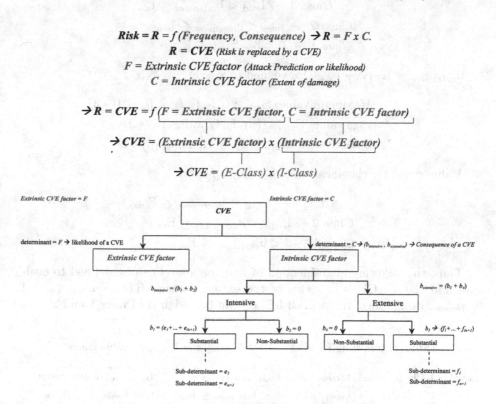

Fig. 2. Itemizing of determinants and sub-determinants of the coherence model.

However, to classify the (C) value and evaluate it according to the criticality of the extent, a scheme with differentiated classes must first be defined, to which the achieved (C) values can be assigned. For this assignment of the achieved (C) value to the individual criticality classes, the $b_{intensive}$ and $b_{extensive}$ determinants are combined in a two-dimensional model.

$b_{intensive} = (e_1 + ... + e_{(n+1)})$: assigned to x-axis

$$Maximum \text{ value: } I_{max} : ((|e_1, e_2, e_3, ... e_{(n+1)}|) * 3)$$
$$Average \text{ value: } I_{mid} : ((|e_1, e_2, e_3, ... e_{(n+1)}|) * 2)$$
$$Minimum \text{ value: } I_{min} : ((|e_1, e_2, e_3, ... e_{(n+1)}|) * 1)$$

$Value$ range for classification of $b_{intensive}$ factors:

$$Class \ 3 \ \rightarrow I_{mid} < b_{intensive} \leq I_{max}$$
$$Class \ 2 \ \rightarrow I_{min} < b_{intensive} \leq I_{mid}$$
$$Class \ 1 \ \rightarrow 0 < b_{intensive} \leq I_{min}$$

$b_{extensive} = (f_1 + ... + f_{(n+1)})$: assigned to y-axis

$$Maximum \text{ value: } E_{max} : ((|f_1, f_2, f_3, ... f_{(n+1)}|) * 3)$$
$$Average \text{ value: } E_{mid} : ((|f_1, f_2, f_3, ... f_{(n+1)}|) * 2)$$
$$Minimum \text{ value:} E_{min} : ((|f_1, f_2, f_3, ... f_{(n+1)}|) * 1)$$

$Value$ range for classification of $b_{extensive}$ factors:

$$Class \ 3 \rightarrow E_{mid} < b_{extensive} \leq E_{max}$$
$$Class \ 2 \rightarrow E_{min} < b_{extensive} \leq E_{mid}$$
$$Class \ 1 \rightarrow 0 < b_{extensive} \leq E_{min}$$

Thus, the following quantification of first meta-level can be defined to evaluate and classify CVEs in terms of the extent damage. Thus, $b_{intensive}$ and $b_{extensive}$ value range, the defined I-Class can be assigned (Tables 1 and 2).

Table 1. Itemizing I-Classes with $b_{intensive}$ and $b_{extensive}$ value range

Level	I-Class value	Border area	$b_{intensive}$ -value range	$b_{extensive}$-value range
Low	1	(E_{min}, I_{min})	$0 < b_{intensive} \leq I_{min}$	$0 < b_{extensive} \leq E_{min}$
High	2	(E_{mid}, I_{mid})	$I_{min} < b_{intensive} \leq I_{mid}$	$E_{min} < b_{extensive} \leq E_{mid}$
Critical	3	(E_{max}, I_{max})	$I_{mid} < b_{intensive} \leq I_{max}$	$E_{mid} < b_{extensive} \leq E_{max}$

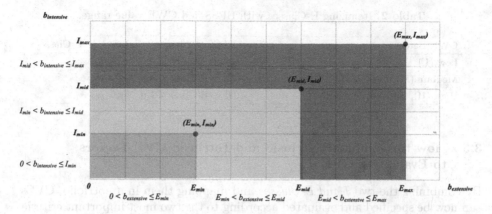

Fig. 3. Coherence computational model and its classification scheme.

3.2 Coherence Model and Its Second Meta-Level (Extrinsic CVE Factors)

In addition to evaluating a CVE according to the assessed extent of damage, the actual frequency at which the CVE is exploited must also be considered. However, this factor is defined as a significant quantity because the frequency and prevalence of exploitation of a CVE is a quantity that can contribute to the true positives (TP) and false negatives (FN), respectively, via pertinent and realistic CVE classification. To define this consideration computationally and methodically, we must use a small trick, in which we first quantify the probability of occurrence of a CVE and then assign them to three criticality classes (E-Class). The background for this is that we use the I-Classes and E-Classes in the later course to visualize these in a portfolio model. For this purpose, we use the publicly available data, which can be determined via First (EPSS model with its EPSS score to represent the probability of exploitation in the wild in the next 30 d) or via the CWE (probability of exploit) and transform these into three classes using our own computational model to classify the probability of occurrence of a CVE according to time criticality. The decision to determine the probability of occurrence via First or CWE has a pragmatic view. In general, not all CVE occurrence probabilities can be immediately quantified with the EPSS model. However, because the CVE information from the NIST NVD is referenced to the equivalent CWE ID, the CWE probability of occurrence can be used as a redundant method to determine the empirical probability of occurrence. For this purpose, the quantified EPSS score [0 - 10] and qualitative CWE score are unified and assigned using the critical E-Class model. For example, if the probability of occurrence of a CVE via the EPSS score is 0.4 (=0.4*100= 40%) is the probability of occurrence, or comparatively for CWE - score at "medium (M)." This score is assigned to the E-Class "high" with the value 2. Therefore, the quantified EPSS score [0–10] and qualitative CWE score are unified as follows:

Table 2. Itemizing E-Classes with EPSS and CWE value range.

CWE Border area	EPSS Border	Level	E-Class
Low (L)	0 < E-Class ≤ 0,3	Low	1
Medium (M), Default (D), Unknown (UK)	0,3 < E-Class ≤ 0,6	High	2
High (H), Not Applicable (NA)	0,6 < E-Class ≤ 1,0	Critical	3

3.3   How to Combine Extrinsic and Intrinsic CVE Factors to Evaluate a CVE

By combining the two *I and E-Classes* and mapping them in a portfolio, CVEs can now be specified and evaluated according to the two most important criteria (CVE damage extent and CVE probability of occurrence). Figure 4 shows the final evaluation and classification of CVEs, as well as the failure consequence estimated by magnitude and time criticality, defined as the treatment strategy and time prioritization of each CVE. The following time priorities are proposed: A (immediate elimination (first 24 h)), B (immediate elimination (first 48 h)), C (prompt elimination (first 120 h)), D (elimination in the first two weeks), E (elimination in the next four weeks), F (elimination in the next eight weeks) and deprioritize, which can be neglected as TN and FP, respectively. Determining the time criticality of each CVE treatment will help target resource allocation more effectively. In this way, the treatments incurred can be contrasted according to the extent and time criticality, a) which CVEs will have major consequences, b) how the individual probability of occurrence is to be defined for the respective, CVE and c) in which chronological order the CVEs can be eliminated most effectively.

I-class	E-class	F-Value	*Treatment strategy*	Classification in terms of information theory "precision and recall"	Prioritization of time criticality
1	1	1	Acceptance	True Negatives (TN)	Deprioritize
1	2	2	Acceptance	True Negatives (TN)	Deprioritize
1	3	3	Reduction	True Positives (TP)	F
2	1	2	Acceptance	True Negatives (TN)	Deprioritize
2	2	4	Reduction	True Positives (TP)	E
2	3	6	Reduction	True Positives (TP)	D
3	1	3	Reduction	True Positives (TP)	C
3	2	6	Reduction	True Positives (TP)	B
3	3	9	Reduction	True Positives (TP)	A

Fig. 4. Portfolio of the I-Class and E-Class.

The time-priority scale (A - F) is an organization-specific variable that must be determined depending on the available personnel and technical resources. With the already defined coherence model, CVEs can now be evaluated and classified organization-specifically and according to facts (independent of the subjective view of the decision-maker). The conceptualized coherence model, computational model, and portfolio can be instantiated according to the above declaration so that each organization can adapt the above procedure and adapt it to its own needs.

3.4   How to Specify Default Sub-determinants

However, to transfer the first meta-level and its sub-determinants of the coherence model to the computational model, the sub-determinants must be quantified in a scaled system using suitable characteristics and definitions.

The global definition of applicability determines (gDoA) the super-ordinate evaluation characteristics of the respective classes. This transfer serves to maintain the logical relation that must be established between the individual partial sub-determinants and gDoA (Fig. 5). This creates the prerequisite that all partial sub-determinants are classified according to a uniform evaluation scheme, and the logical connection can be used as a basic prerequisite for compliance with objective and reproducible evaluation. For this purpose, there are three classes: low, high, and critical. The superordinate definitions of the respective classification levels are shown as follows:

Level	Value	gDoA I (impact level)	gDoA II (treatment level)
Low	1	The quality and quantity of system services and affected assets are not at risk by the incident at any time. This assessment may only be performed if system failures and impairments are excluded.	In terms of prognostics, the decision not to treat (acceptance strategy) has no negative impact on the impact level (gDoA I).
High	2	The quality and quantity of system services and affected assets may be at risk by the incident. This assessment may only be carried out if only marginal system failures and impairments are to be expected, which, however this, can be compensated by personnel and system-relevant redundancies.	In terms of prognostics, the decision not to treat (acceptance strategy) may have a negative impact on and complicates the impact score (gDoA I).
Critical	3	The quality and quantity of system services and affected assets are at risk from incident. This assessment leads to system failures and impairments, which also affect the system-relevant redundancies.	In terms of prognostics, the decision not to treat (acceptance strategy) has a negative impact on the impact level (gDoC I) and favors it.

Fig. 5. Itemizing of gDOA

After determining a global assessment scheme, a total of eight standard intrinsic sub- determinants are defined (Fig. 6), which are classified according to the gDoA logic as follows:

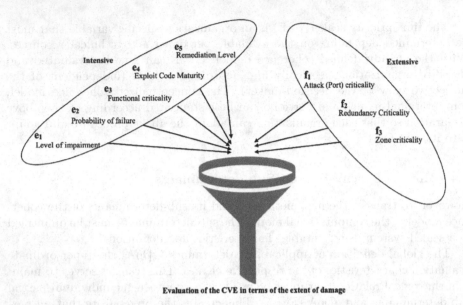

Evaluation of the CVE in terms of the extent of damage

Fig. 6. Itemizing of the intrinsic sub-determinants.

The original objective of the coherence model can be stated through eight sub-determinants (i.e., reliable, objective determination of CVEs). Let us first consider existing methods. Conventional methods for the evaluation of risks from ISO/IEC 27005, ISO/IEC 27035, and NIST SP 800-53 are currently perceived for the most part in practice, with a subjective and person-dependent evaluation of the extent of damage and the probability of occurrence. The methodological approach is clear. The assessment of the extent of damage relates to its negative impact on data and system security. The probability of occurrence represents an empirical analysis, which is often defined on a gut- level basis and not well founded and embedded in the respective analysis. Depending on the experience, personal feelings, perceptions of the current security situation (e.g., pessimism versus optimism), salience, behavioral intention, knowledge, and capability of the assessor, an assessment of a risk can be individual and different. With reference to a CVE assessment, the coherence model is therefore intended to remedy the situation and ensure it is not subjective (independent of the decision-maker), but objective according to facts. To achieve this goal, we use eight objective properties, which are used as sub- determinants for the evaluation of the extent of damage. According to the coherence model, there is a relationship between the intensive and extensive sub-determinants. For this purpose, we postulate that the depth of damage of a CVE is also directly related to the extent of damage of a CVE. The conclusion of this assumption thus represents the possibility that a statement about the damage depth also allows a statement about the extent of damage. If we apply this premise to our sub-determinants, we obtain the possibility to establish a direct connection between them. The first intensive sub-determinant comprises the "level of impairment e_1" and makes a statement about how pronounced the degree of compromise of a CVE is. Here, a correlative consideration stands, which is to be understood as follows: If one assumes that a CVE concerns TCP-Port 445, which becomes, for example, in the network land-scapes several times as network protocols (e.g., used by Windows) and cannot be deactivated easily (i.e., because with a deactivation a multiplicity of network services cannot be executed any longer). It can be assumed that this kind of CVE can achieve a major degree of impairment (accumulation effect), because several systems and areas can be infiltrated by a single CVE. The attack diversity of a CVE can make a statement about its degree of impairment of a CVE. This results in a correlated effect in which the determination of the extensive factor "port criticality f1" simultaneously implies the determination of e1. This is based on the internal configuration of the system architecture and implemented ports. The coherence relationship between e_1 and f_1 is shown in Fig. 7.

Ports Criticality (f_1)

Value		Impact Level	Treatment Level
1	Locked and only inward open ports without access to the Internet (Stand-alone networks)	Low	Low
2	Open ports with access to the Internet, segmented by firewalls and simultaneously monitored by ports security and scanning systems	High	High
3	Open ports with access to the Internet, which are not monitored by Ports Security, as well as multiple use of ports in one or more logical zones	Critical	Critical

Level of Impairment (e_1)

Value		Impact Level	Treatment Level
1	Correlated score: The impairment level of a CVE can be classified as low if the port affected by CVE (f_i) is evaluated with a score of 1.	Low	Low
2	Correlated score: The impairment level of a CVE can be classified as high if the port affected by the CVE (f_i) is evaluated with a score of 2.	High	High
3	Correlated score: The impairment level a CVE can be classified as critical if the port affected by CVE (f_i) is evaluated with a score of 3.	Critical	Critical

Fig. 7. Coherence between e_1 and f_1.

For this purpose, one can make an equivalent inference on the level of impair-ment of systems based on the existing port criticalities. Furthermore, the "prob-ability of failure e_2" also contains a correlated impact, in which the weighting depends on the sub-determinant "redundancy criticality f_2" (business continu-ity). The probability of failure can be classified as "critical" if the systems are physically and logically non-redundant (e.g., without redundancies in separate fire compartments, (geo-)redundancies backups, or possible design of systems that were designed without considering the n-1 criterion). Therefore, if a CVE affects a system with- out redundancies, it can be concluded that such systems are not adequately secured in terms of resiliency and business continuity. In this case, f_2 must be defined as critical, i.e., e_2 also evaluated as critical by the given coherent character. This means that the probability of failure can be classified as critical, because the systems are to be defined as a single point of failure. For example, if a CVE compromises a system that has a backup system in the same logical network segment, the criticality of the system must be considered critical despite the presence of the backup. The reason for this is that an online backup system may be used, which can be encrypted in the event of infiltration, e.g., by ransomware. Thus, if the main system is compromised, there is a very high probability that the existing backup will also be drawn into passion (inheritance effect). The distribution effect should also be considered here. The coherence relationship between e_2 and f_2 is shown in Fig. 8.

Redundancy Criticality (f_2)

Value		Impact Level	Treatment Level
1	ICS have a physical 1:1 mirrored redundancy with an offline backup system - or ICS have a geo-redundancy	Low	Low
2	ICS and online | offline backup systems are physically separated only by different fire cut-offs; a failure can hardly be compensated	High	High
3	ICS have no redundancies and are considered a "Single Point Of Failure" (SPOF) or have redundancies with a backup system in the same logical and physical segment	Critical	Critical

Probability of Failure (e_2)

Value		Impact Level	Treatment Level
1	Correlated score: The probability of failure can be classified as low if the ICSs affected by CVE have a redundancy criticality (f_2) of 1.	Low	Low
2	Correlated score: The probability of failure can be classified as high if the ICSs affected by CVE have a redundancy criticality (f_2) of 2.	High	High
3	Correlated score: The probability of failure can be classified as critical if the ICSs affected by CVE have a redundancy criticality (f_2) of 3.	Critical	Critical

Fig. 8. Coherence between e_2 and f_2.

Furthermore, when classifying the implemented OT systems (i.e., in addition to considering logical and physical segmentation and the presence of redundancy and backup systems), the virtual machines must also be considered.

In addition, "functional criticality e_3" also contains a correlated rating in which the weighting of functional criticality depends on the sub-determinant "zone criticality f_3". According to the logical zone principle, critical systems and applications are integrated into deeper network zones and separated from other networks through firewalls or dedicated security gateways. For example, if the exploit affects an application in the lowest security zone, the coherent evaluation is that critical functionality is affected at the same time. Referring to our example with the CVE, which affects TCP-Port 455, we can assume that because of the multiple occurrences of TCP-Port 455, several logical zones are also affected. To evaluate these constellations, we use the classification theme in Fig. 9.

Zone Criticality (f_3)

Value		Impact Level	Treatment Level
1	If the first logical zone (internal OT network) is affected (first zone - separated by DMZ and/or the firewall or security gateway layer from the IT zone or ERP systems)	Low	Low
2	If the second logical OT zone is affected (second zone - separated by the second firewall or security gateway layer).	High	High
3	i. If the third/fourth/fifth logical OT zone is affected (second zone - separated by the third/fourth/fifth firewall or security gateway layer) ii. or if multiple OT zones are affected ii. or if OT network does not have any sufficient differentiated network zones and segments and thus only one OT zone is defined.	Critical	Critical

Function Criticality (e_3)

Value		Impact Level	Treatment Level
1	Correlated score: The functionality criticality can be classified as low if the CVE infiltration only affects the OT network zone (f_3) with a rating of 1.	Low	Low
2	Correlated score: The functionality criticality can be classified as high if the CVE infiltration only affects the OT network zone (f_3) with a rating of 2.	High	High
3	Correlated score: The functionality criticality can be classified as critical if the CVE infiltration only affects the OT network zone (f_3) with a rating of 3.	Critical	Critical

Fig. 9. Coherence between e_3 and f_3.

The other two intensive sub-determinants relate to the volatile and temporary "exploit code maturity e_4" and "remediation level e_5" which can therefore be fed directly from the dedicated research information via own research by CVSS-methodology:

Exploit Code Maturity (e₄)

Value		Impact Level	Treatment Level
1	Unproven (U)	Low	Low
2	Proof-of-Concept (P)	High	High
3	Functional (F) High (H) Not Defined (X)	Critical	Critical

Remediation Level (e₅)

Value		Impact Level	Treatment Level
1	Official Fix (O)	Low	Low
2	Temporary Fix (T)	High	High
3	Workaround (W) Unavailable (U) Not Defined (X)	Critical	Critical

Fig. 10. Coherence between e_4 and e_5.

Next, we demonstrate how the coherence model can be embedded and operationalized in a software solution "Incident Response Evaluation Tool" (IRET) using John Boyd's OODA loop for this purpose as framework.

3.5   Modified OODA Loop in the Context of Coherence Model

The logic of the OODA loop can be interpreted in many ways (e. g for continuous and dynamic construction of a security awareness program) [22]. Our modified OODA loop adapts the logic of Boyd's OODA loop [20], but changed the three crucial phases, observe, orient, and decide, to implement the specific aspects of the coherence model into the OODA loop. The first modification concerns the observe phase and is performed by integrating the principles of situational awareness. For this purpose, the function add "CVE" will be designed and integrated into the software-based solution "IRET." The second modification concerns the orient and decide phase to integrate other determinants relevant to the coherence model. Thus, the aspects from the "Relationship of objects in an information security incident" of ISO/IEC 27035-1 are adopted, modified, and replaced in an equivalent manner with extrinsic and intrinsic determinants and integrated into the modified OODA loop.

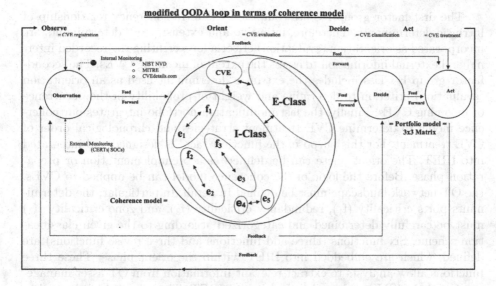

Fig. 11. Modified OODA loop in terms of the coherence model.

To implement the modified OODA loop, the functions "add criticality" and "set criticality" are designed and integrated into IRET (Fig. 12).

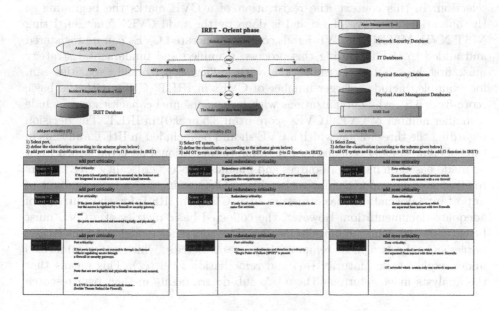

Fig. 12. IRET - how to add criticality.

The first factor group I-Class comprises the intra-coherency relationship of intrinsic determinants. Therefore, intensive and extensive sub-determinants are incorporated as orientation (evaluation) criteria for weighting the recorded internal and external information to assess the extent of incoming CVEs. The second-factor group E-Class includes the extrinsic determinant used as an orientation (evaluation) criterion to determine and weight of probability of the occurrence of incoming CVEs. Finally, the last modification portfolio integrates our coherence model to determine CVE treatment strategies and chronological order of CVE treatment. For this purpose, the function "act" is designed and integrated into IRET. The orient phase can be defined as a preimplementation or preparation phase. Before the logic of the coherence model can be applied to CVEs, the OT network landscape must be defined in detail. In particular, the determinants ports criticality (f_1), redundancy criticality (f_2), and zone criticality (f_3) must be carefully determined and categorized according to the given classification scheme. Six functions (three add functions and three revise functions) are defined, which are embedded into IRET within the orient phase. These three functions allow analysts to extract relevant information from OT asset management tools or ISMS tools and embed it into IRET. The orient phase is used to determine and classify the internal information, which is later correlated with external CVE information to reliably define the extent of damage caused by a CVE. The orient phase thus takes place under the motto: know your OT environment. After the inclusion and classification of extensive determinants, the coherence model and its computational model can be applied to the CVE selection. In this context, the registration of a CVE marks the beginning of the operational observe phase and is done by the "add CVE" function. Using NIST NVD, MITRE, or CVEdetails.com the generated CVEs can be registered and added to IRET. During this process, a unified and fundamental strategy must first be selected. Organizations with sufficient personnel capacities can, for example, include a larger number of CVEs in IRET (CVEs with the basic score from 6.5), while organizations with lower personnel capacities can include a smaller number of CVEs (CVEs score from 8.5 or 9.0) in IRET. The decision regarding the threshold at which a CVE should be included in IRET and thus in the coherence model remains an individual organizational decision, which must be made based on its own resources and business process criticality. IRET offers relevant storage capacities for registering a CVE to include a large amount of important information (basic metrics of a CVE) in IRET for the purpose of adequate documentation. However, the collected basic metrics of a CVE must be extended by using temporally metrics. The coherence model and thus IRET, implements the two most temporal important metrics, which are summarized under exploit code maturity (e_4) and remediation level (e_5). This means that the analysts must determine these two sub-determinants in their own research activities. After registering the CVE, the "set criticality" function can be selected to match the collected external information with the internal information previously determined in the orient phase. Here, the analyst only needs to determine which port, OT system, and zone are affected by the registered CVE. While the analyst transfers this information to IRET, it automatically calculates the damage extent of the registered CVE in the background. In addition, the value of the I-Class is determined here. Finally, the analyst must use EPSS score or CWE probability of the exploit score to determine the probability of occurrence of the CVE. Again, IRET performs calculations in the background and determines the score for E-Class. Subsequently, IRET merges the two classes and integrates the results into the portfolio and determines the final decision. The final decision is treatment strategy and time prioritization, which analysts can use to initiate treatment processes to eliminate vulnerabilities and CVEs. For a better understanding, we show how the coherence model is designed with the modified OODA loop as a software solution and how it can be operationalized using an example to evaluate a CVE.

3.6 Incident Response Evaluation Tool "IRET"

This section presents the final artifact "IRET." As a prototype, IRET takes over the task of realizing and operationalizing the coherence model and attempts to implement it as an efficient solution in an industrial environment. IRET was developed for the first-time using visual basic for application with macro programming. This development is the result of a pragmatic approach to shorten long development times of the prototype.

Another consideration was that almost every organization owns licenses for MS Office products; therefore, the prototype can be used, evaluated, and operated in all system environments, without the clients and test persons having to laboriously embed it in their environment. In addition, handling IRET in this form is user-friendly and self- explanatory. Another advantage is that IRET can be run stand alone. The feasibility of IRET, and thus the model presented above, were tested, and evaluated in two independent OT networks, each with a different analyst, over a period of one year at each stage of method construction. The defined test environments have strict network segmentation and are logically and physically isolated from the respective office networks. In test environment 1, an eight-person decentralized team with two specialized analysts is deployed, and in the second test environment, a five-person centralized team with two analysts is deployed. The first test environment is used in coal mining, power generation (power plants) and power transmission. The second test environment is used in power generation. Both networks use centralized SCADA systems and decentralized programmable logical controllers to efficiently control and monitor their plants and aggregates. Both network landscapes are composed

of a heterogeneous system landscape, which also consists of several system manufacturers and network components. The first test environment works with a
total of approx. 250 people in the OT area, whereas the second test environment
works with only 40 people. These include system operators, administrators, and
electrical engineers in the distribution, collectors, converter, and switching substations. To better understand the use of the coherence model and IRET, the
use cases for the registration and evaluation of a CVE up to its distribution are
as follows:

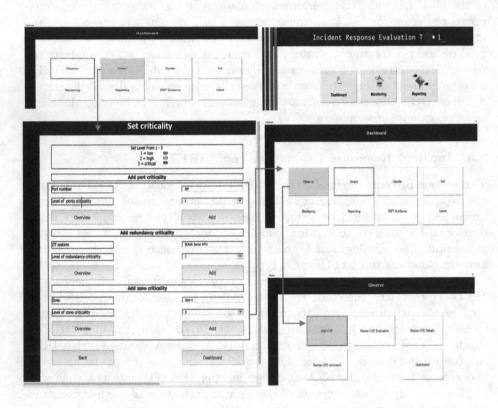

Fig. 13. IRET - navigation and how to set criticality

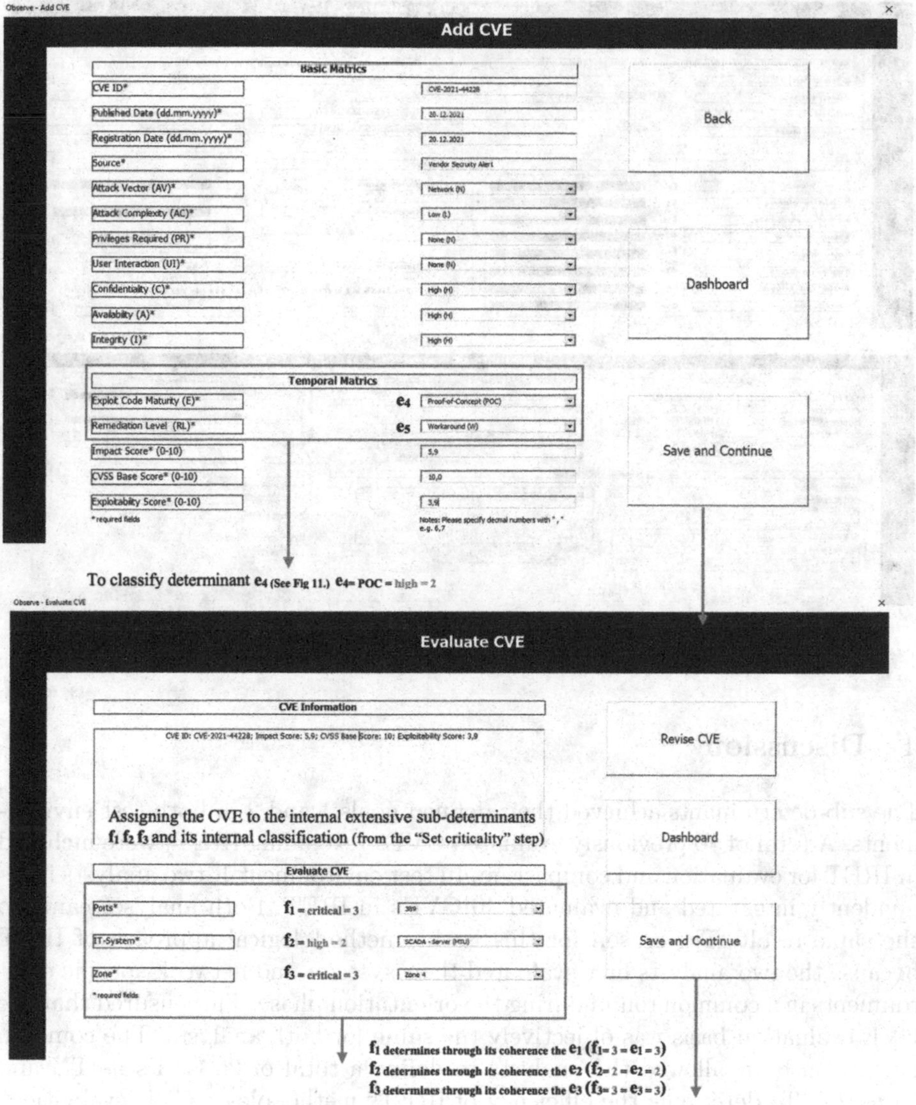

Fig. 14. IRET - how to evaluate a damage of extent of a CVE

114   E. Koza

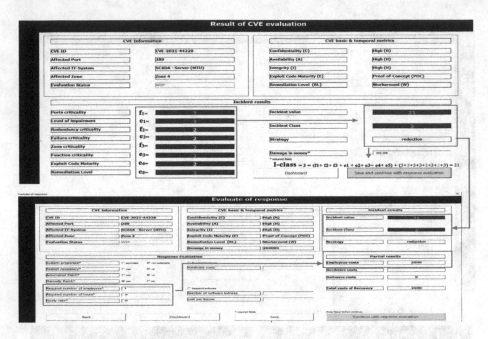

Fig. 15. IRET - result of CVE evaluation

4 Discussion

The sub-determinants achieved their defined goals 1 and 2 in both test environments. A total of 40 previously evaluated CVEs (excluding IRET) were included in IRET for evaluation and comparison. In test environment 1, two analysts independently integrated and evaluated 40 CVEs in IRET. Both analyses came to the same result. The reason for this is the methodological approach of IRET because the two analysts first evaluated their system- and network-specific environments in a common round during the orientation phase. This ensured that the CVE evaluation basis was objectively the same for both analysts. The common evaluation basis allowed the analysts to define a total of 26 CVEs as TN and 14 as TP. To determine the efficiency of IRETs methodology, CVE evaluations with and without IRET are compared. For this comparison, the measurement data of IRET are used as a benchmark for the calculation and comparison. The comparison of the TP (14 versus 21 selected CVEs) shows that with IRET, the efficiency (TP divided by (TP+FP)) of the evaluation increased by approximately 40% compared to evaluations without IRET.

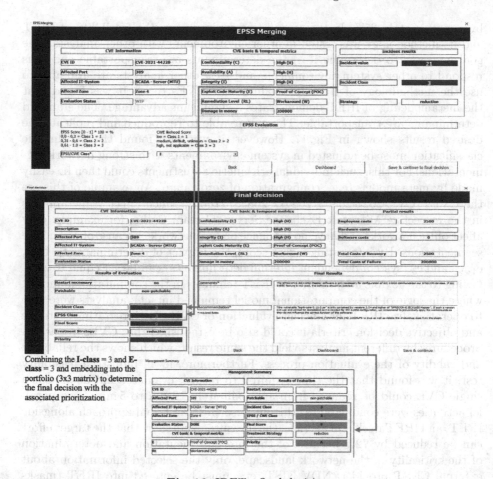

Fig. 16. IRET - final decision

Without IRET (selected for treatment (defined as TP))	21 / 40
Without IRET (Not prioritized (defined as TN))	19 /40
Efficiency (TP / (TP+FP)) * 100 Notes: As FP for this calculation the 14 CVEs are used, which are to be defined as FP according to IRET.	(21 / (21+14)) * 100 = 60%
Coverage (TP / (TP+FN)) * 100 Notes: The FN used for this calculation is the 7 CVEs defined as TP in IRET assessment compared to assessment without IRET. The assessment without IRET eliminates these 7 CVEs and considers them as TN.	(21 / (21+7)) * 100 = 75%
With IRET (selected for treatment (defined as TP))	14 /40
With IRET (Not prioritized (defined as TN))	26 /40
Efficiency of IRET as a benchmark	100%
Coverage of IRET as a benchmark	100%

Fig. 17. IRET - efficiency measurement

The observation was that 21 CVEs (assessment without IRET) included a total of 14 CVEs that are incorrectly defined as TN by evaluation without IRET. This increases the precision resp. coverage of IRET (TP divided by (TP+FN)) by approximately 25%. In the second test environment, the feasibility of IRET and its methodology was tested in other environments with other analysts. The goal here was to determine if a) the determinants are transportable and thus respond to other system environments and b) if other analysts are also able to use the methodology of IRET to evaluate the CVEs to a). It was found that the metamodeling of IRET demonstrates a significant advantage. The standard determinants are transportable. These were able to reproduce and replicate the desired results shown in Fig. 17. However, it was also found that arithmetic classification must be adjusted in system environments with strong network segmentations. For this, such individual arithmetic adjustments could then be easily made by meta-models (e.g., configuration of zero value). An example of this are the CVEs (CVE-2021-26855/26857/ 26858/27065), which affect vulnerabilities in the respective Microsoft Exchange Server. Certain CVEs, for example, only affect office networks and have no influence on OT networks because of restrictive segmentations. By integrating a zero score, the impact of determinants f_1, f_2,f_3, e_1, e_2 and e_3 (system-dependent internal determinants) can be set equal to zero. Owing to the flexible adaptability of IRET (changes in the computational model, where the logic of the computational model remained intact), analysts were able to operationalize IRET for efficient evaluation of CVEs. By integrating systemic and objective decision criteria it could also be established that CVEs in parallel procedures by different analysts yield the same result, which shows the reliability and validity of the evaluation process. Furthermore, in an industrial feasibility test, it was found that the time required to record, evaluate, and document a single CVE could be reduced from approximately 19 min to 5 min. Two parallel activities were conducted for this purpose-the traditional approach alongside IRET, and IRET itself. On average, the measurements show that the target effort can be reduced by 72% because of the internal orientation and determination of the criticality of the network landscape, only the selected information about external CERT provider, NDV NIST, etc. must be entered into IRET (masks add CVE, evaluate CVE, evaluate EPSS). In the background, the evaluation and prioritization of CVEs run automatically. In addition, the time required not only for the evaluation but also for the documentation and reporting of the CVEs is significantly reduced (goals 3, 4, 5). IRET integrates the possibility of making comments and recommendations. Thus, despite the standardized procedure, the evaluation of a CVE can be given certain flexibility to include the subjective expertise and experience values of analysts for the evaluation of a CVE in the documentation and evaluation. One of the unanticipated benefits is that the prioritization of actions over time to address a CVE has enabled the creation of a dynamic internal remediation plan. IRET classifies the extent of damage to a CVE but at the same time determines which temporal prioritization can be assigned to the treatment of a CVE. In addition, CVE reports in the form of management summaries with the necessary information for CVE evaluation and responses can be identified, documented, and sent to the relevant department for remediation. In this context, beyond its methodological and design approaches, this paper serves as an initial point to challenge the research community in linking concepts of security engineering research with the building of pragmatic tools to reach the information security paradigms in an efficient manner. The synergies generated by building efficient tools, such as technical and logical tools (e.g. Intrusion Detection Systems weighted sum model (IDS-WSM), which was honored with best award by German Federal Office for Information Security) [22], represent a valuable and irreplaceable asset that will undoubtedly contribute to enriching and optimizing research on information security.

References

1. Jeong, J., Mihelcic, J., Oliver, G., Rudolph, C.: Towards an improved understanding of human factors in cybersecurity. In: IEEE 2019: Proceedings of the 1st International Conference on Trust, Privacy and Security in Intelligent Systems and Applications, pp. 338–345. IEEE, Piscataway (2019)
2. Hurst, W., Shone, N., Monnet, Q.: Predicting the effects of DDoS attacks on a network of critical infrastructures. In: IEEE 2015: Proceedings of the International Conference on Computer and Information Technology, UK (2015)
3. Wang, H., Chen, Z., Zhao, J., Di, X., Liu, D.: A vulnerability assessment method in industrial internet of things based on attack graph and maximum flow, pp. 8599–8609. IEEE (2018)
4. Alperin, K.B., Wollaber, A.B., Gomez, S.R.: Improving interpretability for cyber vulnerability assessment using focus and context visualizations. In: Proceedings of ViZSec, 2020, USA, pp. 30–30. IEEE (2020)
5. ISO/IEC 27002:2017-06, 2017: Information technology-Security techniques- Code of practice for information security controls, Beuth Verlag, Berlin, Germany (2017)
6. ISO/IEC 27035–1:2016–11: Information technology-security techniques- Information security incident management- Part 1: Principles of incident management, Beuth Verlag, Berlin, Germany (2016)
7. National Institute of Standards and Technology, Computer Security Incident Handling Guide, U.S. Department of Commerce, Washington, D.C., SP 800–61, Revision 1 Mar 2008
8. FIRST, The EPSS Model. Accessed 21 Jan 2022
9. Bolívar, H., Parada, H.D.J., Roa, O., Velandia, J.: Multi-criteria decision making model for vulnerabilities assessment in cloud computing regarding common vulnerability scoring system. In: Proceedings of CONIITI, Bogota, Colombia, 2019, pp. 1-6. IEEE (2019)
10. Vanamala, M., Yuan, X., Roy, K.: Modeling and classification of common vulnerabilities and exposures database. In: icABCD 2020: IEEE, pp. 1–5. Durban, South Africa (2020)
11. Kebande, V.R., Kigwana, I., Venter, H.S., Karie, N.M., Wario, R.D.: CVSS metric-based analysis, classification and assessment of computer network threats and vulnerabilities. In: icABCD 2018: IEEE, South Africa, pp. 1–10 (2018)
12. Almukaynizi, M., Nunes, E., Dharaiya, K., Sennguttuvan, M., Shakarian, J., Shakarian, P.: Proactive identification of exploits in the wild through vulnerability mentions online. In: IEEE 2017: Proceedings of CyCon U.S., United States, pp. 82-88 (2017)
13. Jalali, M.S., Siegel, M., Madnick, S.: Decision-making and biases in cybersecurity capability development: evidence from a simulation game experiment. J. Strateg. Inf. Syst. **28**(1), 66–82 (2019)

14. Gianini, G., Cremonini, M., Rainini, A., Cota, G.L., Fossi, L.G.: A game theoretic approach to vulnerability patching. In: ICTRC 2015: Proceedings of the Information and Communication Technology Research, pp. 88-91 (2015)

15. Islam, C., Babar, M.A., Nepal, S.: An ontology-driven approach to automating the process of integrating security software systems. In: ICSSP 2019: Proceedings of the IEEE/ACM ICSSP, Canada, pp. 54–63 (2019)

16. DiMasse, D., et al.: A holistic approach to cyber physical systems security and resilience. In: IEEE 2020: Proceedings of SSS, Crystal City, VA, USA, pp. 1-8 (2020)

17. Wang, J.A., Guo, M., Wang, H., Xia, M., Zhou, L.: Environmental metrics for software security based on a vulnerability ontology. In: IEEE 2009: Proceedings of the International Conference on Secure Software Integration and Reliability Improvement, China, pp. 159–168 (2009)

18. NIST. National Vulnerability Database. Accessed 21 Mar 2022

19. Pham, V., Dang, T.: CVExplorer: multi-dimensional visualization for common vulnerabilities and exposures. In: IEEE 2018, Seattle, WA, USA, pp. 1296-1301 (2018)

20. Boyd, J.R.: A Discourse on Winning and Losing, pp. 1–400. Maxwell, AFB, Alabama, Edited and Compiled by Dr. Grant T. Hammond (2018)

21. Koza, E., Öztürk, A.: A literature review to analyze the state of the art of virtual power plants in context of information security. In: Wohlgemuth, V., Naumann, S., Behrens, G., Arndt, H.-K. (eds.) ENVIROINFO 2021. PI, pp. 49–69. Springer, Cham (2022). https://doi.org/10.1007/978-3-030-88063-7_4

22. Koza, E.: Information security awareness and training as a holistic key factor - how can a human firewall take on a complementary role in information security? In: Ahram, T., Karwowski, W., (eds) Human Factors in Cybersecurity. AHFE (2022) International Conference. AHFE Open Access, vol 53. AHFE International

23. Koza, E., Öztürk, A.: Entwicklung eines adaptiven Anforderungsanalyse-Tools zur bedarfsgerechten Ermittlung von CERT und IDS Dienstleistungen für die Akteure in der Energiewirtschaft. In: Book: Cyber-Sicherheit ist Chefinnen und Chefsache! - Tagungsband zum 18. Deutschen IT-Sicherheitskongress, Bundesamt für Sicherheit in der Informationstechnik (Hg.), SecuMedia-Verlag Gau-Algesheim (2022)

Towards a Layer Model for Digital Sovereignty: A Holistic Approach

Isabelle Fries[1], Maximilian Greiner[1], Manfred Hofmeier[1], Razvan Hrestic[1(✉)], Ulrike Lechner[1], and Thomas Wendeborn[2]

[1] Universität der Bundeswehr München, Neubiberg, Germany
razvan.hrestic@unibw.de
[2] Universität des Saarlandes, Saarbrücken, Germany

Abstract. Digital sovereignty has gained interest in the political field and in the public discourse. This discussion paper addresses "digital sovereignty" from various academic disciplines in a holistic analysis approach: In the discussion of digital sovereignty, the question arises whose digital sovereignty is being addressed, what digital sovereignty means for the respective entities, how to increase digital sovereignty and how to build a digital sovereign civil society and its critical infrastructures. We present a layered model to conceptualize the meaning of digital sovereignty on three layers: (1) state or supranational institution, (2) organization, (3) individual as well as the relationships between the three layers. This model provides guidance for research and practice - including policy and decision making - on the complex subject of digital sovereignty. It is a living model and can also be expanded and adapted as more insight is added to this relatively new field. With this article, we share the model with the community and open it up for discussion.

Keywords: Digital Sovereignty · Model · Interdisciplinary

1 Introduction

Digital sovereignty has become an increasingly important topic in the political field and in public discourse - primarily driven by geopolitical challenges. Now, it is also gaining interest in scientific research. In most cases when discussing digital sovereignty, the focus is on a state or supranational entity level [44]. But "many other meanings are emphasized when talking about sovereignty" [15]. Sovereign entities could be states or supranational institutions, organizations such as companies, or individuals. Critical infrastructure security efforts are generally related to "the economic lifeblood, social stability, and public interests of countries, and even national security, and involves common concerns of all countries" as Fang rightly points out [18, p. 196]. In German politics this is made clear by the fact that the current coalition agreement enshrines digital sovereignty at both the state and individual layer [43, p. 12 f.]. In this context, the term "digital sovereignty" appears to be used topically, but does not appear to have a clear definition [46, p. 82].

Disentangling the notion of digital sovereignty from informal and political discourse is a challenging task. There are other terms describing the topic, often in the context of cybersecurity: while in the discourse at the level of the European Union (EU) there is talk of "cyber sovereignty" and this seems to refer to a nationally restrictive idea with a view to the policies of China or Russia, there is talk both nationally and supranationally of "data sovereignty", which emphasizes more strongly the handling of data at the level of the individual and the organization [14]. Talk of data sovereignty is also found in particular in the context of the GAIA-X initiative [1], an European attempt to create an alternative to provider-specific commercial cloud platforms. Pertaining to this, the term "strategic autonomy" was found to be used in the EU context [17]. However, one crucial point seems to uniformly presuppose today's discussion in digital sovereignty: digital sovereignty is seen as a desirable good, which at the same time does not seem to exist anymore, not yet, or not to a satisfactory degree. This is especially true at the policy level related to critical infrastructure protection. In the context of political efforts in Germany, for example, the 2013 coalition agreement already states that "technological sovereignty" - referred to here - is to be "regained" [13, p. 103]. At the same time, the pursuit of digital sovereignty is linked to the pursuit of independence and competitiveness. There is talk of the dependence of states and organizations on external hardware and software, which must be overcome, or of the digital literacy of citizens, which has not yet been achieved to a satisfactory degree.

If one goes back and looks for a concept-historical approach to understanding, one quickly comes across state theory. Reference is often made to Thomas Hobbes's "Leviathan" and to a social contract between an absolute sovereign and the people. Although this is initially far from an intuitive understanding of what seems to be meant by digital sovereignty today, it does make one thing very clear: the term sovereignty is accompanied by a relational determination that remains intact even in the digital space. An entity is always sovereign in relation to another entity or thing. This makes it useful to look at various relational constellations in the following in order to make the talk of digital sovereignty tangible. Ultimately, the same applies to the still rather young talk of digital sovereignty as it does to language in general: language changes, is a fluid mass rather than a static construct, and gains its shape in social interaction.

In the interaction of social actors and in the interdisciplinary discourse, open questions regarding digital sovereignty also become conscious. Some of them already appear in research. If one defines digital sovereignty as "the ability to act and make decisions in the digital space" [6, p. 6], it is a construct contextualized from the state's power of disposal. But does the state have a digitally sovereign? When is an individual able to act digitally sovereign? Who or which institution has digital sovereignty? All these and other questions cannot be answered unequivocally [15]. On the other hand, there are different aspects to the effective implementation of digital sovereignty. According to Beyerer [6], these are the sovereignty of infrastructures, sovereignty of data, sovereignty of decision-making and sovereignty platforms.

These aspects accompany our approach to understanding digital sovereignty presented below. To conceptualize the term digital sovereignty for researchers and practice (such as policy and decision making), we developed a layered model using creative techniques. We started from the categories of state, organization, and individual, and present both, them and their respective relational structures. We also include the above-mentioned related idioms, such as of cyber sovereignty or data sovereignty to sharpen understanding.

Our approach is holistic, in that we assume that the various layers of digital sovereignty cannot be viewed in isolation from one another. We assume that the political aspiration to increase digital sovereignty can be met if the latter is thought of as a systemic overall process that encompasses state, organization and the individual in a reciprocal interactive and interrelational context. To approach such an understanding of digital sovereignty, we deliberately work in an interdisciplinary way. Given the breadth of the concept and the different views of the disciplines, we do not believe that an all-encompassing definition of digital sovereignty can (or should) be given. Thus we deliberately avoid a normative framework for the term. Our goal with the resulting model is to provide a flexible frame through few but widely defined categories, which are interconnected by factors either reducing or supporting digital sovereignty. This structure can be scaled by adding depth, e.g. when considering the individual layer; one could state that it composes the aspects culture and formal education, which themselves could be interconnected in the above sense. This creates a self-similar but consistent basis to build upon when further structuring future knowledge regarding digital sovereignty is needed.

2   Research Design

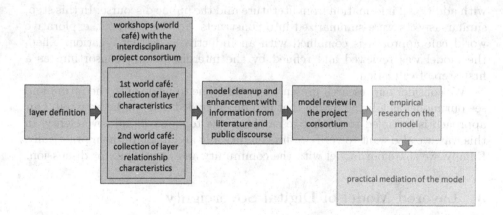

Fig. 1. Model development process

Derived from the domain literature - such as [7,15,27,48] - and from project-internal discussions, we first defined three model layers: (1) state or supranational institution, (2) organization and (3) individual (Fig. 1).

In a second step, we conducted a workshop with the project consortium using the world café method [42] adjusted for a virtual workshop format on the platform Miro. The interdisciplinarity of the consortium with twelve experts including expertise in the fields of computer science, information systems, psychology, education and ethics is the basis for the holistic analysis of the concept of digital sovereignty. Note that various experts of the consortium have expertise in cybersecurity, IT-security for critical infrastructures and resilience as well as serious games as a method for cybersecurity. In addition, there is psychological expertise in negotiating interests and in behavior, in the field of education under the conditions of digitization and in political philosophy and technology ethics. Thus we were able to approach the topic of digital sovereignty on a professional level from multiple perspectives.

In this constellation, two world cafés were performed. The first world café featured three (virtual) tables, each table addressing one layer. In accordance with the world café method, the layer characteristics were collected and written down in three rounds, between which the participants freely changed tables (so that the groups were reformed every round). Participants were asked to add to the model what sovereignty means for them in their individual discipline in relation to each layer. In the second world café, there were three (virtual) tables addressing the relationships between the three layers. Here, the participants collected mutual interactions and dependencies between the respective layers.

The information collected in the world cafés - which also represents the subjective views of the participants and is influenced by previous knowledge, a primarily German context, and the public discourse - was then cleaned up (e.g. removal of duplicates or correction of misplaced characteristics) and enhanced with additional information from literature and the public discourse. In this step, similar aspects were summarized into constructs. So the heuristic, explorative world café approach is combined with an inductive construct creation. Then, the model was reviewed and refined by the interdisciplinary consortium as a first step of validation.

We consider our research presented at this time to be open to the future and see our model as a living model that can be expanded and will be adapted. Our approach is intended to further research on the topic of digital sovereignty. In this way, we also want to verify results empirically and mediate them practically. Finally, we share our model with the community and open it up for discussion.

3   Layered Model of Digital Sovereignty

As mentioned in our research design, we found suggestions in the domain literature that a layered approach to digital sovereignty would better depict its wide-reaching implications than a one-dimensional approach. Wittpahl for instance [27] structures his book in three sections: citizen, company and state. Pohle suggests in [38] that there are individual, state and economic dimensions, the intersection of which falling into the notion of digital sovereignty. The organization BITKOM, representing the IT branch in Germany, also takes a layered approach to describing digital sovereignty, positions it however as a stakeholder-relationship between consumers, enterprise users and state [7].

Our proposed model introduces a novel element in placing the organizational layer on the same level as the individual and the state, both of which represent the main focus of the current literature on the topic of digital sovereignty. We also expand the state dimension to include supranational entities such as the EU since the issue of sovereignty always entails the question of an international determination of relations and the EU in particular can have a great influence on the policies of individual member states (Fig. 2).

4   Model Layers

Our model for digital sovereignty presented in this paper consists of the following three layers: The first layer addresses states and supranational institutions (such as the EU), the second layer addresses organizations including both companies and non-profit organizations, private or governmental and the third layer addresses the individual citizen.

In this section, we describe each of the three levels using statements made in the world cafés as well as broader literature. The following section then proceeds to describe the relationships between layer elements in terms of how they influence each other in terms of digital sovereignty. In this second section, we have also included statements from the world cafés as well as relevant literature.

4.1   State or Supranational Institution Layer

Digital sovereignty on state or supranational level is closely connected to the underlying layers of organization and individuals as the state can be seen as a superordinate entity. The reference points of the state layer can be divided into three areas: international, EU and national. The characteristics differ accordingly from one layer to another, but on the other hand they are strongly branched together, which poses a challenge of classification and demarcation. Moerel and Timmers offer a different view regarding the state perspective by relating the term sovereignty to the dimensions cyber resilience of critical systems, processes and data, control of economic ecosystems as well as trust in the rules of law and democratic processes [32].

The results of the world café focus on the digital policy of a state entity layer on national, EU and international levels, the national education system as well as on dependencies on other states. Workshop participants linked the term digital sovereignty to autarky, interoperability, portability, and open standards.

Digital Policy. In 2021, a letter from ministers of four European countries was written to the president of the European commission explicitly on the subject of

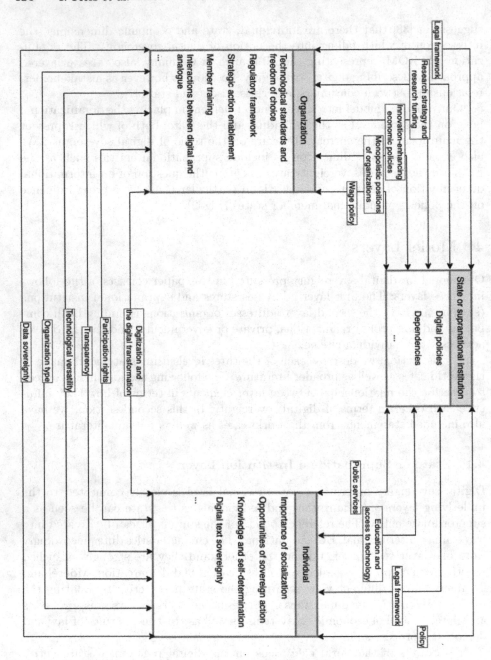

Fig. 2. Layered Model of Digital Sovereignty - Detailed view

digital sovereignty. In addition to concrete deficits and inferential measures, an understanding of digital sovereignty at the European level has been established. In this context, digital sovereignty is outlined as a guiding theme of the digital transformation and digital policy to encompass the interests of society (individuals), business (organizations) and the state (international, EU, national) in equal measure [31]. Considering the political texts above, when referring to technological innovation one can posit that being a top innovator (as a state) makes it easier to remain a top innovator or even increase the advantage. As innovation can be considered a network effect, one may consider investigating preferential attachment (as suggested originally by Barabási and Albert [4]) in innovation networks - in the public and private sector. Furthermore, the education system plays a key role in the context of digital sovereignty on state as well as individual layer. This is confirmed by an expert opinion based on Blossfeld, who describes the Education system as a model of digital sovereignty [8].

Dependencies. According to the results above this is about building on strengths and reducing strategic weaknesses, not excluding other states or taking a protectionist approach. In the context of supranational striving for digital sovereignty, research literature thus also refers to "the creation of a sovereign common good protected by a border and administered by a common rule imposed on incoming actors" [45, p. 144]. It is also about developing a global supply chain in the interests of all participants [31]. This is in accordance with workshop results, where, besides the terms mentioned above, the balance of power and digital access, on mental and material level, were outlined as characteristic in the field of digital sovereignty. Based on the dimensions of Moerel and Timmers, the description of digital sovereignty is outlined on the basis of case studies from different research projects, including deficits and challenges for the Dutch state [32]. Similar views can also be found in the current German coalition agreement, which characterizes digital sovereignty as the self-determined development of digital innovations and the use of digital infrastructure. Furthermore, the topics of digital civil rights and IT security as well as the use of data and data law are discussed [43]. This socio-political demand for digital human rights has long been reflected in scientific discourse [5]. Compared to the results of the workshop, characteristic patterns can be identified as reference was also made to digital rights such as interoperability, portability, as well as open standards and European ecosystems, such as 5G or artificial intelligence.

4.2   Organization Layer

Switching perspectives towards organizations we give an overview of the topic clusters which came up during our world café. This is supplemented by a discussion correlating these statements again to findings in the literature.

Technological Standards and Freedom of Choice. This includes concerns regarding e.g. the dependency of an organization upon specific technologies, data formats or standards. These concerns were quite frequent and supporting and developing standards is a discussion that has been going on for decades. For instance the question of flexible standards and how some healthcare information systems (HMIS) support them has been raised in [10].

Regulatory Framework. This refers to governance issues, norms and laws within which any organization exists. Our participants mentioned these issues less frequently and in rather generic fashion e.g. *What are the legal requirements?*. Ranchordas takes note in [40, p. 202] that legislation still has trouble in keeping up with technological advancement. This is highly apparent in the issue of autonomous driving, the vision of which goes back to 1935[1]. Even after relevant technologies appeared in the late 1960s, a significant period of time passed until the issue was first embedded in a legal framework in Germany (2017) and later in other states.

Strategic Action Enablement. Points included here refer to the longer term ability of organizations to act strategically and where technology is a key enabler e.g. which financial resources are allotted to technology purchasing. We also discuss this below with respect to small and medium enterprises (SMEs) which arguably have more limited strategic resources as was painfully demonstrated by their performances during the COVID-19 pandemic. This has surfaced multiple weak points in the organizations' strategies (or lack thereof) in dealing with remote work.

Member Training. A core pillar of the organization is represented by its members. As will be mentioned in the section concerning the individual, they need to be supported and trained in new technologies introduced by the organization. We will not specify this point further as it is covered in more depth in Sect. 4.3.

Interactions Between Digital and Analogue. Even though this cluster was smaller, there have been questions about the way the digital and the analogue interact and coexist within organizations. This opens the field of further questions, for instance the question of whether such interactions can be intentionally modelled or whether this should or even can be a binary choice.

Another interesting fact we encountered while doing literature research was that there are very few results[2] which refer both to digital sovereignty and to organizations in general. An exception with regard to scientific reflection is the work of Hartmann [24,25]. He understands digital sovereignty of organizations in analogy to digital sovereignty of individuals and wants to make it measurable in terms of the degree of agency and control in the digital space. In this sense, Lehmann and Dörr also understand digital sovereignty with regard to SMEs as being able to inform oneself independently about relevant technologies and new technical possibilities, in order to be able to choose between several options - so

---

[1] In the General Motors film *The Safest Place* by Jam Handy.

[2] Search performed on Google Scholar - "digital sovereignty" (title only) from 2015 to 2022. Only four out of two hundred fifty seven results could fall into the category organizational digital sovereignty.

that the questions "What does digitization mean for my company and how do I set the strategic course?" can be answered [30, p. 14]. In doing so, the authors conceptually include the training of digital skills of managers and employees [30, p. 23]. Nevertheless, the vast majority of literature results have either individual or political focus. This may be interpreted as a sign that organizations do not think of their work in this direction in terms of "digital sovereignty" or prefer not to use the term in public discourse. It may also be that very few organizations see this as an overarching strategic goal, and thus simply do not frame their work in these terms. When used in a political context, digital sovereignty is usually limited to the contexts of data sovereignty or technological sovereignty. In the literature too little focus is set on the fact that organizations are part of ecosystems and thus digital sovereignty discussions should be focused on the entire chain. We argue that the chain perspective is a more consistent one and thus the single-organization perspective, while valid, has to be evaluated in the context of its chain. The type of chain is here a criterion which the researcher should use at her own discretion. For instance, in a logistics context, the supply chain perspective would be relevant and one would thus choose to look at the suppliers, customers and other partners of a chosen organization.

Our search suggests that organizations currently do not approach digital sovereignty at a strategic level. One needs to switch perspectives from the strategic to the more tactical or operative layers. Our workshop results suggest that technological and data sovereignty are topics of interest for organizations (e.g. the question of how dependent an organization is on a software provider or the question of proprietary digital formats and standards). When comparing these with the literature we see mixed results.

Like Hartmann, Dörr und Lehmann, which have already been mentioned, Pentenrieder, Bertini and Künzel also frame digital sovereignty in the context of SMEs as the ability to maintain an overview of new technical capabilities in order to be able to choose the best among different digital options [37, pg. 2]. They further argue that some technologies can serve as enablers more than others for continued self-determination of business processes and name artificial intelligence (AI) technologies as an example in the context of the machine tool industry. A frequent association between the companies' ability to innovate and digital sovereignty is also suggested in previous work. For example Bogenstahl and Zinke in [9] focus on trends such as intelligent algorithms, Big Data, artificial intelligence (machine learning) or the Internet of Things. Competence development in these areas has enjoyed a wider attention, for instance regarding Machine Learning in [36].

4.3 Individual Layer

The concept of sovereignty is also a way of comprehending the human individual - to be understood as an open system - in its entirety. In this perspective sovereignty is a term that reflects the real wealth of human beings. It can be linked and supplemented with terms from a wide variety of sciences. These include terms such as subject and subjectivity, individual and individuality, personality and personal development, autonomy and maturity. These terms are closely related to issues and problems of the society, communities, families and parents, as well as issues of education and formation. The associated assumptions allow people to use the possibilities for self-realization and individual development. In the discourse on digital sovereignty, these fundamental thoughts are reflected particularly in the topic of self-sovereign identity (SSI), which incorporates the idea of sovereignty in its very name. This is followed, especially in the German discourse, by a striving for free self-determination in the digital space that is seen as worthy of protection and that is also subject to corresponding legal regulations.

Importance of Socialization. The socialization process is particularly important for the quality of development opportunities. However, socialization can only take place within the framework of opportunities given to an individual. "Even under the assumption of different social and cultural conditions in large parts of the world, the political and economic conditions in many countries of the world differ considerably and thus also the development opportunities for individuals".

Opportunities of Sovereign Action. In increasingly digital societies, this becomes particularly relevant when individuals of all ages are confronted with very specific requirements. This includes the acquisition of mechanisms, techniques for accessing and using digital technologies [39]. Above all, this creates associations with questions about the acquisition of knowledge and skills. But, it is more than just consuming content. In particular, the focus is on the means that individuals have to realize themselves in an increasingly digital world, to pursue personal goals and to fulfill tasks. Regarding to this, it is important to identify what opportunities an individual has to assert themselves in a digitally shaped world and to get involved (or not) in social reproduction processes. The concept of digital sovereignty - so far almost exclusively used in legal terms and anchored especially in political theory as mentioned before - has become an important concept in politics and is more and more the subject of scientific analysis. It attempts to describe a very ambivalent structure of state control mechanisms, economic and political interests, and the personal development of individuals at different levels of action. It is evident that these developments are associated with qualitatively new challenges for people of all ages in the 21st century.

Knowledge and Self-determination. In our world cafés, we discussed in more detail the extent to which digitization affects the sovereignty of the individual - in a positive or possibly negative way. Indeed, it is less evident whether the digital separates people from sovereignty or connects them to it. Can sovereignty be digital at all? Can people act and make sovereign decisions in the digital world? What about data sovereignty and data ownership [26]: does data belong to the person to whom it refers or to those who collect it? It does not seem to make sense to try to find out how the individual can maintain sovereignty over his or her digital traces. Rather, the question arises as to how individuals can be put in a position of knowing and sovereign self-determination [21]. Two fundamental perspectives emerge: on the one hand, an individual, very human perspective. Because first of all, each individual independently decides whether or not to use digital technologies. For example, in our world café, the question arose: *Can digital sovereignty also mean that an individual sovereignly chooses to remain analog, and should there be a legal provision for this?* In practice, individuals are free to use an analog watch or a smartwatch. Or very recently: individuals can request a digital vaccination certificate or use a printed version. Other examples can certainly be found. However, in an increasingly digitized world, it is also more difficult to evade digital technologies. This brings us to the second perspective. Because on the other hand, it is the design of the framework conditions in a digital world in which individuals act. These framework conditions refer to a digital text world. In this digital text world, skills are required that enable the individual to work with texts that were generated under the conditions of **digitization** [20]. These texts differ significantly from those texts that are typographically and scriptographically generated.

Digital Text Sovereignty. "Digital text sovereignty" [20] as a terminus technicus is an essential variable for coping with these changes at the individual layer. As mentioned before regarding SSI, digital text sovereignty already addresses the issue of sovereignty by name. In our workshop, we discussed the various implications of this skill. Following the approach of digital text sovereignty has various advantages in this context. Because in international educational policy discourse and international educational research reference is clearly made to the digital world. But the associated aspects of ability are derived in very different terminology. In the international discourse, the main focus is on "skills" [35, pg. 6] and "digital literacy" [34, pg. 32]. In Germany, for example, the terms "digital competencies" and "digital education" are used. In this context, the construct of digital sovereignty has gained importance in educational policy, educational research and educational theory. Closely related to this is digital text sovereignty, which is differentiated by Frederking and Krommer [20] in an 8-level model (e.g. the semantic level of digital texts, the level of the source code of digital texts, the level of intentionally of digital texts). The challenges for the individual can be summarized with the sovereign functional-technical use of digital texts and a sovereign personal-reflective attitude compared to digital texts.

5 Layer Relationships

While digital sovereignty is characterized differently on three layers, the layers are not isolated from each other. Rather, there are various connections between them such as dependencies, empowerment or even conflicts. Following, the relationship characteristics are described.

5.1   Relationship Between State and Organization

According to the characteristics of the previous chapters, the relationship between the state institution layer and organizations can be seen from two opposing perspectives. On the one hand, the positive or negative influence of the state on organizations must be taken into account. On the other hand, one should consider how the digital sovereignty of organizations can be influenced by the state: The state cannot make society digital sovereign - it is the organizations who build the digital infrastructure that may facilitate digital sovereignty.

However, the workshop results suggest that in discourse the participants differentiated between organizations within a state (jurisdiction) and organizations outside it (as e.g. supranational organizations as the UN). While international legal frameworks exist (such as the International Trade Law), they are often difficult to navigate and some organizations then tend to adhere to local laws when uncertain. In addition, the following five potential mutual were identified:

Legal Frameworks. Central guidelines and standards can be defined and passed, by the state institution layer in consultation with organizations and ideally support in making the information base or decision-making basis for companies transparent. Within the workshop, data protection and data security specifications were also given as examples in this regard: they determine how personal data can be processed and why cybersecurity investements and technologies are necessary to be compliant with regulations. Regulations shape the competition in the markets and the competitiveness of organizations in a global market. This contributes to shaping the digital sovereignty of organizations as these will not need additional assistance in identifying or implementing standards, but rather use the embedded guidelines provided by the state. An example of this is basic IT Security Guidance which in some states[3] is implemented as a certifiable standard. On the other hand, such regulation also tends to be implemented as required, no more and no less. Hence, if the regulation itself is watered down in a political compromise or is loosely enforced, its implementation will tend to have the same quality.

Research Strategy and Research Funding. Research programs are designed to add value to the digital sovereignty of both state and organization layer. Close cooperation between research and practice, i.e. modern ecosystems should facilitate novel technologies and innovation enables innovations in order to bring new innovations, e.g. block chains, and the resulting business models in the market to create value. This effect of public research and development (R&D) funding has been the object of public evaluation under general additionality[4] principles, leading to mixed results according to [19]. The results also vary by state, so it would be interesting to investigate potential correlations of positive additionality and digital sovereignty in the future.

---

[3] Examples are the Minimum Cyber Security Standards (MCSS) in the United Kingdom or the BSI IT-Grundschutz in Germany.

[4] A specific term used to describe the benefits resulting from public sector funding.

Innovation-enhancing Economic Policies. On the one hand, this can promote the availability of alternative products or services and thus positively influence self-determined action at national, EU and international level. On the other hand, these types of regulations can act as barriers to innovation. Organizations are thus restricted in their right of co-determination and cannot contribute to technological diversity. Furthermore, economic policies support the state layer in understanding and expanding its own options for action through innovations by organizations. Social networks have been voiced as an example. Due to the strong increase in users, the state has become aware of a need for action with regard to regulation and control.

Monopolistic Positions of Organizations. A balance of power defines the relation between state and organization. Our participants expressed concerns that modern platforms or digital organizations may yield monopolistic positions. Examples include social media platforms and tech companies. Through technologies, standards and patents large corporations can encroach upon the sovereignty of the state layer. Especially when regulation lags behind technical advances.

Wage Policy. Both the relationship between the individual and the state as well as between the state and organization become clear within this topic. As a rule, IT professionals are higher paid in the private sector than in public sector. This can lead to an imbalance of digitally sovereign competencies that culminates in the business sector at national, EU as well as international level.

5.2   Relationship Between State and Individual

The Karlsruhe theses on the digital sovereignty of Europe [6] place digital sovereignty in the context of individuals, companies and the European community of states in the digital space. The theses show very clearly that the perspective of the individual on digital sovereignty must always be linked to the perspective of the state. However, democratic states and democratically elected governments are made up of the people. The state represents the people. The constitution of democratic states is constituted by the basic rights of the citizens. The people can assert this against the state. Therefore, the individual development of digital sovereignty is strongly linked with the development of the democracy of the states. This relates to the following fields of interaction between state and individual.

Policy. As part of the political decision-making process and political control, the state creates a framework for action in which the people can make digitally sovereign decisions. Political decisions should protect the rights of citizens in the digital space [39]. This includes the prevention of comprehensive communication surveillance of citizens, the surveillance of government members (e.g. from the opposition), spying on companies and media up to the infiltration of the entire network communication structure. Without political decisions, there is a high risk of an attack on the fundamental rights and freedoms of citizens and a threat of an open, free and democratic society.

Legal Framework. In an open and democratic society it is presupposed that there are spaces in which individuals can move and communicate without being observed [39]. In this context, probably the most important aspect for securing or developing digital sovereignty is the adoption of the European General Data Protection Regulation (GDPR). The GDPR ensures a high level of data protection throughout Europe. All providers who offer their services in Europe are subject to this [41]. In addition, terms such as data security, data protection, patent and copyright law, cloud computing, the regulation of e-commerce and the consideration of general contractual and business conditions in the digital economy can be described as part of the legal framework. However, the recent years have shown that the dynamic development of technology, media and communication is far ahead of the development of appropriate regulatory concepts. This means that digital sovereignty must always be linked to the underlying legal framework.

Education and Access to Technologies. Education is one of the key parameters for achieving digital sovereignty. In particular, the institutionalized, compulsory general education with a focus on acquiring digital skills is a basic requirement for sovereign participation in society. Training and adult education is also important [23]. A certain level of digital competence is the prerequisite for digital sovereignty [8]. It is the liability of the state to create framework conditions in and outside of educational institutions (e.g. schools, colleges, universities) in which citizens can acquire digital skills. This does not only refer to the linking of education and digitization in general. Rather, it requires a profound and sustainable implementation of this topic in the curriculum of general school education, as well as university study programs. However, access to digital technologies must also be made possible. For example, achieving data sovereignty requires knowledge of different media, relevant security aspects and potential risks of their use. Furthermore, certified IT products, systems and network infrastructures that guarantee secure data transmission are also required.

Public Services. Public services can be seen as an interface between the obligations of the state and the interests of the citizens. It shows that citizens are increasingly demanding transparency, efficiency and responsiveness from public authorities, public administration and public organizations in the context of digitization. Thus, the increasing adoption of digital technologies represents a key element of governments' response to such requirements. The use of digital technologies to edit and process sensitive citizen data also requires completely new concepts in terms of data security, availability and communication. This not only relates to the technical perspective of the IT systems, but also to the ICT competencies (e.g. knowledge of current IT technologies and support processes, understanding of technology, knowledge of software architecture) of the involved people. In the interaction of political decisions, legal framework conditions, the design of educational processes in a digital world and the granting of access to digital technologies, public services are an important instance of sovereign acting citizens in democratic states.

5.3   Relationship Between Organization and Individual

As we have seen in Sect. 4.2 the political and scientific discourse around digital sovereignty appears to primarily revolve around the state and the individual. Our workshop findings seem to confirm this gap in the area of relationships between organizations and individuals: we have markedly less input on that level compared to any of the others discussed in Sects. 5.1 and 5.2.

In structuring future research paths we need to be able to better phrase research questions regarding how organizations and individuals influence each other's digital sovereignty.

Emerging from our workshop are six candidates for criteria, which we present in the following paragraphs. These criteria constitute early results and therefore we also propose relevant research question for follow-up work.

Digitization and the digital transformation are terms often mentioned in the context of digital sovereignty of organizations. Low digital competencies of workers may mean less possibilities for organizations to become more digitally sovereign. The converse is thus also possible when the organization itself is more digitally sovereign as a result of external or internal pressure and thus influences workers or collaborators to also become more digitally sovereign as a result. There are hints of these in the efforts of governments to improve planning outcomes for local regions in Australia [2]. A recent Italian study for public organizations suggests that there may be a significant downside for these organizations when workers do not possess e-skills required from the digital transformation [12]. In assessing the role of digital competencies in work engagement, Oberländer and Bipp [33] suggest that digital communication and collaboration are central competencies at work, both in theory and practice and that more work is needed in this area in order to understand the exact implications of said digital competencies.

Participation Rights. Another question arising from the workshop is whether or not there is a correlation among workers or associates having a say in the organization decisions and the digital sovereignty of said organization. In other words: Do more participation rights result in more digital sovereignty? This question may prove to be very challenging to answer. A literature review on the topic of participation suggests that there are vast amounts of scholarly material and views available on this topic [29]. Thus one has to be very careful and specific in choosing an interpretative framework for this in order to frame it for the context of digital sovereignty. In any case, the question of the extent to which individuals want to act with digital sovereignty at all is also highly relevant to security. It could be that individuals would rather hand over responsibility to a technical system than take responsibility themselves and thus become a security risk themselves (so considered in [22]).

Transparency is also interesting from multiple points of view and at different levels. At the level of enterprise architecture for instance, we would posit that a transparent application landscape plays an important role when needing to decide which digital tool to use for a given task. At a higher level, market transparency seems to play a role. There are, for instance, companies[5] as well as governmental agencies[6] helping consumers get better overviews of several different offers in markets with high information asymmetry. This suggests that organizations can positively influence the digital sovereignty of individuals if no other non-trivial downsides are used. A platform can use its positioning to take advantage of the information asymmetry by placing sponsored offers or by manipulating prices.

Technological versatility represents the experience and know-how in a wide spectrum of technologies and offerings (e.g. open source software or multiple potential providers for cloud computing of employees or associates could enable organizations themselves to become more digitally sovereign as this capability may enable better strategic choices. The converse may also hold true when organizations apply anti vendor lock-in strategies and thus themselves opt to use open source software. In turn, the members of the organization are trained and so they can also apply these strategies in their personal software choices. An interesting question here is how such organizations perform in the long term, compared with organizations without these strategies.

Organization type may be an important factor in how digital sovereignty is represented. One should differentiate between commercial and non-profit companies, between NGOs, clubs and government agencies. Also their internal structure - centralized versus decentralized - may affect how they perceive and act with respect to digital sovereignty.

Data sovereignty reflects in the ability of organization to control their data. An organization with a high degree of control may mean more data protection for individuals. Low capabilities in organizations however could lead to choosing providers with low quality or obscure data protection practices. We also consider good IT security practices as part of data sovereignty.

6   Discussion and Limitations

Particularly in interdisciplinary approaches to digital sovereignty, the question arises whose digital sovereignty is being addressed and what digital sovereignty means for the respective entities. We developed a layered model to conceptualize the meaning of the term digital sovereignty on three layers (state or supranational institutions, organization, individual) as well as the relationships between the layers. This model attempts to provide guidance for research and practice - including policy and decision making - on the complex subject of digital sovereignty.

---

[5] e.g. Check24 for financial offers, clevertanken.de for gas prices, Expedia for travel offers.
[6] For instance consumer protection agencies.

When operating with the notion of digital sovereignty at any level, the question of measurement arises: is it possible to quantify or somehow probe specific aspects thereof? Some have proposed dimensions of digital sovereignty. In [3] for instance, three dimensions are proposed: privacy, cybersecurity and strategy. We cannot and should not assume that there is an exhaustive list of dimensions, but rather that the researcher should select the relevant dimensions for her own research questions.

Nevertheless, the proposed layered model does not claim to be fully exhaustive, but is seen as a suitable way to conceptualize digital sovereignty. Other characteristics are possible that have not been included here. The model is a theoretical approach and does not directly serve the purpose to measure digital sovereignty. Further subsequent steps are necessary for this (see outlook), but these are enabled by this model.

7   Outlook

The goal of our research on a model for digital sovereignty is to provide guidance and orientation on how to achieve the political goal of digital sovereignty. We employ the well-established model as a kernel with the three layers of state, organization, and individual. Furthermore, we pay special attention to the relationship between the levels in favor of an increase in digital sovereignty when located in an overall systemic process. We explored it from various academic perspectives, drawing on expertise in cybersecurity, security of critical infrastructures, and resilience, as well as educational, psychological, and philosophical expertise. The method of world café allowed us to capture the ideas and concepts various disciplines associate, justify, and emphasize with sovereignty or digital sovereignty. The existing model bridges political discourse with design-oriented, empirical, and hermeneutic disciplines and provides an idea of what various academic disciplines can offer for achieving digital sovereignty.

We have further plans to refine our holistic approach and make it a living model that takes into account the respective socio-political circumstances. For example, we already were able to consider the Covid19 pandemic and its consequences in terms of digital sovereignty. The intensification of the Ukraine crisis at the end of February 2022, which has been accompanied by a massive cyber war since 2014 (annexation of Crimea) on Ukraine's digital infrastructure [16], now increasingly shows us how important the topic of digital sovereignty is for scientific and overall social orientation. Reports of suspected targeted disruptive attacks on satellite communications [28] and the GPS system [47] with collateral damage beyond Ukraine reinforce the urgency of advancing research that focuses on digitization, particularly with regard to critical infrastructure. The fact that many countries, including Germany [11], have warned against the use of Kaspersky products, for example, also represents a reflex in favor of digital sovereignty. One way our project team would like to advance such research is to invite more disciplines and experts to contribute to the model and enhance interdisciplinarity. A second way forward is to use our approach in practice. For example, in our research project, this scientific basis will guide further technology development. We want to continue the theorization of digital sovereignty towards a set of Key Performance Indicators that allow assessing the level of digital sovereignty from, e.g., digital products, services, supply chains, critical infrastructures and processes, and design guidelines on building digital sovereignty. We will do more work on harmonizing the research on digital sovereignty with the extant understanding of security and resilience.

Acknowledgements and Contributions. The Project LIONS is funded by dtec.bw - Digitalization and Technology Research Center of the Bundeswehr which we gratefully acknowledge. We also thank the LIONS consortium and our research partners for their contributions to this research activity.

Authors have been listed in alphabetical order. The contributions can be attributed to the coauthors as described below:

– Isabelle Fries contributed additions from a philosophical point of view, as well as for general coherence, and mainly wrote the introduction.

– Maximilian Greiner moderated world café tables and contributed mainly the relationship between state and organization and the state layer.

– Manfred Hofmeier prepared and conducted the world café and contributed research design, discussion and limitations to this article.

– Razvan Hrestic co-organized the world café, and wrote mainly organization layer and relationship between the organization and the individual.

– Ulrike Lechner contributed to the research design, to data collection, data interpretation and the revisions of the article.

– Thomas Wendeborn contributed the individual layer and state of the art on digital sovereignty and definitions of digital sovereignty.

References

1. Gaia-X European Association for Data and Cloud AISBL: Gaia-X Dataspaces (2021). https://gaia-x.eu/what-is-gaia-x/deliverables/data-spaces/. Accessed 20 Apr 2022
2. Alam, K., Erdiaw-Kwasie, M.O., Shahiduzzaman, M., Ryan, B.: Assessing regional digital competence: digital futures and strategic planning implications. J. Rural. Stud. **60**, 60–69 (2018)
3. Baischew, D., Kroon, P., Lucidi, S., Märkel, C., Sörries, B.: Digital sovereignty in Europe: a first benchmark. Wik-consult report, Bad Honnef (2020). http://hdl.handle.net/10419/251539
4. Barabási, A.L., Albert, R.: Emergence of scaling in random networks. science **286**(5439), 509–512 (1999)
5. Benedek, W.: International organizations and digital human rights. In: Wagner, B., Kettemann, M.C., Vieth, K. (eds.) Research Handbook in Human Rights and Digital Technology. Global Politics, Law and International Relations, pp. 364–375. Edward Elgar Publishing (2019)
6. Beyerer, J., Müller-Quade, J., Reussner, R.: Karlsruher Thesen zur Digitalen Souveränität Europas. Datenschutz und Datensicherheit - DuD **42**(5), 277–280 (2018). https://doi.org/10.1007/s11623-018-0940-2

7. BITKOM: Digitale Souveränität. Datenschutz und Datensicherheit - DuD **42**(5), 294–300 (2018). https://doi.org/10.1007/s11623-018-0944-y
8. Blossfeld, H.P., et al.: vbw – Vereinigung der Bayerischen Wirtschaft e.V. [Hrsg.]: Digitale Souveränität und Bildung. Gutachten (2019). https://doi.org/10.25656/01:16569
9. Bogenstahl, C., Zinke, G.: Digitale Souveränität - ein mehrdimensionales Handlungskonzept für die deutsche Wirtschaft. Digitale Souveränität, p. 65 (2017)
10. Braa, J., Hanseth, O., Heywood, A., Mohammed, W., Shaw, V.: Developing health information systems in developing countries: the flexible standards strategy. Mis Quarterly, pp. 381–402 (2007)
11. Bundesamt für Sicherheit und Informationstechnik: BSI warnt vor dem Einsatz von Kaspersky-Virenschutzprodukten (2022). https://bit.ly/3w6Zllo. Accessed 04 May 2022
12. Casalino, N., Saso, T., Borin, B., Massella, E., Lancioni, F.: Digital competences for civil servants and digital ecosystems for more effective working processes in public organizations. In: Agrifoglio, R., Lamboglia, R., Mancini, D., Ricciardi, F. (eds.) Digital Business Transformation. LNISO, vol. 38, pp. 315–326. Springer, Cham (2020). https://doi.org/10.1007/978-3-030-47355-6_21
13. CDU, CSU, SPD: Deutschlands Zukunft gestalten: Koalitionsvertrag zwischen CDU, CSU und SPD (2013)
14. Chin, Y.C., Li, K.: A comparative analysis of cyber sovereignty policies in China and the EU (2021). https://doi.org/10.2139/ssrn.3900752
15. Couture, S.: The diverse meanings of digital sovereignty (2020). https://bit.ly/3kCDVYa. Accessed 13 Apr 2022
16. Eichensehr, K.: Ukraine, cyberattacks, and the lessons for international law (2022)
17. European Political Strategy Centre (European Commission): Rethinking strategic autonomy in the digital age (2019). https://bit.ly/3MSarkW. Accessed 23 Apr 2022
18. Fang, B.: Cyberspace Sovereignty. Springer, Singapore (2018). https://doi.org/10.1007/978-981-13-0320-3
19. Fantino, D., Cannone, G.: Evaluating the efficacy of European regional funds for R&D. Evaluating the efficacy of European regional funds for R&D, pp. 165–196 (2014)
20. Frederking, V., Krommer, A.: Digitale Textkompetenz: Ein theoretisches wie empirisches Forschungsdesiderat im deutschdidaktischen Fokus (2019). https://bit.ly/38fJoRU
21. Friedrichsen, M., Bisa, P.J.: Digitale Souveränität. Vertrauen in der Netzwerkgesellschaft (2016)
22. Fries, I.: "In Code We Trust"? Zur Vertrauens-Verheißung der Blockchain-Technologie. Zeitschrift für Evangelische Ethik (2022)
23. Gegenfurtner, A., Schmidt-Hertha, B., Lewis, P.: Digital technologies in training and adult education. Int. J. Train. Dev. **24**, 1–4 (2020). https://doi.org/10.1111/ijtd.12172
24. Hartmann, E.A.: Digitale souveränität in der wirtschaft – gegenstandsbereiche, konzepte und merkmale. In: Hartmann, E.A. (ed.) Digitalisierung souverän gestalten, pp. 1–16. Springer, Heidelberg (2021). https://doi.org/10.1007/978-3-662-62377-0_1

25. Hartmann, E.A.: Digitale souveränität: soziotechnische bewertung und gestaltung von anwendungen algorithmischer systeme. In: Hartmann, E.A. (ed.) Digitalisierung souverän gestalten II, pp. 1–13. Springer, Heidelberg (2022). https://doi.org/10.1007/978-3-662-64408-9_1

26. Hummel, P., Braun, M., Dabrock, P.: Own data? Ethical reflections on data ownership. Philos. Technol. **34**(3), 545–572 (2020). https://doi.org/10.1007/s13347-020-00404-9

27. Wittpahl, V. (ed.): Digitale Souveränität. Springer, Heidelberg (2017). https://doi.org/10.1007/978-3-662-55796-9

28. Knopp, A.: Satellitenkommunikations-System: Vermutlicher Cyberangriff (2022). https://bit.ly/3w3I24S. Accessed 04 May 2022

29. Lee, C.W.: Participatory practices in organizations. Sociol. Compass **9**(4), 272–288 (2015)

30. Lehmann, C., Dörr, L.: Digital souveräne gestaltung von services – ein marktfähiger mehrwert? In: Hartmann, E.A. (ed.) Digitalisierung souverän gestalten II, pp. 14–24. Springer, Heidelberg (2022). https://doi.org/10.1007/978-3-662-64408-9_2

31. Merkel, A., Frederiksen, M., Marin, S., Kallas, K.: DE-DK-FI-EE: Letter to COM President on Digital Sovereignty (2021). https://politi.co/3FfWdrs

32. Moerel, L., Timmers, P.: Reflections on digital sovereignty. SSRN Scholarly Paper ID 3772777, Social Science Research Network, Rochester, NY (2021). https://papers.ssrn.com/abstract=3772777

33. Oberländer, M., Bipp, T.: Do digital competencies and social support boost work engagement during the COVID-19 pandemic? Comput. Hum. Behav. **130**, 107172 (2022)

34. OECD: PISA 2009 results: students on line (2011). https://doi.org/10.1787/9789264112995-en

35. OECD: Skills for a digital world. Tech. rep., OECD (2016)

36. Panusch, T., Büscher, J., Wöstmann, R., Deuse, J.: Konzept zur zielgerichteten kompetenzentwicklung für initiativen des maschinellen lernens. In: Hartmann, E.A. (ed.) Digitalisierung souverän gestalten II, pp. 93–109. Springer, Heidelberg (2022). https://doi.org/10.1007/978-3-662-64408-9_8

37. Pentenrieder, A., Bertini, A., Künzel, M.: Digitale Souveränität als Trend? Digitalisierung souverän gestalten (2021). https://doi.org/10.1007/978-3-662-62377-0_2. Accessed 24 Mar 2022

38. Pohle, J.: Digitale Souveränität. Handbuch Digitalisierung in Staat und Verwaltung (2020). https://doi.org/10.1007/978-3-658-23669-4_21-1

39. Pohle, J., Thiel, T., et al.: Digital sovereignty. In: Practicing Sovereignty: Digital Involvement in Times of Crises, pp. 47–67. Bielefeld: transcript Verlag (2021)

40. Ranchordas, S.: Innovation-friendly regulation: the sunset of regulation, the sunrise of innovation. Jurimetrics **55**, 201 (2014)

41. Regulation, G.D.P.: General data protection regulation (gdpr). Intersoft Consulting. Accessed 24 Jan 2018

42. Schieffer, A., Isaacs, D., Gyllenpalm, B.: The world café: Part pne. World Business Acad. **18**(8), 1–9 (2004)

43. Scholz, O.: Koalitionsvertrag 2021–2025: Mehr Fortschritt Wagen (2021). https://bit.ly/3seGljP. Accessed 09 Apr 2022

44. Seidel, I., Bös, P.K.: Grundlagen, Inhalte und Implikationen 18(November) (2009)

45. Amedzro St-Hilaire, W.: Digital Risk Governance. Springer, Cham (2020). https://doi.org/10.1007/978-3-030-61386-0

46. Steinbach, J.: Souveränitätsfragmente. Ein Beitrag zur Literaturgeschichte der Souveränität und gegenwärtigen Herausforderungen der Rechtswissenschaften im Spiegel der Digitalisierung. Mohr Siebeck (2019)
47. Universität der Bundeswehr München: Störquellen: Setzt Russland Störangriffe gegen das GPS ein? (2022). https://bit.ly/3LKeLTt. Accessed 04 May 2022
48. Weber, H.: Digitale Souveränität. Informatik Spektrum **45**, 62–69 (2022). https://doi.org/10.1007/s00287-022-01439-2

Building Collaborative Cybersecurity for Critical Infrastructure Protection: Empirical Evidence of Collective Intelligence Information Sharing Dynamics on ThreatFox

Eric Jollès[1] , Sébastien Gillard[2,3] , Dimitri Percia David[1,4] ,
Martin Strohmeier[1,5] , and Alain Mermoud[1(✉)]

[1] Cyber-Defence Campus, armasuisse Science and Technology, Zurich, Switzerland
mermouda@ethz.ch
[2] Information Science Institute, Geneva School of Economics and Management,
University of Geneva, Geneva, Switzerland
[3] Department of Defense Economics, Military Academy at ETH Zurich, Zurich,
Switzerland
[4] Institute of Entrepreneurship and Management, University of Applied Sciences
HES-SO Valais-Wallis, Sierre, Switzerland
[5] Department of Computer Science, Oxford University, Oxford, UK

Abstract. This article describes three collective intelligence dynamics observed on ThreatFox, a free platform operated by abuse.ch that collects and shares indicators of compromise. These three dynamics are empirically analyzed with an exclusive dataset provided by the sharing platform. First, participants' onboarding dynamics are investigated and the importance of building collaborative cybersecurity on an established network of trust is highlighted. Thus, when a new sharing platform is created by abuse.ch, an existing trusted community with 'power users' will migrate swiftly to it, in order to enact the first sparks of collective intelligence dynamics. Second, the platform publication dynamics are analyzed and two different superlinear growths are observed. Third, the rewarding dynamics of a credit system is described - a promising incentive mechanism that could improve cooperation and information sharing in open-source intelligence communities through the gamification of the sharing activity. Overall, our study highlights future avenues of research to study the institutional rules enacting collective intelligence dynamics in cybersecurity. Thus, we show how the platform may improve the efficiency of information sharing between critical infrastructures, for example within Information Sharing and Analysis Centers using ThreatFox. Finally, a broad agenda for future empirical research in the field of cybersecurity information sharing is presented - an important activity to reduce information asymmetry between attackers and defenders.

Keywords: Information Sharing and Analysis Center · Threat Intelligence · Sharing Platform · Security Information Sharing · Collaborative Cybersecurity · Collective Intelligence · Indicator of Compromise

© The Author(s) 2023
B. Hämmerli et al. (Eds.): CRITIS 2022, LNCS 13723, pp. 140–157, 2023.
https://doi.org/10.1007/978-3-031-35190-7_10

1   Introduction

Cybersecurity Information Sharing (CIS) is an important activity to reduce the information asymmetry between attackers and defenders [1]. This activity also allows the production of Cyber Threat Intelligence insights, which enables organizations to proactively detect cyberrisks and prevent malicious activities [2]. More than two decades ago, the first Computer Emergency Readiness Teams (CERT) [3] and Information Sharing and Analysis Centers (ISACs) [4] were established to allow critical infrastructure operators to share important information about cyberthreats [5]. Today, threat intelligence platforms help organizations aggregate, correlate, and analyze threat data from multiple sources in quasi real-time to support defensive actions [6,7]. In addition, open-source solutions, such as the MISP[1] Threat Sharing platform [8] or the AlienVault Open Threat Exchange[2] (OTX), have been proposed to counterbalance the influence of large cybercriminal networks and organizations. In March 2021, abuse.ch launched the ThreatFox[3] project, a platform used to collect and share IoCs to help IT-security professionals and threat analysts protect their customers from cyberthreats.

In this article, three collective intelligence dynamics observed on ThreatFox are empirically investigated, with the goal of better understanding the institutional rules that enact such collective intelligence dynamics. First, participants' onboarding dynamics are investigated and the importance of building collaborative cybersecurity on established networks of trust is highlighted. Second, the platform publication dynamics are analyzed and superlinear growth is observed during the first one hundred days. Third, a rewarding dynamic of a credit system is described—a promising incentive mechanism to improve information sharing in open-source intelligence communities.

The remainder of this article begins by providing a brief overview in Sect. 2 of CIS and collaborative cybersecurity. In Sect. 3, an empirical analysis of the three dynamics is conducted before presenting the obtained results in Sect. 4. Section 5 discusses this work and brings some improvement recommendations for the platform. Section 6 presents a broad research agenda on CIS and collective intelligence in cybersecurity, and Sect. 7 concludes this work.

2   Related Work

The constant evolution of cyberthreats has forced organizations and governments to develop new strategies [2] to reduce the risks of security breaches [9]. In this regard, the development of collaborative platforms as governance-strategy and knowledge-management tools has highlighted the importance of information sharing [10]. Hence, the World Economic Forum has recently recognized the fact that CIS is critical to helping improve collective security in the digital ecosystem on which society increasingly relies [11]. However, CIS faces multiple barriers.

---

[1] https://www.misp-project.org.

[2] https://otx.alienvault.com.

[3] https://threatfox.abuse.ch/.

First, these challenges have a social aspect; human beings tend not to optimize organizational goals [12] without selective incentive [13] and—in the case of collective action—might behave selfish in ways that do not support the overall goal of information sharing [14], leading to situations such as the prisoner's dilemma [15]. In this situation, it is in the interest of two players to cooperate on an issue; however, in the absence of communication between them, each will choose to betray the other [16]. As a result, cybersecurity professionals likely share less information than is desirable, resulting in knowledge asymmetry that benefits the attackers [1]. In particular, stakeholders strategically select their contributions to share, leading to truncated and imperfect information sharing.

In the absence of trust, commitment, and a shared vision among stakeholders, organizations are reluctant to share information for fear of disclosure, reputational risk, or loss of competitive power [17]. In this respect, information sharing can be understood as a marketplace in which transactions take place and knowledge is transferred [9].

2.1 Collective Intelligence Dynamics in Cybersecurity

The scientific literature confirms that sharing information security among human agents operating information systems is conducive to improving cybersecurity [1]. However, empirical analysis shows that 'sharing centers', such as ISACs do not always function optimally [18]. To improve CIS, the computer science technical literature generally focuses on getting the exchange format right, through data models, the adoption of specific technologies [19], or sharing conventions, such as the Traffic Light Protocol (TLP). This approach neglects the fact that information sharing is a human activity needing incentive mechanisms [13], which is not related to technology. Hence, CIS can be viewed as a collective intelligence process through which group intelligence emerges from repeated collaboration and collective efforts through crowdsourcing and peer-reviewing [20].

2.2 Linking Institutional Economics and Information Sharing

Institutional economics focuses on understanding the role of the evolutionary process and institutions in shaping economic behavior. With this study, a better understanding of the institutional rules enacting collective intelligence dynamics in cybersecurity is sought. By understanding and measuring these rules, an attempt is made to explain the success of abuse.ch compared with other platforms that are less successful and use different rules, such as OTX[4]. Therefore the assumption is made, that the success of sharing platforms is directly linked to the rules implemented from its creation. Hence, an institutional economics framework is used to describe the three identified dynamics. Studying these three dynamics leads to the hope that, at the same time, this study contributes to the institutional economics literature from a cybersecurity perspective, as was done in previous interdisciplinary work using a similar approach [12].

---

[4] The success of abuse.ch is publicly visible on Twitter, especially through the number of followers (more than 25.5K in less than a year of existence). https://twitter.com/abuse_ch.

Analyses have already been conducted on various information security sharing platforms. An analysis of the widely used open source threat sharing platform MISP [7] shows how collective action in this type of platform can increase the efficiency in the time required to fully characterize a cybersecurity threat. Their results generally informs how collective actions can be organized online at scale and in a modular fashion to address a large number of time-critical tasks.

3   Data and Methodology

3.1   abuse.ch: Community Driven Threat Intelligence

abuse.ch is a project created years ago by Roman Hüssy[5]. Initially, personally recovered malware samples were documented and shared via a blog called 'The Swiss Security Blog', which paved the way for the emergence of abuse.ch as it is known today. Subsequently, multiple platforms used to track different malware were created on the website to help participants fight cybercrime. A community and a network of trust slowly emerged behind abuse.ch, which helped feed the different datasets of the different projects. Today, abuse.ch is a web-based platform specialized in open-source threat intelligence and is composed of multiple projects used by many public and private actors to protect themselves and/or their clients against cyberthreats. Most of the threat information is generated by the community on four important platforms:

- URLHaus, launched in 2018, is a project with the goal of sharing URLs used for malware distribution.
- MalwareBazaar, launched in 2020, is a project that aims to collect and share malware samples—not easily accessible before this initiative.
- ThreatFox, launched in early 2021, is an open-source threat intelligence platform used to share, store, and collaborate on cybersecurity incidents, known as IoCs. Despite its young age, ThreatFox already has an active community.
- YARAify, launched in June, 2022, is a project from abuse.ch that allows anyone to scan suspicious files such as malware samples or process dumps against a large repository of YARA rules. With YARAhub, the platform also provides a structured way for sharing YARA rules with the community.

Overall, the goal of these platforms is to facilitate access to threat information by removing as many barriers to sharing as possible and to reduce executional costs, as described in [17]. Therefore, there is no need of a platform account to access the data.

3.2   ThreatFox Dataset Description

ThreatFox is an open-data threat intelligence platform, launched in March 2021 and operated by abuse.ch, on which participants can collaborate by sharing artifacts of cybersecurity incidents in the form of IoCs. These IoCs contain basic

---

[5] Roman Hüssy is a research associate at the Bern University of Applied Sciences (BFH) https://www.bfh.ch/fr/la-bfh/personnes/7364w3jin4k5/. The abuse.ch project has been hosted by this institution since June 1, 2021.

144   E. Jollès et al.

information, such as a URL, IP address, or a hash of a malware sample (see Table 1 for an overview of relevant fields), which can be reused by other investigators to discover the same evidence on their systems. Therefore, sharing these data with as many users as possible through sharing platforms is important. However, other platforms are either closed (only selected participants can share and receive IoCs), fee-based, or require some form of registration. From an economic perspective, these platforms can be considered as a club good (excludable and nonrivalrous). In contrast, ThreatFox is one of the first platforms to offer a public good approach (nonexcludable and nonrivalrous) with its free and open-data mindset. Moreover, ThreatFox attempts to minimize barriers and create new incentives for IoC sharing. Consequently, the user interface and API used to retrieve IoCs do not require any form of registration, and these IoCs can be downloaded in the most used formats, e.g. JSON, CSV, MISP events, and others.

ThreatFox was also built on a pre-existing community from former abuse.ch platforms, such as URLHaus or MalwareBazaar, and has used all of the experiences and best practices to create a new platform that encourages sharing, such as a credit system used to reward the user for sharing an IoC.

In this article, ThreatFox data published from March 8, 2020 to July 4, 2022, is used for the analysis. During this period, 767,396 IoCs were published by anonymous users and 106 identifiable users, also called reporters. These IoCs are accessible via a web interface (see Fig. 1) or via API requests to be easily accessible. Roman Hüssy from abuse.ch kindly provided additional data (e.g., credits of the IoCs) that are not directly available on the website.

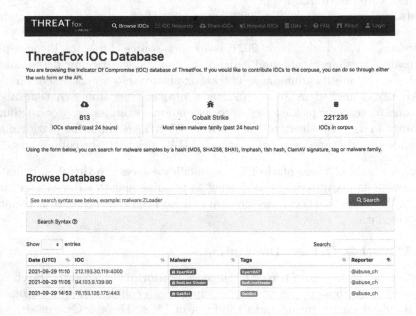

Fig. 1. Web interface of ThreatFox

The important fields in the ThreatFox dataset are visible in Table 1.

Table 1. Important fields of the ThreatFox dataset.

Field name	Description
IoC value	The value of the IoC. This can be a hash (sha1, sha256, sha3 or md5), a url, a domain, or an ip:port pair
IoC type	The corresponding type of the IoC (hash, url, domain, or ip:port pair)
Threat type	The threat type of the IoC (payload, command & control)
Malware	The name of the corresponding malware
Timestamp	IoC post time (UTC+0)
Confidence level	Value between 25 and 100 characterizing the confidence of the contributor toward the shared IoC
Reference	Link to a web page (often tweets or MalwareBazaar pages) that gives more information and features about the IoC
Reporter	Pseudo (Twitter account) of the user who shares the IoC
Anonymous	Whether or not the IoC is shared anonymously
Credits earned	Number of credits earned by the reporter with the posted IoC

3.3 Methodology

Fitting methods are used on the dataset to highlight the dynamics of organizational integration and the cumulative dynamics of event production. In particular, the data are fitted using the most probable growth functions, starting with a visual inspection: (i) a linear growth function takes the form: $y = a \cdot x + b$, while (ii) a superlinear growth function is represented $y = x^{\beta} \Rightarrow log(y) = \beta \cdot log(x)$ for $\beta > 1$. Linear and superlinear relations are most commonly found in open collaboration platforms [21–23]. Once identified, the function is calibrated according to the data in this study by non-linear least squares.

4 Results

4.1 Onboarding Dynamics of Reporters

When considering information sharing, a key aspect is the number of participants in the collective action process because each participant is expected to contribute to the collective good. It is not the case here, since 10% of users contribute to around 98% of the IoCs, which is highly skewed. We can thus conclude that, although it is admitted, free-riding [24] (e.g., leeching) occurs.

From that, we produce the Fig. 2a that shows the cumulative number of new reporters as a function of the date on which the first organization was created once the platform was launched. ThreatFox is based on an existing community, which is why a massive arrival of new reporters in Fig. 2a in the first five days is observed. This arrival corresponds to onboarding reporters who were already present and active on previous abuse.ch platforms. The arrival of new reporters is observed to indicate a slow, linear growth after the first five days (see equation (1)), which could mean that the platform's attractiveness remains the same over time. Joining curve of reporters' arrival is:

$$A_{\text{reps}}(t) \sim a_{\text{reps}} \cdot t \quad \text{with} \quad a_{\text{reps}} = 0.19 \tag{1}$$

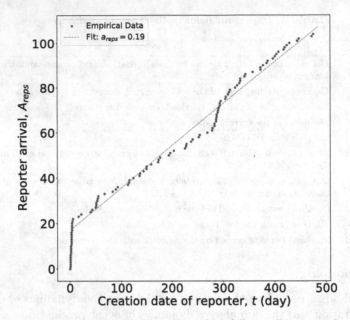

(a) Arrival of reporters in ThreatFox, which follows a linear growth with slope $a_{\text{reps}} = 0.19$ (see equation 1).

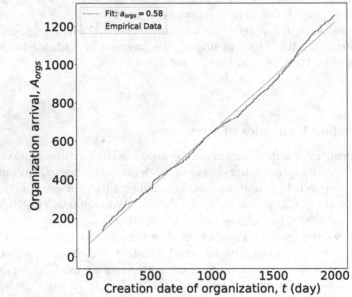

(b) Arrival of reporters in Computer Incident Response Center Luxembourg (CIRCL) MISP, which follows a linear growth with slope $a_{\text{orgs}} = 0.58$ (Data taken from Gillard et al. paper [7]).

Fig. 2. Onboarding dynamics of new reporters in ThreatFox and CIRCL MISP.

In Fig. 2b, a similar pattern is observed with the CIRCL MISP community, which was also built on a pre-established community.

Goldenberg and Dean [25] argued that successful information sharing depends on a combination of a common mission, a shared identity, familiarity, and trust. Trust facilitates data sharing, which in turn enhances trust itself, and is thus necessary on information sharing platforms [16]. Indeed, data on these platforms will be used, for example, in monitoring systems; therefore, they must be reliable. Lack of trust within the community can lead to collaboration issues [26] (e.g., sharing information with rivals could improve their competitive position).

Trust cannot come from anywhere; it must be built through pre-existing personal relationships [16] developed over time through formal and informal networks [25]. Thus, information sharing must rely on a core of trusted individuals, who interact formally for the information sharing process but also informally to build trust among themselves.

In this way, the suggestion is made that pre-established communities create a foundation of trust that then encourages newcomers to become more involved.

4.2   Publication Dynamics of Indicator of Compromise

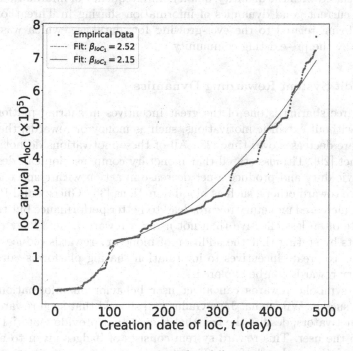

Fig. 3. Arrival of IoCs in ThreatFox, which first follows a superlinear growth function with $\beta_{IoC_1} = 2.52$ (see Eq. 2) for the first 111 d, then follows a superlinear growth function with $\beta_{IoC_2} = 2.15$ (see Eq. 3). The repeated pattern of strong/flat growth in the figure could be explained by the grouped arrival of new users from other pre-existing communities of trusted networks on abuse.ch.

Figure 3 shows the cumulative number of IoCs created over time. The publication of IoCs is composed of two distinct growth phases.

When a new sharing platform is created by abuse.ch, an existing trusted community with 'power users' will migrate swiftly to it, in order to enact the first sparks of collective intelligence dynamics.

During the first 111 d, the number of shared IoCs is observed to grow superlinearly (faster than the linear function) with the number of days since the opening of ThreatFox (and, thus, with the number of reporters) (see equation (2)).

$$A_{IoC}(t) \sim t^{\beta_{IoC_1}} \quad \text{with} \quad \beta_{IoC_1} = 2.52 \tag{2}$$

This first step could consist of transferring the events already collected by the different reporters.

After the first 111 days, the number of IoCs published begins a second slower growing phase, also superlinear. This behavior shows a strong positive dynamics, as indicated in Eq. (3). The majority of the IoCs published in this section could correspond to new cyber events that are shared after their detection.

$$A_{IoC}(t) \sim t^{\beta_{IoC_2}} \quad \text{with} \quad \beta_{IoC_2} = 2.15 \tag{3}$$

As reported by Müller et al. [27], a high degree of social interaction is positively associated with the quantity, quality, and frequency of information sharing. Thus, the current good dynamics of information sharing in ThreatFox is suggested as being related to the ever-growing IoC database, which was initially populated by the pre-existing community.

4.3   Credit System Rewarding Dynamics

Easy and free sharing is one of the great incentives in sharing platforms [16]. However, without extrinsic motivations, such as money or rewards, the motivation to share decreases over time [28]. All of these motivations do not have the same impact [29]. Titmuss stated that monetary compensation can destroy the sense of civic duty and produce a net decrease in action with respect to acts of benevolence toward others, such as blood donations [30]. Gneezy and Rustichini found that increased monetary rewards lead to better performance but that small rewards are often less effective than not using a reward at all. They explained their results by stating that the addition of monetary rewards reduces intrinsic motivation. To create incentives to information sharing platforms, alternatives to monetary rewards can be explored.

Purely symbolic rewards can affect user behavior on information sharing platforms, such as Wikipedia. Jana Gallus [31] showed that such rewards can be powerful motivators, despite the fact that they do not provide material goods or benefits to the user. This reward system consists of badges given to new users if they are active on the platform. These symbols were observed to increase the number of active contributors and their number of contributions over a long period. These rewards allow users to identify as members of the Wikipedia community and gain a reputation and recognition from other community members, creating a new motivation to share.

ThreatFox introduces a credit system used to reward the sharing of IoCs in which a user earns credits when he shares an IoC. An IoC earns more credits if requested by another user. However, the credits are only symbolic and cannot be used to buy anything yet. Hence, they rather support the gamification of sharing. They are only present in the list of 'richest reporters', which is available on the ThreatFox website. Wikipedia used a similar leaderboard. Gallus et al. [31] showed that such leaderboards have a positive impact on information sharing.

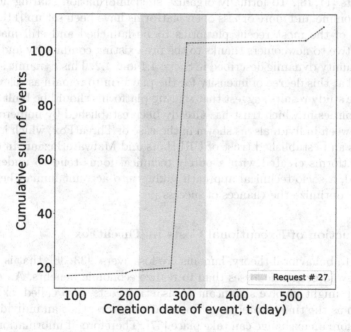

Fig. 4. Cumulative sum of the number of domains linked to Formbook botnet shared. The corresponding IoC request is represented by gray area.

Of the 105 IoCs requests made since the launch of ThreatFox, only 62 received at least one response, which results from the low number of users sharing information and the fact that IoCs are not items that the user can easily obtain or create. Instead, they are items that the user already has (e.g., because of previous incidents) or has recently received. However, the credit system seems to have—for some attacks and some users—some impact. Another explanation could be that there is an underlying cause, such as an ongoing attack, resulting in an increase of requests and share IoCs simultaneously. Indeed, Fig. 4 shows that 80% of the sharing of domains linked to Formbook botnet malware are made when a request is made. The apparition of the IoC request (IoC request #27) is linked with the apparition of a peak in the number of IoC shared. ThreatFox is still a young platform with few participants and little sharing; therefore, repeating this analysis in the future is recommended, when more data are available for analysis. However, the credit system is a good, free incentive and could be promoted more on abuse.ch website.

5   Discussion and Recommendations

Building collaborative cybersecurity through information sharing has been considered a critical path to keeping up with increasingly pervasive and innovative cyberthreats [11,18]. To formally organize such information sharing activity, a number of online and more or less open platforms have been set up [11]. ThreatFox is one of the most recent platforms to be launched and still manages to stay attractive to newcomers thanks to the pre-existing community and the positive community dynamic described in Sects. 4.1 and 4.2. This dynamic should be maintained at this degree of intensity for the platform to remain as relevant as it is now. The study results suggest that sharing platforms should be built on existing communities in which trust has already been established by numerous interactions between individuals, as shown in the case of ThreatFox, which is built on the success and established trust of URLHaus and MalwareBazaar. In contrast, sharing platforms created with a purely technical focus tend to underperform [32]. Indeed, a socio-technical approach taking into account human behavior is essential to optimize the chances of success [9].

5.1   Reduction of Executional Costs in ThreatFox

According to behavioral theory, humans are loss averse [33–36]; that is, they try harder to avoid economic losses than to realize economic benefits. An exchange relationship might involve significant transaction costs, also called 'executional costs', such as the time, material, or financial resources, that an individual must commit before an exchange can take place [37]. Therefore, if information sharing takes too long, is too laborious, or requires too much effort, individuals likely avoid the necessary resource commitments and, thus, reduce or terminate their participation [38]. Yan et al. argued, for example, that knowledge sharing is inhibited when it is time consuming [39]. The European Union's cybersecurity agency also warns that an abundance of procedures blocks information sharing activity [40]. Thus, high executional costs are likely to deter users of a sharing platform from participating [16]. ThreatFox attempts to minimize the execution cost because everyone can share without too much time, hardware, or financial resources (simple API requests, no registration required, etc.).

5.2   Anonymity in ThreatFox

One of the biggest obstacles to sharing for companies and individuals is the threat of reputational damage [41] and privacy issues. Indeed, if an incident becomes public, customers' trust in an entity can be severely affected, resulting in a loss of customers and, thus, revenue. One solution is to anonymize the shared data, an option offered by some information sharing platforms, such as ThreatFox or AlienVault OTX.

As Murdoch and Leaver [18] pointed out, members of sharing communities sometimes have to hide their identities using anonymity-enabling design principles because of legal restrictions (e.g., GDPR), public relations concerns, or the sensitive nature of the information. However, anonymizing the contributor can lead to a deterioration of trust in the shared data because its origin cannot be confirmed [42]. Furthermore, anonymity is not enough to allow a cyber event to be shared. In fact, some IoCs might still contain information about a company and its users [43] and must be shared with care as defined by the TLP[6] to avoid legal issues (e.g., GDPR).

Some platforms, such as ThreatFox, only allow data to be published when marked with the TLP:WHITE flag to avoid problems; this flag means that the data cannot be abused. Others, such as MISP, create special closed communities that share these data. In both cases, these solutions do prevent the data from being abused. Therefore, events containing personally identifiable information (PII) cannot be shared freely, which creates a form of censorship. Before these events can be openly shared they must first be modified into something shareable by anonymizing the content of the shared data [43, 44]. The U.S. National Institute of Standards and Technology (NIST) published a list of recommendations in its Guide to Cyber Threat Information Sharing [45] to maximize anonymity for contributors by removing sensitive information from the shared data that is not necessary for describing an incident (e.g., masking IP/MAC addresses in network packets, masking names in phishing email samples, masking user identifiers in application logs). The problem with this technique is that PII identification, extraction, and obfuscation might be incomplete, which can lead to unauthorized disclosure of intellectual property or trade secrets [45]. Disclosing this information could result in financial loss, violation of sharing agreements, legal action, or reputational damage to an organization.

In some cases, data cannot be anonymized without losing the utility of sharing (e.g., because too many fields are deleted); alternatively, anonymization via a third party might not be reliable for everyone. In these cases, alternatives to sharing information exist, such as distributed threat intelligence learning. This solution was explored by [46, 47], who attempted to find a compromise in the information-sharing trade-offs between the benefits of improved threat response capability and the drawbacks of disclosing national security-related information to foreign agencies or institutions. Their solution enables secure collaboration with valuable, sensitive data that are not normally shared. Each institution

---

[6] The TLP was created in the early 2000s by the U.K.'s National Infrastructure Security Coordination Centre to encourage the sharing of sensitive information between individuals and organizations in a reliable and controlled manner. The data are classified into one of four classes that regulate the conditions of its disclosure https://www.cisa.gov/tlp.

retains full control of its data records, which never leave the platform's secure perimeter, whereas computations are protected by efficient and highly scalable multi-party homomorphic encryption techniques [48]. However, this solution is not flawless because the data are no longer shared and can thus only be used for specific computations. This solution also adds some overhead to the complexity of the computations, which is not addressed in this article.

5.3   Implications for ThreatFox and Generalization to Other Sharing Platforms

In a broad sense, this study has implications for the design of CIS platforms. Fundamentally, the success of abuse.ch is argued as being related to its ease of use (reduction of the main barrier 'executional cost' to sharing described in [49]), its privacy, and the trust created over the years by an existing community. Thus, when a new sharing platform is created by abuse.ch, an existing trusted community with 'power users' will migrate swiftly to it and bring the necessary critical mass to enact collective intelligence dynamics. For instance, in June, 2022, abuse.ch launched a new platform called 'YARAify'[7], which allows anyone to scan suspicious files such as malware samples or process dumps against a large repository of YARA rules. With YARAhub, the platform also provides a structured way for sharing YARA rules with the community.

These fundamental institutional rule may explain the success of abuse.ch and might be generalizable to other platforms. In a narrower way, this research also has direct implications for abuse.ch. The first recommendation is that the platform improve its statistical processing by collecting its data in the following ways.

Indeed, at the moment, the IoCs that earn the most are those requested by other users. This system seems to have some limitations because users cannot create specific IoCs on demand. The reward system could be improved by introducing new ways to earn credits, such as a system that awards credits based on the exclusivity of an IoC. The double-blind peer review process for IoCs could be improved with more reviewers to ensure quality and to improve user confidence across IoCs. This activity could also be rewarded with a credit system to encourage review.

The 'confidence level' field of shared IoCs (see Table 1), which characterizes the confidence of the contributor in the shared IoC, seems interesting at first sight. However, this field is defined by the contributor, who might have a biased view of the shared object. When possible, the level of trust should be assessed by other ThreatFox users. This field could also be combined with a new 'utility' field, which would represent the number of times a specific IoC has been used by other ThreatFox users to detect cyberattacks in their system. This new field could be very valuable in measuring the usefulness of an IP and, thus, could detect interesting patterns, such as the existence of a best performance area (inverted U-curve) of sharing communities based on the optimal number of participants in

---

[7] https://yaraify.abuse.ch.

the sharing community [50]. Next, in the same vein, future work could investigate if a Ringelmann effect exists on cybersecurity sharing platforms [51].

6   Research Agenda

The development of open and free sharing platforms and ThreatFox in particular opens up many research opportunities in the growing field of CIS. This study identified numerous research gaps in the literature, such as a lack of research about patterns on onboarding dynamics, a lack of research about publication dynamics, and a lack of research about reward systems to incentivize information sharing. A 'universal' performance indicator to measure the influence of institutional rules on CIS is a remaining gap in the literature. In the future, it would also be interesting to study the abuse.ch community structure with new "community analysis" methods adapted from the International Data-driven Research for Advanced Modeling and Analysis (iDRAMA Lab)[8]. At the technical level, building response incident rate indicators based on ThreatFox data would be interesting. At a socio-technical level, investigating the optimal size of sharing communities and the role of pre-existing communities would be interesting. In the future, it will also be necessary to better characterize the data and the users, for example by identifying associated distributions. Finally, the assumption that 'open' sharing communities share IoCs better and faster could be benchmarked, such as against MISP data or even other sharing communities, such as COVID-19 large threat intelligence communities [14].

7   Conclusion

This study used an exclusive ThreatFox dataset to describe how pre-existing communities and pre-established networks of trust have an important impact on the success of newly created information sharing platforms. An initial study of ThreatFox's promising credit system is also provided and some IoC requests were shown to be effective in creating new IoC sharing. However, this incentive, although rarely found on such information sharing platforms, is not mature enough and could be improved to be more impactful. Finally, this study sheds light on the onboarding dynamics of both reporters and a publication of IoCs. Overall, the results of this study provide a better understanding of the institutional rules enacting collective intelligence dynamics in cybersecurity. Finally, a broad agenda is presented for future empirical research in the field of CIS, which is an important activity to reduce information asymmetry between attackers and defenders.

Acknowledgments. We would like to thank abuse.ch and especially its founder, Roman Hüssy, for the technical support and data availability, as well as Enago.com for the English language review. Comments received from Vincent Lenders, Thomas Maillart, Marcus Keupp, Philipp Fischer, William Lacube, Michael Tsesmelis and three anonymous reviewers all helped to improve previous versions of this article.

---

[8] https://idrama.science.

References

1. Laube, S., Böhme, R.: Strategic aspects of cyber risk information sharing. In: ACM Computing Surveys 50.5 (2017). https://doi.org/10.1145/3124398
2. Meier, R., et al.: FeedRank: a tamper- resistant method for the ranking of cyber threat intelligence feeds. In: 2018 10th International Conference on Cyber Conflict (CyCon) (2018). https://doi.org/10.23919/CYCON.2018.8405024
3. Sridhar, K., et al.: Cybersecurity information sharing: analysing an email corpus of coordinated vulnerability disclosure. In: The 20th Annual Workshop on the Economics of Information Security (2021)
4. Gal-Or, E., Ghose, A.: The economic incentives for sharing security information. Inf. Syst. Res. **16**(2) (2005). https://doi.org/10.1287/isre.1050.0053
5. EricWeiss, N.: Legislation to facilitate cybersecurity information sharing: economic analysis. In: Econ. Anal. (2015)
6. He, M., Devine, L., Zhuang, J.: Perspectives on cybersecurity information sharing among multiple stakeholders using a decision-theoretic approach: cybersecurity information sharing. Risk Anal. **38**(2) (2018). https://doi.org/10.1111/risa.12878
7. Gillard, S., et al.: Efficient collective action for tackling time-critical cybersecurity threats. Tech. rep. arXiv:2206.15055. [physics] type: article. arXiv, (2022)
8. Wagner, C., et al.: MISP: the design and implementation of a collaborative threat intelligence sharing platform. In: Proceedings of the 2016 ACM on Workshop on Information Sharing and Collaborative Security. (2016). https://doi.org/10.1145/2994539.2994542
9. Percia David, D., Matthias Keupp, M., Mermoud, A.: Knowledge absorption for cyber-security: the role of human beliefs. Comput. Human Behav. **106** (2020). https://doi.org/10.1016/j.chb.2020.106255
10. Sohrabi Safa, N., Von Solms, R.: An information security knowledge sharing model in organizations. Comput. Hum. Behav. **57** (2016). https://doi.org/10.1016/j.chb.2015.12.037
11. World Economic Forum. Cyber Information Sharing: Building Collective Security. Tech. Rep. (2020)
12. Mermoud, A., MatthiasKeupp, M., Percia David, D.: Governance models preferences for security information sharing: an institutional economics perspective for critical infrastructure protection. Critical Inf. Infrastruct. Secur. (2019). https://doi.org/10.1007/978-3-030-05849-4_14
13. Oliver, P.: Rewards and punishments as selective incentives for collective action: theoretical investigations. Am. J. Sociol. **85**(6) (1980). Publisher: The University of Chicago Press. https://doi.org/10.1086/227168
14. Bouwman, X., et al.: Helping hands: measuring the impact of a large threat intelligence sharing community. In: Proceedings of the 31st USENIX Security Symposium (2022)
15. Poundstone, W.: Prisoner's Dilemma/John Von Neumann, game theory and the puzzle of the bomb. Anchor (1993)
16. Mermoud, A.: Three articles on the behavioral economics of security information sharing: a theoretical framework, an empirical test, and policy recommendations". PhD Thesis. Université de Lausanne, Faculté des hautes études commerciales, (2019)
17. Mermoud, A., et al.: Incentives for human agents to share security information: a model and an empirical test. In: 17th Workshop on the Economics of Information Security (WEIS) (2018)

18. Murdoch, S., Leaver, N.: Anonymity vs trust in cyber-security collaboration. In: Proceedings of the 2nd ACM Workshop on Information Sharing and Collaborative Security (2015). https://doi.org/10.1145/2808128.2808134
19. Burger, E., et al.: Taxonomy model for cyber threat intelligence information exchange technologies. In: Proceedings of the 2014 ACM Workshop on Information Sharing & Collaborative Security - WISCS '14 (2014). https://doi.org/10.1145/2663876.2663883
20. Miorandi, D., Maggi, L.: Programming Social Collective Intelligence. In: IEEE Technology and Society Magazine, Conference Name: IEEE Technology and Society Magazine vol. 33. no. 3 (2014). https://doi.org/10.1109/MTS.2014.2345206
21. Sornette, D., Maillart, T., Ghezzi, G.: HowMuch is the whole really more than the sum of its Parts? 1 + 1 = 2.5: Superlinear Productivity in Collective Group Actions. In: PLoS ONE 9.8 (2014). https://doi.org/10.1371/journal.pone.0103023
22. Scholtes, I., Mavrodiev, P., Schweitzer, F.: From aristotle to ringelmann: a large-scale analysis of team productivity and coordination in open source software projects. Tech. Rep. Gesellschaft für Informatik e.V. (2016)
23. Muri, G., et al.: Collaboration drives individual productivity. In: Proceedings of the ACM on Human-Computer Interaction 3.CSCW (2019). https://doi.org/10.1145/3359176
24. Anesi, V.: Moral hazard and free riding in collective action. Soc. Choice and Welfare 32(2) (2008). https://doi.org/10.1007/s00355-008-0318-8
25. Goldenberg, I., Dean, W.: Enablers and barriers to information sharing in military and security operations: lessons learned. In: Enablers and Barriers to Information Sharing in Military and Security Operations: Lessons Learned (2017). https://doi.org/10.1007/978-3-319-42819-2_16
26. Koepke, P.: Cybersecurity information sharing incentives and barriers. In: Working Paper CISL (2017)
27. Müller, J.M., Veile, J.W., Voigt, K.-I.: Prerequisites and incentives for digital information sharing in industry 4.0 an international comparison across data types". In: Computers & Industrial Engineering 148 (2020). https://doi.org/10.1016/j.cie.2020.106733
28. Zibak, A., Simpson, A.: Cyber threat information sharing: perceived benefits and barriers. In: Proceedings of the 14th International Conference on Availability, Reliability and Security (2019). https://doi.org/10.1145/3339252.3340528
29. Wagner, T.D., et al.: Cyber threat intelligence sharing: survey and research directions. Comput. Secur. 87 (2019). https://doi.org/10.1016/j.cose.2019.101589
30. Mellström, C., Johannesson, M.: Crowding out in blood donation: was titmuss right? J. Eur. Econ. Assoc 6(4) (2008). https://doi.org/10.1162/JEEA.2008.6.4.845
31. Gallus, J.: Fostering Public good contributions with symbolic awards: a large-scale natural field experiment at wikipedia. Manage. Sci. 63(12)(2017). https://doi.org/10.1287/mnsc.2016.2540
32. Stojkovski, B., et al.: What is in a cyber threat intelligence sharing platform? A mixed-methods user experience investigation of MISP. Ann. Comput. Secur. Appl. Conf. (2021). https://doi.org/10.1145/3485832.3488030
33. Kahneman, D., Tversky, A.: Prospect theory: an analysis of decision under risk. In: World Scientific Handbook in Financial Economics Series, vol. 4 (2013). https://doi.org/10.1142/9789814417358_0006
34. Tversky, A., Kahneman, D.: Loss aversion in riskless choice: a reference-dependent model. Q. J. Econ. 106(4) (1991). https://doi.org/10.2307/2937956

35. Tversky, A., Kahneman, D.: Advances in prospect theory: cumulative representation of uncertainty. J. Risk Uncertain. **5**(4) (1992). https://doi.org/10.1007/BF00122574
36. Tom, S.M., et al.: The neural basis of loss aversion in decision-making under risk. Science **315**(5811) (2007). https://doi.org/10.1126/science.1134239
37. Williamson, O.E.: The economics of organization: the transaction cost approach. Am. J. Sociol. **87**(3) (1981). https://doi.org/10.1086/227496
38. Luiijf, E., Klaver, M.: On the sharing of cyber security information. In: Critical Infrastructure Protection IX, vol. 466. Series Title: IFIP Advances in Information and Communication Technology (2015). https://doi.org/10.1007/978-3-319-26567-4_3
39. Yan, Z., et al.: Knowledge sharing in online health communities: a social exchange theory perspective. Inf. Manage. **53**(5) (2016). https://doi.org/10.1016/j.im.2016.02.001
40. Alkalabi, W., Simpson, L., Morarji, H.: Barriers and incentives to cybersecurity threat information sharing in developing countries: a case study of Saudi Arabia. In: 2021 Australasian Computer Science Week Multiconference (2021). https://doi.org/10.1145/3437378.3437391
41. Mavroeidis, V., Bromander, S.: Cyber threat intelligence model: an evaluation of taxonomies, sharing standards, and ontologies within cyber threat intelligence. In: 2017 European Intelligence and Security Informatics Conference (EISIC) (2017). https://doi.org/10.1109/EISIC.2017.20
42. Danezis, G., et al.: Privacy and data protection by design - from policy to engineering. In: arXiv:1501.03726 [cs] (2014). https://doi.org/10.2824/38623
43. Pang, R., et al.: The devil and packet trace anonymization. ACM SIGCOMM Comput. Commun. Rev. **36**(1) (2006). https://doi.org/10.1145/1111322.1111330
44. Fathi, Z., Rafsanjani, A.J., Habibi, F.: Anon-ISAC: anonymity-preserving cyber threat information sharing platform based on permissioned blockchain. In: 2020 28th Iranian Conference on Electrical Engineering (ICEE) (2020). https://doi.org/10.1109/ICEE50131.2020.9261029
45. Johnson, C.S., et al.: Guide to cyber threat information sharing. Tech. rep. NIST SP 800–150. National Institute of Standards and Technology (2016). https://doi.org/10.6028/NIST.SP.800-150
46. Froelicher, D., et al.: Truly privacy-preserving federated analytics for precision medicine with multiparty homomorphic encryption. Nat. Commun. **12**(1) (2021). Publisher: Nature Publishing Group
47. Trocoso-Pastoriza, J., et al.: Orchestrating collaborative cybersecurity: a secure framework for distributed privacy-preserving threat intelligence sharing. In: ACM Digital Threats: Research and Practice, Special Issue on Information Sharing (2023)
48. Froelicher, D., et al.: DRYNX: decentralized, secure, verifiable system for statistical queries and machine learning on distributed datasets (2020). arXiv:1902.03785
49. Mermoud, A., et al.: To share or not to share: a behavioral perspective on human participation in security information sharing. J. Cybersecurity 5.tyz006 (2019)
50. Dejean, S., Pénard, T., Suire, R.: Olson's Paradox Revisited: an empirical analysis of incentives to contribute in p2p file-sharing communities. SSRN Scholarly Paper (2010). https://doi.org/10.2139/ssrn.1299190
51. Maillart, T., Sornette, D.: Aristotle vs. Ringelmann: on superlinear production in open source software. Physica A: Stat. Mech. Appl. **523** (2019). https://doi.org/10.1016/j.physa.2019.04.130

Automatic Concrete Bridge Crack Detection from Strain Measurements: A Preliminary Study

Rudy Milani[1]([✉])(iD), Tarik Sahin[2](iD), Max von Danwitz[2](iD), Maximilian Moll[1](iD), Alexander Popp[2](iD), and Stefan Pickl[1](iD)

[1] University of Bundeswehr Munich, Institute for Computer Science, Werner-Heisenberg-Weg 39, Neubiberg 85577, Germany
rudy.milani@unibw.de
[2] University of the Bundeswehr Munich, Institute for Mathematics and Computer-Based Simulation, Werner-Heisenberg-Weg 39, Neubiberg 85577, Germany

Abstract. The detection of cracks is a fundamental task for maintaining the security of a concrete bridge. The data used in our analysis are gathered from four-point bending test of a concrete beam that serves as a simplified model of a bridge. In this paper, we present a preliminary study using a new method for identifying cracks in strain measurements obtained by fiber optical sensors. The proposed approach consists of three main phases: in the first part, the data are decomposed considering the usual deformation of the beam; in the second, we statistically analyse the difference curve obtained by subtracting the fit of the previous step and the real one to detect outliers relative to crack regions. Lastly, by applying the K-means algorithm it is possible to find the center of each crack. The results obtained confirm the accuracy of the considered method in identifying cracks from fiber Bragg strain measurements.

Keywords: Crack detection · Data analysis · Concrete bridge

1 Introduction

Concrete bridges are designed to carry great loads of moving traffic that can lead to the deterioration of some components. For this reason, cracks are fundamental signs for the discrimination of the durability of these infrastructures. Therefore, reliable crack detection methods are important for avoiding possible disasters. Thank to today's digital sensors, a goal arises: to directly receive all the fundamental information gathered without even personally inspecting the infrastructure. One major problem is generating an automated algorithm that can detect cracks from these measurements. In this way, there will be a reduction also in the cost of the maintenance since the periodic inspection of all bridges could be done remotely. For this reason, in the last years, high importance was given to the digitalization of infrastructures and the creation of the well-known Digital Twins [1,2].

B. Hämmerli et al. (Eds.): CRITIS 2022, LNCS 13723, pp. 158–163, 2023.
https://doi.org/10.1007/978-3-031-35190-7_11

In this paper, we present a novel method for the automatic detection of cracks in a concrete beam (that simulates the concrete bridge) from digital measurement. In detail, the approach consists in finding first a curve that fits the continuum strains of the beam, and then, after subtracting it from the initial dataset, statistically analysing the extreme values.

2   Literature Review

Several approaches have been proposed to detect cracks in concrete structures and identify their location and crack length using data from embedded sensors or images. In the following short review, we will focus on three examples.

Many recent methods for crack identification in concrete structures are based on image processing and deep learning. E. g., Kim et al. [3] propose a method based on a genetic algorithm (GA) to optimize the parameters of image processing and they train a convolutional neural network (CNN) to distinguish cracks and non-crack areas in images of concrete.

Another approach for crack detection is based on the eigenfrequency shifts. E.g., Young-Shin Lee et al. [4] proposed a method using the natural frequency data of a one-dimensional beam-type structure. They combined the Finite Element Method (FEM), different crack detection techniques based on eigenfrequency, such as Armon's technique [5], and the experimental natural frequency data for identifying the crack position.

Further methods are based on embedding of sensors in concrete structures to monitor changes occurring in the parameters of the domain. Gkantou et al. [6] applied microwave sensors to compare the crack propagation and electromagnetic signals. They recorded structural performance and signal measurements using microwave sensors and found a strong correlation between cracks and signals.

In the following, we propose a method for crack detection in concrete structures based on spatially-resolved fiber optical strain measurements.

3   Data Collection

The physical experiment to obtain the considered measurement data was carried out by Braml et al. [7]. For the sake of completeness, the setup of the experiment is summarized in the following paragraph.

A four-point bending test with a cyclic load is carried out on a steel-reinforced concrete beam specimen to evaluate the crack initiation and crack propagation as illustrated in Fig. 1a and 1b. The casted steel-reinforced concrete beam has a dimension of $300\,cm \times 15\,cm \times 30\,cm$. It is simply supported at $25\,cm$ from the free ends and the load is applied at two positions symmetrically at $85\,cm$ from the supports using the loading machine. One fiber optical sensor is placed on the compression side and five fiber optical sensors are placed on the tension side of the beam. They are aligned with the longitudinal axis of the beam by attaching them to the steel bars and to the concrete surface. During the cyclic loadings, strains are measured at a frequency $10\,Hz$.

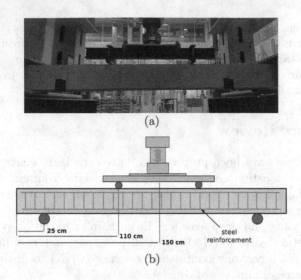

(a)

(b)

Fig. 1. (a) Four-point bending test under cyclic loading. (b) Geometry specifications of the steel-reinforced concrete beam and locations of fiber-optical sensors.

4   Analysis and Discussion

The dataset we use in this analysis consists of values at a fixed time-step, i.e., time-step = 0 as represented in Fig. 2, relative to only one of the sensors. In particular, by plotting the values it is possible to distinguish clearly three peaks that are generated by the presence of a crack in that x-coordinate. The main problem is relative to automatically detecting these peaks without any intervention from a human user.

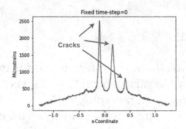

Fig. 2. Plot of a fixed time-step ($t = 0$) data-point.

In particular, we want also a method that can be easily generalised to different measurements and experiments. For this reason, the first step of the proposed approach consists in eliminating the component given by the continuous deformation of the beam.

In fact, in this way, it is possible to consider not only beams that are subjected to different forces but also analyse the measurements independently of the time. Therefore, we can study in the same way all the possible density distributions associated with the problem of detecting the cracks by eliminating this deformation component and analysing the corresponding probability density function.

For the identification of the best function that could approximate the strains due to the bulk deformation of the beam, we used different approaches: we considered first the application of Ordinary Least Squares (OLR) using polynomials of degree 3 and 4, exponential function and the square root of the Microstrain values. As can be noticed in Fig. 3a, all the approximated curves found are always giving more importance to the peaks, creating a greater concavity in their proximity. This leads to a decrease in the extremity of the peaks that are related to the cracks, so to a more difficult detection since they will have values that are similar to the normal points. For this reason, we tried a different approach, consisting of interpolating the data using splines. In particular, we decided to use only 5 nodes, since the interpolation should only understand the shape of strains due to the bulk deformation. Furthermore, we did not fix the position of the nodes but we allowed them to change if they were near a peak region. In fact, in that scenario, the spline obtained would present an accentuated concavity that we want to avoid. Therefore, we checked before the fitting of the curve if the nodes selected were in a region where there was a high increment in absolute value, and we slightly moved them away from there in the positive case. Thus, it is possible to obtain a spline interpolation that can respect all the requirements that we need.

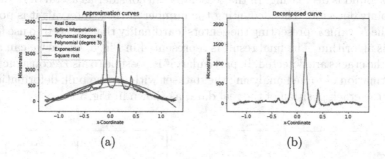

(a)   (b)

Fig. 3. (a) Approximation of the deformation of the beam. (b) Difference between the approximation and the initial data.

Now that the trend of the strains is derived, it is possible to calculate the difference between the initial data and the spline interpolation in order to obtain the relevant information curve that we have to analyse. In Fig. 3b the values are reported after the subtraction.

It is also possible to notice that the distribution obtained after the decomposition is different from the initial one, and most importantly, independent of the magnitude of the force applied and the time of the measurement. The distribution found after this first step, shown in Fig. 4b, has only a major peak near the value of 0 while the initial one presented a slightly moved center, caused by the deformation, as can be noticed in Fig. 4a.

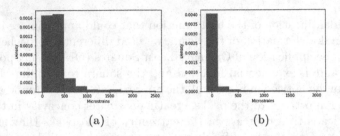

(a)   (b)

Fig. 4. Histograms of the density probability function of (a) Initial data, and (b) Decomposed data.

From these data, it is finally possible to statistically analyse the outliers using a half-normal density function with a cut percentage of 80%; thus the crack regions are found. However, the optimal percentage can be increased to 95% if an iterative approach is operated. In fact, if we use this cut value in the first step we will identify only two cracks, but, then, we can eliminate from the dataset these points, saving them as crack values, and statistically analyse the remaining data by refitting the distribution and applying the same percentage cut. We can iterate this process for a fixed number of iterations or until we obtain that the number of intervals found is decreasing. In that case, we will consider as useful only the previous points detected. Then, counting the number of these intervals it is possible to find the K value representing the centers' cardinality that we need to use for the K-Means algorithm. The final result is represented in Fig. 5, where we can notice that all the cracks are detected. In particular, it is possible to also reconstruct from the information obtained analysing the dataset without the bulk deformation (in Fig. 5a) the crack position of the real data, as shown in Fig. 5b.

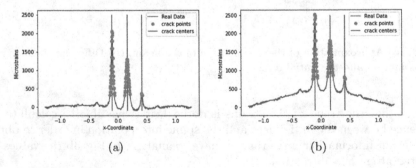

(a)   (b)

Fig. 5. Detection of cracks in the dataset (a) without deformation, and (b) real measurements.

5   Conclusion and Future Work

In this paper, we presented a novel method that can automatically detect cracks from digital measurements. In our experiment, we used a concrete beam to simulate a concrete bridge, which was subjected to a cyclic load to simulate the stress caused by traffic. We analysed in detail only data from one of the 6 sensors, and only for a fixed time-step. The results achieved are satisfying since all the cracks could be automatically detected using a simple methodology.

In the future, we will study this dataset considering also the time dependencies and the information gathered by the other sensors. In fact, combining the analysis of fixed position and fixed time values could lead to an increment in the accuracy of the crack detection. An interesting study can be also done with real measurements of concrete bridges, in order to understand the actual efficiency of the proposed approach.

Acknowledgments. This research is funded by dtec.bw - Digitalization and Technology Research Center of the Bundeswehr project RISK.twin.

References

1. Ye, C., et al.: A digital twin of bridges for structural health monitoring. In Structural Health Monitoring 2019: Enabling Intelligent Life-Cycle Health Management for Industry Internet of Things (IIOT), In: Proceedings of the 12th International Workshop on Structural Health Monitoring, Stanford University: Stanford, CA, USA, 1, 1619–1626 (2019)
2. Braml, T., et al.: Digitaler Zwilling: Verwaltungsschale BBox als Datenablage über den Lebenszyklus einer Brücke. Bautechnik **99**(2), 114–122 (2021)
3. Kim, C.N., Kawamura, K., Nakamura, H., Tarighat, A.: Automatic Crack Detection for Concrete Infrastructures Using Image Processing and Deep Learning. In IOP Conference Series: Materials Science and Engineering, **829**(1), 012027 (2020)
4. Lee, Y.S., Chung, M.J.: A study on crack detection using eigenfrequency test data. Comput. Struct. **77**(3), 327–342 (2000)
5. Armon, D., Ben-Haim, Y., Braun, S.: Crack detection in beams by rank ordering of eigenfrequency shifts. Mech. Syst. Signal Process. **8**(1), 81–91 (1994)
6. Gkantou, M., Muradov, M., Kamaris, G.S., Hashim, K., Atherton, W., Kot, P.: Novel electromagnetic sensors embedded in reinforced concrete beams for crack detection. Sensors **19**(23), 5175 (2019)
7. Braml, T., Wimmer, J., and Varabei, Y.: Erfordernisse an die Datenaufnahme und -verarbeitung zur Erzeugung von intelligenten Digitalen Zwillingen im Ingenieurbau (Requirements to data acquisition and processing for the generation of intelligent digital twins in civil engineering). In Innsbrucker Bautage eds Berger, J. Studia 31–49 (2022)

Mapping Cyber-Physical Threats
for Critical Infrastructures

Michael Mundt[1](✉)[iD] and Harald Baier[2][iD]

[1] Esri Deutschland, Kranzberg, Germany
`m.mundt@esri.de`
[2] Universität der Bundeswehr München – FI CODE, Munich, Germany
`harald.baier@unibw.de`
https://www.esri.de, https://www.unibw.de/digfor

Abstract. Critical infrastructures in general and Industry Control Systems (ICS) in particular need specific protection. For instance, Advanced Persistent Threats (APT) are a well-known modus operandi of attackers to penetrate enterprise IT systems with the consequence of a severely disrupt production. The typical arms race leads to new, updated attack vectors (https://thehackernews.com/2022/07/hackers-distributing-password-cracking.html.). Hence critical infrastructures in general are vulnerable, and consequently our society, too. In this paper we propose an approach in the scope of ICS, which chains Cyber Threat Intelligence with the spatiotemporal analytical capabilities of a Geographic Information System (GIS). Our goal is an improved defense approach addressing the risk that a cyber-physical attack disrupts parts of the critical infrastructure. We furthermore quantify the threat and the extent of potential effects by providing reliable data on the expected level of risk/damage. Our approach of interlinking Cyber Threat Intelligence, incident response, and GIS operational models is evalutated using a prototype within a sample use case. For the implementation of the prototype, market-available products are used such as the Security Information and Event Management (SIEM) of the company LogPoint, the GIS of the company Esri and the MITRE ATT&CK framework. Our work shows how critical infrastructure protection can be improved through the optimized concatenation of existing procedures and technologies to make available knowledge actionable for defense. Our solution offers a unique starting point to combine the existing knowledge of Cyber Threat Intelligence with the knowledge of operational processes of critical infrastructures and put it at the service of the defender.

Keywords: Cyber Threat Intelligence · Critical Infrastructure · Industry Control Systems · Geographic Information System · Cyber-physical Attack

1 Introduction

Critical infrastructures have been under attack for years. This is impressively demonstrated by the report on the attack on the electricity grid in Ukraine,

B. Hämmerli et al. (Eds.): CRITIS 2022, LNCS 13723, pp. 164–179, 2023.
https://doi.org/10.1007/978-3-031-35190-7_12

published by Electricity Information Sharing and Analysis Center (E-ISAC) in cooperation with the Escal Institute of Advanced Technologies (SANS) ICS team on March 18, 2016 [18]. The effects comprise several outages that caused 225,000 customers to lose power across various areas [18, p. 1]. The E-ISAC reports gives details on the attackers' techniques and procedures [18, pp. 4–6] and maps the multi-layered complex attack to the ICS kill chain[1] [18, pp. 7–13]. Furthermore the report highlights lessons learned and measures to optimize defense [18, pp. 21–24].

In recent years, structures and semantics have been developed to describe such incidents in a common language. An example of a best practice approach is the MITRE Adversarial Tactics Techniques and Common Knowledge (ATT&CK) framework[2]. Its focus is on Advanced Persistent Threats (APT), more specifically on analyzing the behavior of the APT based on recent, actual incidents and describing them in a uniform way. Finally, incidents are assigned to so-called'Tactics and Techniques', e.g. with respect to an Iranian Cyber Espionage Group named APT 39 [6]. Due to the open and free availability of the MITRE ATT&CK framework, recent attack vectors are available as a database for Cyber Threat Intelligence (CTI)[3]. The current release of the MITRE ATT&CK framework includes a special version of the'Tactics and Techniques' matrix for the domain specific context of ICS[4].

Manufacturers of cyber security solutions implement and make use of the MITRE ATT&CK framework, e.g., the enterprise Logpoint in its SIEM and User Entity and Behaviour Analytics (UEBA) solution [14]. Logpoint maps basic queries to the corresponding building blocks of the MITRE ATT&CK framework, thus if configured appropriately, all alert rules of the framework are covered. Every single enabled alert rule will return an alert record that already includes the relevant MITRE ATT&CK ID. This ID makes it easy for an analyst to see whether the raised alerts are matching with a single attack, which follows the established sequence [14, p.8]. All the Tactics and Techniques that are covered may be seen within an adapted Navigator[5]. The technology behind UEBA enables to match the detection capability with the tactical methods in the framework [14, p.8]. In contrast to the previous process to evaluate reports by cyber analysts, the use of the MITRE ATT&CK framework leads to an assignment based on raw data as it comes from SIEM data sources (or Extended Detection and Response solution (XDR) [17] [16] data lakes in future installations [5]).

On the other hand, Geospatial Information Systems (GIS) are used to map a critical infrastructure [7, pp. 266–267] and to provide a georeferenced digital representation of it. The locations of the assets of the critical infrastructure are identified, for example based on current aerial and satellite images. Machine and deep learning methods are increasingly used [7, p.277], however,

---

[1] https://www.sans.org/white-papers/36297/.
[2] https://attack.mitre.org/.
[3] https://mitre-attack.github.io/attack-navigator/.
[4] https://attack.mitre.org/matrices/ics/.
[5] https://www.logpoint.com/mitre/.

assets are still entered manually, such as long-distance connection lines (power lines, pipelines) [7, p. 272]. It is already common practice today to assess the cyber attack risks of a critical infrastructure on the basis of geographic features in the areas [7, p. 278].

An attack on ICS pursues the goal of having an effect. For this purpose, cyber attacks are carried out that have physical effects such as the destruction of important assets [12, pp. 1–2,60,100,109,169]. Our work puts forward the hypothesis that the skillful combination of cyber security solutions on the one hand and operational GIS systems on the other makes it possible to better assess the risks posed by APTs and thus protect the critical infrastructure more proactively. Cyber-physical attack targets are geographically localized and potential effects are recorded more holistically. In our paper, we evaluate this statement on base of a sample infrastructure to demonstrate the basic feasibility of our approach. So far, threat models only show the direct impact of cyber attacks, however, the MITRE ATT&CK framework as used by our approach supports to identify the techniques used and to directly quantify the impact (such as the destruction of a PLC). That is, we provide a far more differentiated picture of the situation via the analytical possibilities of the underlying GIS. Instead of the simple direct impact, it is possible to determine exactly which areas of the critical infrastructure can no longer be supplied; connections that will no longer be supplied in the event of the attack can be quantified in this manner.

The remainder of this paper begins by reviewing some related work in Sect. 2. The following Sect. 3 elaborates on the localization of physical assets and the connection to the GIS data model. Then Sect. 4 shows how to concatenate both data models followed by Sect. 5 to present a use case. We conclude this work with a summary and an outlook in Sect. 6.

2   Related Work

In this section we review competing literature to our approach. The idea of using a GIS in the context of the ICS is by no means completely new. This integration is currently discussed in various papers, for instance Tariq's and Sultan's approach to use GIS in Industry 4.0 digital twins [21]. Also, the essential property of modeling an operational production environment in GIS is used: GIS-Based ICS-IIoT Digital Twins with Spatio-Temporal Topology Control of Production Flows [21, 137(3)]. We too use these spatiotemporal analytical properties of the GIS, however, our solution aims to better protect against cyber-physical attacks from APT, while Tariq's and Sultans's approach focuses on a heterogeneity and interoperability tunnel [21, 136(4)].

As early as 2019, a work was published that sometimes considers some possibilities for modeling critical infrastructures with a GIS [7, 265 Chap. 3]. This investigation points out the ability to construct and validate the topology of a power system and their interconnections with a GIS. They mention that it is possible to generate network topology of a system using satellite imagery by utilizing a GIS. Furthermore, it is mentioned that finding the topology of a power system with GIS can be automated through machine learning and image processing techniques. In addition, tagging power structures and power networks can be crowd sourced. This intention is mentioned to be followed by an Open Street Map (OSM)[6] subproject [7, p. 267]. This work confirms the existence, or at least the possibility of collecting the data we need for our approach. The infrastructure data, the topology of the networks of the critical infrastructure (e.g. electricity grids) is provided in the GIS and managed there. Our solution uses this data in the GIS to map it to a cyber attack defense.

There are some works regarding the analysis of cyber threats in the context of ICS on base of the MITRE ATT&CK framework. For example, Choi et al. deal with the question of how a test bed can be extended to check cyber security [4]. They use the Techniques of the MITRE ATT&CK framework to specifically check the effectiveness of the protection. In addition to this approach, we link it to GIS data.

Threat scenarios for specific critical infrastructures have already been devised and tested. Lykou, Anagnostopoulou and Gritzalis devised and evaluated threat scenarios for specific critical infrastructures [15]. They investigated the implementation rate of cybersecurity measures in commercial airports, malicious threats that evolve due to IoT and smart devices installed, and they evaluated risk scenario analysis for IoT malicious attacks with threat mitigation actions. Finally, they presented a systematic and comprehensive analysis of malicious attacks in smart airports, to facilitate airport community comprehend risks and proactively act, by implementing cybersecurity best practices and resilience measures [15, p .2].

To our best knowledge, our solution approach goes beyond previous work by considering cyber security holistically for enterprise IT, operational IT, including GIS analysis capabilities.

3 Localization of Cyber-Physical Assets

In this section we explain our use of the MITRE ATT&CK framework and the geodata information to localize relevant assets of the critical infrastructure.

We use the taxonomy of the MITRE ATT&CK framework in our work. This taxonomy is commonly understood by offense and defense to classify individual adversary actions and goals [20, pp. 23,34]. Here, the term and the dimensions of "threat" are determined by the effects of an attack matrix that is spanned by Tactics and Techniques and is described in further detail by Software, Groups and Mitgations. In its current version, campaigns are added in the framework. All the entities mentioned are related to each other. Together, they specify the threat posed by the attackers' current objective (Tactic) [20, pp. 6,8].

Second, we agree on the use of the term "cyber-physical" in this context. This term is indirectly described for the definition of an ICS as: "[...] systems that enable efficient (and most of the time, safe) automation of the physical processes

---

[6] https://www.openstreetmap.org/.

that we all rely on (e.g. electric power delivery from generation to load, water and wastewater management, manufacturing, and other similar cyber-physical processes)" [20, pp. 7,21].

If you want to find out which cyber-physical points of attack an ICS offers, then the so-called Purdue Model [1, pp. 16–21] is a first entry point. The Purdue Enterprise Reference Architecture (PERA) defines six different levels of a critical infrastructure used in production lines [23]. The core idea was to define best practices for the relationship between ICS and business networks. A key aspect is the boundary point between the ICS/Operational Technology (OT) systems represented at Levels 0–3 as listed in Table 1 and the IT systems of the enterprise network at Levels 4 and 5. The boundary point must ensure, that the connection between these levels is carefully controlled with demilitarized zones (DMZ) [1, pp. 61–92]. The IT business component of the organization provides an untrusted zone towards the ICS/OT in the same manner as the internet does for the IT business network[7].

Table 1. Physical Assets and corresponding PERA levels

Level	Description	Asset
Level 3: Site-Wide Supervisory	Monitoring, supervisory, and operational support for a site or region	Management servers, Human-machine interfaces (HMIs), Alarm servers, Analytic systems, Historians (if scoped for an entire site or region)
Level 2: Local Supervisory	Monitoring and supervisory control for a single process, cell, line, or distributed control system (DCS) solution. Isolate processes from one another, grouping by function, type, or risk	HMIs, Alarm servers, Process analytic systems, Historians, Control room (if scoped for a single process and not the site/region)
Level 1: Local Controllers	Devices and systems to provide automated control of a process, cell, line, or DCS solution. Modern ICS solutions often combine Levels 1 and 0	Programmable Logic Controllers (PLCs), Control processors, Programmable relays, Remote terminal units (RTUs), Process-specific microcontrollers
Level 0: Field Devices	Sensors and actuators for the cell, line, process, or DCS solution. Often combined with Level 1	Basic sensors and actuators, Smart sensors/actuators speaking fieldbus protocols, Intelligent Electronic Devices (IEDs), Industrial Internet-of-Things (IIoT) devices, Communications gateways, other field instrumentation

We first look at the issue of cyber-physical assets from the IT business network side. The key question is: which attack vectors does the MITRE ATT&CK framework identify for physical assets? It can be seen here that the assets, i.e. the question of whether a server or a client is being attacked, are not modeled directly. Neither are the locations where the hardware is operated, e.g. by recording the location coordinate as a geographical reference.

---

[7] https://www.sans.org/blog/introduction-to-ics-security-part-2/.

There is no mandatory field that could hold this location information [20, pp. 10–12,14,15–17]. Furthermore, we have searched through the ICS-specific parts and found references to physical assets [1, pp. 27–28]. The physical assets of PERA levels 0–3 correspond to the assets class of the underlying object model of the MITRE ATT&CK ICS matrix. An asset class is associated with a technique if there is a documented case of an adversary using the technique against an asset. They are also associated on a functional level with the Purdue Model as well as with the physical hardware asset [3, p. 10]. The asset data field is mandatory anchored in the ICS Tactics Object model. Designated physical assets are shown in Table 1 with the corresponding PERA level.

```
import mitreattack.attackToExcel.attackToExcel as
    attackToExcel

attackToExcel.export("ics-attack","v11.3","Path_to_folder")

import pandas as pd
xlsx_file = "Path_to_folder\\ics-attack-v11.3\\ics-attack-v11
    .3-techniques.xlsx"
df = pd.read_excel(io=xlsx_file,sheet_name="techniques")

def get_unique_platforms(df):
    unique_platforms = []
    for platform in df.platforms:
        assets = platform.split(",")
        for asset in assets:
            asset = asset.strip(" ")
            unique_platforms.append(asset)
    return set(unique_platforms)

unique_platforms = get_unique_platforms(df)
print(unique_platforms)
# results
{'Device Configuration/Parameters', 'Engineering Workstation',
    'None', 'Input/Output Server', 'Data Historian', 'Human-
    Machine Interface', 'Field Controller/RTU/PLC/IED', '
    Control Server', 'Safety Instrumented System/Protection
    Relay'}
```

Listing 1.1. Assessing the assets from the MITRE ATT&CK framework

The actual entries of the MITRE ATT&CK framework can be checked, for example, using an API access (current version is 11.3). Listing 1.1 shows a Python script snippet that opens previous values stored in a local Excel file, the corresponding values are in the "platforms" field during access via this API[8]. The physical assets are entered. However, multiple names, separated by "/", have often been used for entries (there are "None" values, too). The assets were

---

[8] https://github.com/mitre-attack/mitreattack-python.

assigned to different Techniques. This is the first connection between cyber-physical assets and Techniques within the ICS specific attack vectors.

In the next step we review how the assets are modeled in the geographic information system. Here it is particularly important to check whether these assets are provided with a georeference in a GIS. Within a small test data set we model the critical infrastructures gas, water and electricity in the GIS for a small town. This is often done, mostly by the operator, e.g. to justify a situation picture in operations [7, p. 267].

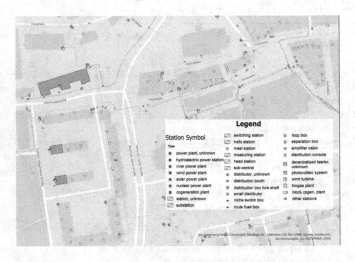

Fig. 1. Mapping the cyber-physical ICS assets in a GIS

We describe the data model of the test data set in form of a UML diagram. All entities contained in the sample town are stored in a GIS database and are managed there. The special feature is that a so-called geometry is saved for many entities constituting the clear geographic reference. This geometry is the prerequisite for the representation of the respective entities on the digital map as shown in Fig. 1 or in a 3D scene. So-called stations are identified as objects in the object model of the electricity network considered here, in all 30 different types are assigned. Listing 1.2 shows a sample specification of the spatial reference and the coordinates are projected in the give spatial reference system. The schema of the database is based on a vendor specific XML specification[9].

---

[9] https://www.loc.gov/preservation/digital/formats/fdd/fdd000295.shtml.

```
1  <SpatialReference xsi:type="esri:ProjectedCoordinateSystem">
2  <WKT>PROJCS["DHDN_3_Degree_Gauss_Zone_4",GEOGCS["
     GCS_Deutsches_Hauptdreiecksnetz",DATUM["
     D_Deutsches_Hauptdreiecksnetz",SPHEROID["Bessel_1841"
     ,6377397.155,299.1528128]],PRIMEM["Greenwich",0.0],UNIT["
     Degree",0.0174532925199433]],PROJECTION["Gauss_Kruger"],
     PARAMETER["False_Easting",4500000.0],PARAMETER["
     False_Northing",0.0],PARAMETER["Central_Meridian",12.0],
     PARAMETER["Scale_Factor",1.0],PARAMETER["
     Latitude_Of_Origin",0.0],UNIT["Meter",1.0],AUTHORITY["EPSG
     ",31468]]</WKT>
3  ...
4  <LatestWKID>31468</LatestWKID>
5  </SpatialReference>
```

Listing 1.2. Sample specification of spatial reference and domain for types of the stations

The precision of the geographical localization of individual assets and the logic that was anchored in the data model specifically for the type of geometric network now allow further spatial analyses. For example, it can be analyzed which industrial complexes and households can no longer be supplied with electricity if certain stations should fail. This position data is processed in the GIS so that the georeference information is available directly.

The key to connecting the object models of the MITRE ATT&CK framework and the GIS database is the information security concept. Here, infrastructure and IT components are related. This makes it possible to indirectly assign which ICS assets are used in the associated stations. For critical infrastructures and ICS, information security concepts, as a manifesto of an orderly Information Security Management System (ISMS) [11] [9] [10], are required by default today [19, pp. 2–16,6–14,6–19,6–29,B-3]. The four elements of technical, organizational, personnel and infrastructural measures [8, 2.4 p.12,3.3.4 p.26–27,7.3 p.59,8.1.4 p.71,8.1.5 p.74] are described here. Physical assets are assigned to a spatial location mandatorily. At least the building and the room number are given. This information is sufficient to derive the location information in the GIS through intersection with the building plan. Such data is provided as Computer Aided Design or Building Information Model dataset.

4   Concatenation of the Object Models

After the explanation of the localization of cyber-physical assets in Sect. 3, we are now able to connect attack vectors directly to GIS modeling of critical infrastructure and vice versa. Figure 2 shows the concept how we accomplish the concatenation of the object models. The concatenation provides the following two key added values. First, by means of a GIS analysis, it is possible to find out the stations that will cause damage if they fail. For these stations, a cyber analysis based on the MITRE ATT&CK ICS should be performed to prioritize protection against APT.

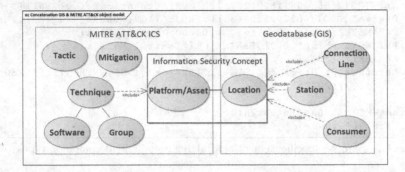

Fig. 2. Concatenation of the object models

Second if the use of MITRE ATT&CK Framework Techniques are now reported via a cyber security solution in the course of incidents, conclusions about the attack vector and the failures to be feared can be analyzed in the GIS. The concatenation is implemented in a graph database to map the corresponding logical connections and to perform the indicated analyses as shown in Fig. 3. Modern graph databases support entities and their relations among each other and the georeferencing of objects.

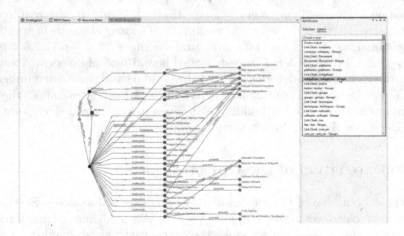

Fig. 3. Implementing the concatenation in a graph database

To transform the data model of the MITRE ATT&CK framework towards the graph entities and graph relations, a data pipeline is built. For example, the data pipeline can be set up and operated efficiently using professional software tools[10]. As a result, we get a knowledge graph that maps the logical connection of the data models. During our consideration in Sect. 5, we make use of a sample software product[11] available on the market. Our evaluation reveals that on the basis of a knowledge graph the concatenation of the two object models of the MITRE ATT&CK ICS and the GIS object model of the electricity network is succesful with respect to both the APT cyber threats and the effects in the operational business of the electricity network.

5   Use Case: Incident by SIEM

To further explain the logical linking of both object models and to show the success of our concatenation introduced in Sect. 4, we present a use case evaluation in this section. The assumed situation is that the SIEM [1, pp. 140–141] solution reports the execution of a Scheduled Task. This is assigned to the Techniques with ID 1053. Adversaries may use task scheduling to execute programs at system startup or on a scheduled basis for persistence. These mechanisms can also be abused to run a process under the context of a specified account (such as one with elevated permissions/privileges)[12]. This Technique is assigned to two Tactics in the Enterprise IT Matrix: Execution, Privilege Escalation(Figure 4). Now it is essential to clarify whether the attackers have already established themselves in the target system. The Tactic Persistence lies between the two Tactics to which the current incident is assigned.

According to the MITRE ATT&CK nomenclature [20, p. 10], the cyber attacker is preparing to bypass system protections (Tactic Defense Evation) and will attempt to acquire additional credentials (Tactic Credential Access). Both Tactics have Techniques whose execution can now be monitored with high priority, e.g., the tactic "Defense Evasion" displays the technique "Process Injection T1055[13]". In combing through the Procedure Examples of this Technique, specific comments are made on individual APTs, such as: "APT32 malware has injected a Cobalt Strike beacon into Rundll32.exe". For detection it is recommended to monitor the execution of API methods of the operating system. Specifically, these API methods can be used to hijack a thread and inject the malicious Dynamic Link Library (DLL): CreateRemoteThread, SuspendThread-/SetThreadContext/ResumeThread, QueueUserAPC/NtQueueApcThread and those that can be used to modify memory within another process, such as VirtualAllocEx/WriteProcessMemory. Experienced cyber defenders can take further proactive measures to avoid other ways to inject a DLL such as controlling the DLL Search Order[14], among others. It is now possible to search specifically

---

[10] https://www.safe.com/.

[11] https://www.esri.com/en-us/arcgis/products/arcgis-knowledge/overview.

[12] https://www.logpoint.com/mitre/.

[13] https://attack.mitre.org/techniques/T1055/.

[14] https://docs.microsoft.com/en-us/windows/win32/dlls/dynamic-link-library-search-order.

for further signs of which Tactic the perpetrators are currently pursuing. The
MITRE ATT&CK framework guides to prioritize the search[15].

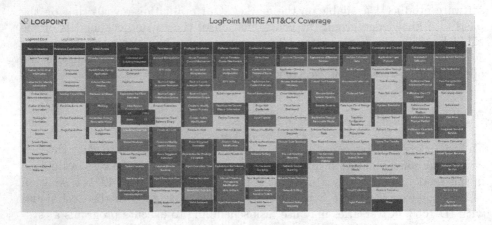

Fig. 4. SIEM reporting a Technique of the MITRE ATT&CK framework

In the next step, we identify all groups (Listing 1.3) that use the reported
Technique and find out about the Tactics' "impact" of these groups to better
understand the risk involved in the event of a successful attack. The preceding
tactics "Inhibit Response Function" and "Impair Process Control" provide further information on this. They identify the techniques that will later cause the
damage in the Enterprise IT. The software used by the perpetrators can also be
derived from this. Last but not least, we also use the identified groups to select
the Techniques that were used in the "Initial Access" tactic. It must be determined afterwards how the perpetrators were able to penetrate the Enterprise IT
to close this entry point. At this point, however, we still know very little about
the attacker; this generates a large number of hits. The results are only a guide.
So far, we have looked at Enterprise IT. The Technique has been reported by the
SIEM here. However, it must also be assumed that the attack on enterprise IT
is used to gain access to the ICS and cause damage to the critical infrastructure
there. Now it is equally important to check whether the ICS has already been
influenced. Through extensive searching, we have now discovered that suspicious
methods of the operating system's API were being executed. Adversaries may
directly interact with the native OS application programming interface (API)
to access system functions. Native APIs[16] provide a controlled means of calling
low-level OS services within the kernel, such as those involving hardware/de-
vices, memory, and processes. Here we are in the ICS Matrix[17] in the Tactic
"Execution". It is now checked whether one of the APT previously identified

---

[15] https://www.logpoint.com/mitre/.

[16] https://attack.mitre.org/techniques/T0834/.

[17] https://attack.mitre.org/matrices/ics/.

in Enterprise IT is also known to attack ICS with this technique. All groups that are entered both for the reported technique in the context of Enterprise IT (SIEM) and for the ICS attack are extracted(Listing 1.3). In this example there are 9 APTs: APT 33, APT 38, Dragonfly, FIN6, FIN7, Lazarus Group, OilRig, TEMP.Veles, Wizard Spider.

```
1  attackToExcel.export(''enterprise-attack", ''v11.3", ''
      Path_to_folder")
2
3  xlsx_file = os.path.join(myfolder, ''enterprise-attack-v11.3\\
      enterprise-attack-v11.3-techniques.xlsx")
4  df = pd.read_excel(io=xlsx_file,sheet_name=''procedure
      examples")
5  procedures_Technique = df[df[''target ID"].str.contains(''
      T1053")]
6  groups = procedures_Technique[procedures_Technique[''source
      type"]==''group"]
7  software = procedures_Technique[procedures_Technique[''source
      type"]==''software"]
8  groups[''source ID]
9
10 xlsx_file = os.path.join(myfolder,''ics-attack-v11.3\\ics-
      attack-v11.3-groups.xlsx")
11 df = pd.read_excel(io=xlsx_file,sheet_name=''groups")
12
13 import re
14 matches = [re.escape(value) for value in groups[''source ID"]]
15 ICS_APT = df[df[''ID"].str.contains('|'.join(matches), case=
      False, regex=True, na=False)]
16 ICS_APT
```

Listing 1.3. First impression of APTs

No groups are assigned for the recognized technique "Native API T0834".

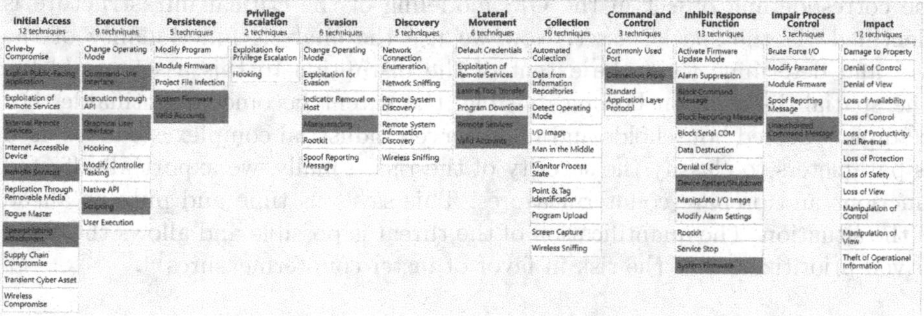

Fig. 5. Sandworm Team Attack Vector

Nevertheless, further research into the question of which of the 9 groups is capable of such an attack could certainly further limit the number of hits of the APTs in question. You see one of the APTs Sandworm Team and its attack vector in Fig. 5. The consideration of the attack vectors provides the first visual information on the expected risk of the further penetration of the APT into the ICS. In the course of further investigations, we secure additional digital traces. Each technique that can be identified further narrows down the number of attack vectors and intents pursued. Certain connections can now also be specifically worked out with the knowledge graph (Fig. 6).

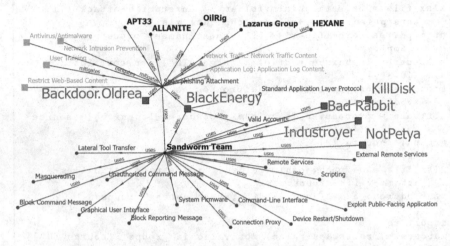

Fig. 6. Sandworm Team Graph

The further investigations, during which the harmful activities also appear on the ICS, also provide information on which physical assets are affected (e.g. Programmable Logical Controller (PLC) or Human Interface (HI)). This is where the logical linking of the object models comes into play. The location and thus the corresponding object in the GIS modeling of the critical infrastructure is identified via the special asset. Now we use the analysis functionality of the GIS and determine what the extent of the disruption to this asset would be. The spatial distribution becomes visible, the extent becomes quantifiable. For example, affected households and underserved industrial complexes can be used as parameters to classify the severity of the risk. Finally, we export all affected junctions and prepare countermeasures. This saves us time and puts us ahead of the situation. The quantification of the threat is possible and allows the data-driven prioritization of the risk in favor of faster countermeasures[18].

---

[18] https://mitre-attack.github.io/attack-navigator/.

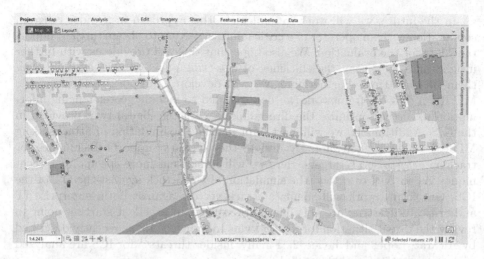

Fig. 7. GIS analysis to foster risk assessment of power outage in case of cyber-physical attack

6   Conclusion and Future Work

When considering the protection of today's critical infrastructures, we find that enterprise IT and operative IT are connected. The transition is well protected, but the connection means a risk. National initiatives for better cyber protection require the operation of an ISMS for the critical infrastructure, often also required by law. In the course of the ISMS, all assets that must be considered for the IT network are localized directly as infrastructure or in relation to it. In addition, more and more assets are sending their position independently, or the current position can be determined via a service.

The connection to GIS is established via the georeferencing of the assets. Enterprise IT, operational IT and the spatial objects in the GIS are logically linked. On the one hand, the cyber threat by APTs is assessed using the Cyber Threat Intelligence (CTI) approach. On the other hand, disruptions in the operational network are analyzed in the GIS. Damage is quantified, by counting the spatial objects concerned. Both sides interlock and allow the development of more precise, data-driven risk assessment and incident response processes. The approach is evaluated using a knowledge graph in the GIS[19]. Although it has not been considered in this document, it is obvious that further insights can be gained using this enhanced approach of risk assessment. Cyber threats are only one dimension of today's hybrid threat vectors for critical infrastructures. Examination of the environment such as the elevation model or the ownership situation of the land around the critical infrastructure will rule out additional threats such as signal intelligence or potential impact of extreme natural events caused by climate change [13].

---

[19] https://www.esri.com/en-us/arcgis/products/arcgis-pro/overview.

In the future, we will work to implement this approach in a wider range in cooperation with an operator of a critical infrastructure to obtain further, important data for the evaluation. We also hope that this will provide us with further insights into increasing the efficiency of detecting cyber attacks and assessing them in good time. Furthermore, we will develop a proposal as to how the MITRE ATT&CK framework can be expanded to include georeferencing information to further optimize the direct linking with the digital twin provided in the GIS. Additionally, we will start implementing a simulation of attacks using MITRE Caldera[20] software. By design, the software supports Techniques for tracking enterprise IT targets. Here we will implement more specific ICS Techniques via an API to extend the simulation of the attack against the OT of the ICS. Our future work will simulate attack vectors against both, enterprise IT and critical infrastructure OT. The work will be an excellent starting point to review the threat situation for digital twins in industry 4.0 as recently described by Alcaraz, Lopez and Javier [2]. Finally, insider threats[21] for ICS are analyzed with special attention [22, pp. 8–13].

Acknowledgments. Supported by Research Institute CODE of Universität der Bundeswehr München.

References

1. Pascal Ackerman. Industrial Cybersecurity, Second Edition, Efficiently monitor the cybersecurity posture of your ICS environment. Number ISBN 978-1-80020-209-2. Packt (2021)
2. Alcaraz, C., Lopez, J.: A comprehensive survey of security threats. IEEE Commun. Surv. Tutorials, Digital twin (2022)
3. Alexander, O., Belisle, M., Steele, J.: Mitre att&ck for industrial control systems: Design and philosophy. MITRE Cooperation. https://attack.mitre.org/docs/ATTACK_Design_and_Philosophy_March_2020.pdf
4. Choi, S., Choi, J., Yun, J.-H., Min, B.-G., Kim, H.C.:. Expansion of ICS testbed for security validation based on MITRE ATT&CK Techniques (2021). https://www.usenix.org/system/files/cset20-paper-choi.pdf
5. Mitre Corporation. Ticket: 473822, incident: tangerine yellow (2019). https://attack.mitre.org/docs/training-cti/ticket-473822
6. Fire Eye and Mitre.org. Apt39: an iranian cyber espionage group focused on personal information (2019). https://attack.mitre.org/docs/training-cti/FireEye
7. Gritzalis, D., Theocharidou, M., Stergiopoulos, G.: Critical infrastructure security and resilience: theories, methods, tools and technologies - serie: advanced sciences and technologies for security applications (2019). https://link.springer.com/content/pdf/10.1007/978-3-030-00024-0.pdf
8. Federal Office for Information Security (BSI). Bsi-standard 200–2, it-grundschutz methodology - version 1.0 (2017). https://www.bsi.bund.de/SharedDocs/Downloads/EN/BSI/Grundschutz/International/bsi-standard-2002_en_pdf.html?nn=128640

---

[20] https://caldera.mitre.org/.
[21] https://ctid.mitre-engenuity.org/our-work/insider-ttp-kb/.

9. International Electronical Commission (IEC) International Standard Organization (ISO). Inf. Secur. Manage. (2013). https://www.iso.org/isoiec-27001-information-security.html
10. International Electronical Commission (IEC) International Standard Organization (ISO). Information technology - security techniques - code of practice for information security controls (2013). https://www.iso.org/isoiec-27001-information-security.html
11. International Electronical Commission (IEC) International Standard Organization (ISO). Information technology - security techniques - information security management systems - overview and vocabulary (2018). https://standards.iso.org/ittf/PubliclyAvailableStandards/c073906_ISO_IEC_27000_2018_E.zip
12. Jenkinson, A.: Ransomware and cybercrime (2022). https://www.taylorfrancis.com/books/mono/10.1201/9781003278214/ransomware-cybercrime-andrew-jenkinson
13. Kumara, N., Poon, V., Gupta, B.B., Goyal, M.K.: A novel framework for risk assessment and resilience of critical infrastructure towards climate change (2021). https://www.sciencedirect.com/science/article/abs/pii/S0040162520313585
14. LogPoint. Technical whitepaper - how logpoint uses mitre att&ck (20190. https://www.logpoint.com/en/resources/mitre-attack-framework/
15. Lykou, G., Anagnostopoulou, A., Gritzalis, D.: Smart airport cybersecurity: threat mitigation and cyber resilience controls (2018). https://www.mdpi.com/1424-8220/19/1/19
16. PR Newswire. Global xdr (extended detection and response) market report 2021: Vendors and end-users need to see beyond marketing claims (2021). https://eds.s.ebscohost.com/eds/detail/detail?vid=26&sid=6bcfe3cb-db80-41c0-bcbf-6921d11a202d%40redis&bdata=Jmxhbmc9ZGUmc2l0ZT11ZHMtbGl2ZQ%3d%3dAN=202108111030PR.NEWS.USPR.IO71820&db=bwh. (Visited 27 Oct 2021)
17. Security-Insider. Xdr - extended detection and response (2022). https://www.security-insider.de/xdr-extended-detection-and-response-d-626fe93eb2c58/
18. Electricity Information Sharing and Analysis Center (E-ISAC). Analysis of the cyber attack on the ukrainian power grid (2016). https://nsarchive.gwu.edu/sites/default/files/documents/3891751/SANS-and-Electricity-Information-Sharing-and.pdf
19. Stouffer, K., Pillitteri, V., Lightman, S., Abrams, M., Hahn, A.: Guide to industrial control systems (ICS) security, national institute of standards and technology (NIST) special publication 800–82 revision 2, us department of commerce (2015). https://dx.doi.org/10.6028/NIST.SP.800-82r2
20. Strom, B.E., Applebaum, A., Miller, D.P., Nickels, K.C., Pennington, A.G., Thomas, C.B.: Mitre att&ck: design and philosophy. MITRE Cooperation. https://attack.mitre.org/docs/ATTACK_Design_and_Philosophy_March_2020.pdf
21. Tariq, H., Sultan, S.: A secure interoperable API wrapper tunnel for integration of gisbased ics-iiot and digital twins in industry 4.0 clouds (2022). https://wseas.com/journals/computers/2022/a365105-015(2022).pdf
22. MITRE Engenuity Center for Threat informaed Defense. Design principles and methodology for the insider threat tactics, techniques and procedures knowledge base (2022). https://github.com/center-for-threat-informed-defense/insider-threat-ttp-kb/releases/download/v0.0.1/design-principles-and-methodology.pdf
23. Williams, T.J.: The purdue enterprise reference architecture (1993). https://www.sciencedirect.com/science/article/pii/S1474667017485326

Identifying Residential Areas Based on Open Source Data: A Multi-Criteria Holistic Indicator to Optimize Resource Allocation During a Pandemic

G. Oliva[1,2]([✉]) [ID], S. Guarino[1], R. Setola[1,2], G. De Angelis[3], and M. Coradini[3]

[1] Universitá Campus Bio-Medico di Roma, via Álvaro del Portillo 21,
Rome 00128, Italy
g.oliva@unicampus.it
[2] Consorzio Nazionale Interuniversitario per i Trasporti e per la Logistica (NITEL),
via Palestro, 95, 00185 Rome, Italy
[3] Space Systems Solutions Ltd., Lordos Vyronos Ave. 36, Nicosia 1096, Cyprus

Abstract. COVID-19 has changed the very way we live our lives, from how we learn and work to how we interact. It has also brought a number of challenges including the management of building utilities under such conditions. In fact, during a lockdown, it makes sense to allocate the available resources based on the density of population, e.g., preferring residential areas over commercial or financial districts. The identification of residential areas is relevant also to prioritize emergency activities in the presence of major natural disaster and it can be the basis to identify which area should be supplied of electricity and gas in case of scarcity of energetic resources. However, given the complexity of the urban landscape, pinpointing residential areas might be difficult. In this paper, based on open source intelligence and multi-criteria decision-making, we aim to develop a holistic indicator to quantify the likelihood that a zone is residential, in order to orient the optimization of the distribution of resources such as power, gas or water. In order to show the effectiveness of the proposed approach, the paper is complemented by a case study set in Nicosia, Cyprus.

Keywords: COVID-19 · Resource Allocation · Residential Area Identification · Multi-Criteria Decision-Making · Incomplete Analytic Hierarchy Process · Logarithmic Least Squares

1 Introduction

Given the complexity of the urban landscape, especially in the case of major cities, assessing the likelihood that a given zone is residential could prove a difficult endeavor. Yet, being able to quantify such a measure could be highly beneficial, especially during a major crisis or when energy resources should be rationed [4]. In particular, consider the case of a strict lockdown due to a pandemics, a scenario which–sadly–has been experienced in most countries at the beginning of the COVID19 pandemics and that has recently occurred in Shanghai due to the surge of infections. In this case, being able to estimate the actual demand of resources such as food or water in a zone would allow to implement tailored and effective resource distribution policies. In the same way, a halt to the import of petroleum and/or gas from Russia due to the conflict in Ukraine might force governments to adopt rationing policies; therefore, they might be interested to identify residential areas in order to estimate potential negative impacts on the welfare of the population.

In this paper, based on open source intelligence, we aim to develop a holistic indicator to quantify the likelihood that a zone is residential, in order to orient the optimization of the distribution of resources such as power, gas or water. Specifically, we resort to open source intelligence data obtained from OpenStreetMap [20] via the OverPass APIs [17], in order to identify a set of indirect indicators such as the ramification of the road network or the number of shops, entertainment, worship or financial facilities. Moreover, we combine such data relying on the experience of human decision-makers. Specifically, the decision-makers assess the relative relevance of such indicators (e.g., "The level of road ramification is twice as important as the number of food shops"), and we resort to the Incomplete Analytic Hierarchy Process technique [2,3,18,19] (specifically, to the Logarithmic Least Squares approach [2,3,18], considering multiple decision-makers at once) in order to distill absolute utility values for the different indicators. Such values become the cornerstone for the proposed holistic index, which amounts to a weighted sum of the score obtained by a zone according to the specific indicators. Notice that, in the literature, GIS based systems have been quite popular for a wide variety of applications. In [1], authors proposed a GIS-based decision support system (DSS) for planning urban transportation policies on the Greater Athens Area in Greece. In [14,15] a web-based Multi-criteria Spatial Decision Support System (MC-SDSS) for land suitability evaluation (LSE) has been developed. In [7] a DSS in the context of coastal zone watershed has been developed. In [23] a DSS aiming at protecting natural and cultural heritage has been presented.

Moreover, given its rich availability of features, OpenStreetMap has been extensively used to support decisions and to identify complex features. For instance, in [16] an approach to automatically detect vandalise acts has been developed; in [9] OpenStreetMap data is used to generate a 3D model for a city; in [10] satellite images from OpenStreetMap are the basis for the identification of urban land use; in [5] flooding risk is evaluated based on OpenStreetMap data; in [6,11] OpenStreetMap data is the key ingredient in order to identify Critical Infrastructures.

With respect to previous literature, the original contribution of the proposed approach is the development of a novel multi-criteria decision model that is able to combine different features extracted from open source data in order to quantify the likelihood that a give zone is residential.

The paper is organized as follows. Section 2 provides the necessary background and describes the methodological tools adopted in the paper; Sect. 3 presents the proposed Multi-Criteria Decision Model; Sect. 4 is devoted to discuss the proposed case study; Sect. 5 draws some conclusions and lays ideas for future work.

2   Material and Methods

2.1   Notation

We denote vectors via boldface letters, while matrices are shown with uppercase letters. We use A_{ij} to address the (i,j)-th entry of a matrix A and x_i for the i-th entry of a vector $\mathbf{x}$. Moreover, we write $\mathbf{1}_n$ and $\mathbf{0}_n$ to denote a vector with n components, all equal to one and zero, respectively; similarly, we use $1_{n \times m}$ and $0_{n \times m}$ to denote $n \times m$ matrices all equal to one and zero, respectively. We denote by I_n the $n \times n$ identity matrix. Finally, we express by $\exp(\mathbf{x})$ and $\ln(\mathbf{x})$ the component-wise exponentiation or logarithm of the vector $\mathbf{x}$, i.e., a vector such that $\exp(\mathbf{x})_i = e^{x_i}$ and $\ln(\mathbf{x})_i = \ln(x_i)$, respectively.

2.2   Elements of Graph Theory

Let $G = \{V, E\}$ be a *graph* with n nodes $V = \{v_1, \ldots, v_n\}$ and e edges

$$E \subseteq V \times V \setminus \{(v_i, v_i) \mid v_i \in V\},$$

where $(v_i, v_j) \in E$ captures the existence of a link from node v_i to node v_j. A graph is said to be *undirected* if $(v_i, v_j) \in E$ whenever $(v_j, v_i) \in E$, and is said to be *directed* otherwise. In the following, when dealing with undirected graphs, we represent edges using unordered pairs $\{v_i, v_j\}$ in place of the two directed edges $(v_i, v_j), (v_j, v_i)$. A graph is *connected* if, for each pair of nodes v_i, v_j, there is a path over G that connects them. Let the neighborhood $\mathcal{N}_i$ of a node v_i in an undirected graph G be the set of nodes v_j that are connected to v_i via an edge $\{v_i, v_j\}$ in E. The *degree* d_i of a node v_i in an undirected graph G is the number of its incoming edges, i.e., $d_i = |\mathcal{N}_i|$. The *degree matrix* D of an undirected graph G is the $n \times n$ diagonal matrix such that $D_{ii} = d_i$. The *adjacency matrix* Adj of a directed or undirected graph $G = \{V, E\}$ with n nodes is the $n \times n$ matrix such that $\text{Adj}_{ij} = 1$ if $(v_i, v_j) \in E$ and $\text{Adj}_{ij} = 0$, otherwise. The *Laplacian matrix* associated to an undirected graph G is the $n \times n$ matrix L, having the following structure.

$$L_{ij} = \begin{cases} -1 & \text{if } \{v_i, v_j\} \in E, \\ d_i, & \text{if } i = j, \\ 0, & \text{otherwise.} \end{cases}$$

It is well known that L has an eigenvalue equal to zero, and that, in the case of undirected graphs, the multiplicity of such an eigenvalue corresponds to the number of connected components of G [8]. Therefore, the eigenvalue zero has multiplicity one if and only if the graph is connected.

2.3   Kendall's Correlation Index

Given two pairs of values (a_i, b_i) and (a_j, b_j), we say they are *concordant* if both $a_i > a_j$ and $b_i > b_j$ or if both $a_i < a_j$ and $b_i < b_j$; similarly the pairs are *discordant* if $a_i > a_j$ and $b_i < b_j$ or if $a_i < a_j$ and $b_i > b_j$. If $a_i = a_j$ or $b_i = b_j$ the pairs are neither concordant nor discordant. Given two vectors $\mathbf{a} \in \mathbb{R}^n$ and $\mathbf{b} \in \mathbb{R}^n$, the *Kendall's correlation index* [12] τ is defined as

$$\tau = \frac{|\mathcal{C}| - |\mathcal{P}|}{n(n-1)/2},$$

where $\mathcal{C}$ and $\mathcal{P}$ are the sets of concordant and discordant pairs (a_i, b_i) and (a_j, b_j), respectively.

When $\mathbf{b}$ is a permutation of the components of $\mathbf{a}$, the Kendall's tau can be interpreted as a measure of the degree of shuffling of $\mathbf{b}$ with respect to $\mathbf{a}$, between minus one and one. In this sense $\tau = 1$ implies $\mathbf{a} = \mathbf{b}$, while $\tau = -1$ represents the fact $\mathbf{b}$ is in reverse order with respect to $\mathbf{a}$. The closer is τ to (minus) one, therefore, the more the two rankings are (anti-) correlated, while the closer is τ to zero the more the two rankings are independent.

2.4   Incomplete Analytic Hierarchy Process for Multiple Decision-Makers

We now review the methodology presented in [18] to quantify the importance of a set of alternatives based on multiple criteria, considering incomplete relative preference information provided by multiple decision-makers, which are in charge of evaluating the relevance of the different criteria.

In particular, let us consider a set of k alternatives, e.g., the zones to be ranked based on the likelihood that they are residential. For each zone, we consider a set of n metrics or indicators describing the importance of a zone according to a specific criterion. In this view, referring to $w_i > 0$ as the weight associated to the i-th criterion and to c_{ij} as the value assumed by the j-th residential zone according to the i-th criterion (possibly normalized between zero and one), the *holistic score* associated to the j-th residential zone is given by

$$C_j = \sum_{i=1}^{n} w_i c_{ij}.$$

Notice that, since the different metrics may have different scales, the scores c_{ij} are normalized in the interval $[0, 1]$. In particular, for each criterion h, we normalize the raw values c_{ij}^{raw} via the min-max normalization technique [21] a popular approach for normalizing features in machine learning applications. Specifically, we set

$$c_{ij} = \begin{cases} \frac{c_{ij}^{\text{raw}} - \min_j\{c_{ij}^{\text{raw}}\}}{\max_j\{c_{ij}^{\text{raw}}\} - \min_j\{c_{ij}^{\text{raw}}\}}, & \text{if } \max_j\{c_{ij}^{\text{raw}}\} > \min_j\{c_{ij}^{\text{raw}}\} \\ 0, & \text{otherwise.} \end{cases}$$

Notably, if the values w_i are known, the problem trivially reduces to ranking the alternatives based on a weighted sum of the score of the different criteria. However, when such weights are unknown, the problem becomes challenging. The classical approach when the weights are not directly available is to resort to the help of decision-makers, in charge of assessing their relative preferences over the metrics.

Specifically, Let us consider a set of n criteria or metrics, and suppose that each criterion is characterized by an unknown utility or value $w_i > 0$. Suppose m decision-makers provide values $\mathcal{A}_{ij}^{(u)} = \epsilon_{ij}^{(u)} w_i/w_j$ for selected pairs of criteria i, j; such a piece of information corresponds to an estimate of the ratio w_i/w_j provided by the u-th decision-maker, where $\epsilon_{ij}^{(u)} > 0$ is a multiplicative perturbation that represents the estimation error. For all the available entries $\mathcal{A}_{ij}^{(u)}$, we assume that $\mathcal{A}_{ji}^{(u)} = \left(\mathcal{A}_{ij}^{(u)}\right)^{-1} = \left(\epsilon_{ij}^{(u)}\right)^{-1} w_j/w_i$, i.e., the available terms $\mathcal{A}_{ij}^{(u)}$ and $\mathcal{A}_{ji}^{(u)}$ are always consistent and satisfy $\mathcal{A}_{ij}^{(u)} \mathcal{A}_{ji}^{(u)} = 1$.

Let us represent the information provided by the u-th decision-maker via a graph $G^{(u)} = \{V, E^{(u)}\}$ with $|V| = n$ nodes; in this view, each criterion i is associated to a node $v_i \in V$, while the knowledge of $\mathcal{A}_{ij}^{(u)}$ corresponds to an edge $(v_i, v_j) \in E^{(u)}$. Clearly, since we assume to know $\mathcal{A}_{ji}^{(u)}$ whenever we know $\mathcal{A}_{ij}^{(u)}$, the graph G is undirected. Let $\mathcal{A}^{(u)}$ be the $n \times n$ matrix collecting the terms $\mathcal{A}_{ij}^{(u)}$, with $\mathcal{A}_{ij}^{(u)} = 0$ if $(v_i, v_j) \notin E$. Moreover, denote by $\widehat{G} = \{V, \bigcup_{u=1}^{m} E^{(u)}\}$ the *multigraph* corresponding to the overall information provided by the m decision makers (i.e., a graph featuring the union of the edges provided by all decision makers, where repeated edges are allowed). In [18], the unknown utility vector is computed as the global optimal solution w^* of the following unconstrained and convex optimization problem

$$w^* = \exp\left(\underbrace{\underset{y \in \mathbb{R}^n}{\arg\min} \frac{1}{2} \sum_{u=1}^{m} \sum_{i=1}^{n} \sum_{j \in \mathcal{N}_i} \left(\ln\left(\mathcal{A}_{ij}^{(u)}\right) - y_i + y_j\right)^2}_{\kappa(y)}\right), \qquad (1)$$

which amounts to computing the global optimal y^* value and then setting $w^* = \exp(y^*)$, where $\exp(\cdot)$ is the component-wise exponential of a vector. In particular, by evaluating $\partial \kappa(y)/\partial y_i = 0$ at $y = y^*$ for all i, it can be shown that the global optimal solution to the above problem y^* satisfies

$$\sum_{u=1}^{m} L(G^{(u)})y^* = \sum_{u=1}^{m} P^{(u)} \mathbf{1}_n, \qquad (2)$$

where $L(G^{(u)})$ is the Laplacian matrix associated to $G^{(u)}$ and $P^{(u)}$ is an $n \times n$ matrix collecting the logarithm of the nonzero entries of $\mathcal{A}_{ij}^{(u)}$, i.e., $P_{ij}^{(u)} =$

$\log\left(\mathcal{A}_{ij}^{(u)}\right)$ for $\mathcal{A}_{ij}^{(u)} > 0$, while $P_{ij}^{(u)} = 0$ when $\mathcal{A}_{ij}^{(u)} = 0$. Moreover, $exp(\boldsymbol{y}^*)$ is unique up to a scaling factor if and only if $\widehat{G}$ is connected.

2.5 OpenStreetMap and Overpass APIs

OpenStreetMap [20] is used in order to retrieve geospatial information from a user-defined geographical area. It is an open source editable map database which allows users to access map images and all of underlying map data. Such data are organised in features which represent physical elements on the ground; these can include both natural and man made objects such as rain-forests and buildings, in general. OpenStreetMap provides these information in well structured xml files where features are uniquely identified by specific tags. In this way, we can retrieve useful geo-referenced data underlying the maps which can be indirectly related to the amount of population residing in a specific geographical area, such as the number of supermarkets, clinics or cinemas. Such information can be downloaded thanks to a read-only API, called OpenStreetMap Overpass API [17], which serves up custom selected parts of the OpenStreetMap map data. It acts as a query API; thus the user sends a request about the geodata of a specfic geographical area and it gets back an xml file reporting such information. In this paper, this process has been implemented in MATLAB™ language [13].

```
1 function [num_features] = getDataByType(bounding_box,type):
2     area_to_request = bounding_box %area defined by two
      longitudes and two latitudes
3     url = strcat('https://overpass-api.de/api/map?bbox=',
      area_to_request);
4     map = urlread(url); %response from OSM
5     data=xml2struct(map);%transforms xml into a Matlab
      Struct data type
6     features = get_features_from_tags(data,type) %number of
       features of given type found in the specified area
7     num_features = count_features(features) %number of
      occurrences per feature
```

As described in the above code snippet, the MATLAB function requests a specific geographical area based on a bounding box, described by two pairs of latitudes and longitudes. The OpenStreetMap server returns the requested geo-referenced data in the form of an xml file which is parsed into a Struct data type. Then, the available features are retrieved based on predefined tags available on the OpenStreetMap website[1]. Eventually, the function returns the number of occurrences per feature; such as the number of clinics, theaters or restaurants.

Notice that, in order to reconstruct the topology of the road network in the zone, it is possible to select the features with type = node (i.e., the nodes of the network) and type = way (a way is a path, passing through a set of nodes). Moreover, for each way is possible to obtain several attributes, e.g., the length in

---

[1] https://wiki.openstreetmap.org/wiki/Map_features.

kilometers. Finally, by building the road network as a graph $G = \{V, E\}$ based on the above features, it is possible to identify those nodes that correspond to actual traffic intersections, by selecting the nodes with degree larger than two (as some node is just a connector between two traits of a way).

3 Proposed Multi-Criteria Decision Model

In this section, we present the proposed Multi-Criteria Decision Model, i.e., the set of metrics considered in this study and the weights that are the result of the interaction with the decision makers. In particular, we remark that the metrics considered in this study represent indirect measures of how much a zone of interest is residential and are based on public information obtained from OpenStreetMap via the Overpass APIs.

Let us consider a specific location j, described in terms of latitude $\mathtt{lat}_j$ and longitude $\mathtt{lon}_j$. Moreover, let us consider an *area of interest* surrounding the location, i.e., the set of points h such that $\mathtt{lat}_h \in [\mathtt{lat}_j - \varDelta\mathtt{lat}, \mathtt{lat}_j + \varDelta\mathtt{lat}]$ and $\mathtt{lon}_h \in [\mathtt{lon}_j - \varDelta\mathtt{lon}, \mathtt{lon}_j + \varDelta\mathtt{lon}]$. Notice that, in this study we consider values of $\varDelta\mathtt{lat}$ and $\varDelta\mathtt{lon}$ that correspond to a bounding box of one square kilometer, centered at the considered location. Specifically, the indicators considered in this study are as follows:

1. **Road Ramification:** Number of nodes of the road network in the area of interest (for instance, a highway tends to have few nodes, while a densely populated neighborhood tends to have roads interjected by several nodes, even though not every node is conceptually a proper road intersection).
2. **Road Intersections:** Number of nodes of the road network in the area of interest that correspond to actual road intersections (i.e., the subset of nodes with degree larger than two).
3. **Road Coverage:** Total length of the roads in the road network in the area of interest (again, a highway tends to have only one main road, while a densely populated neighborhood tends to have several intersections).
4. **Food:** total number of food-related shops (e.g., supermarkets, groceries, restaurants) in the area of interest.
5. **Financial:** total number of finance-related facilities (e.g., atms, banks, bureau de change) in the area of interest.
6. **Education:** total number of education-related facilities (e.g., colleges, driving schools, kindergardens) in the area of interest.
7. **Healthcare:** total number of healthcare-related facilities (e.g., hospitals, clinics, dentists) in the area of interest.
8. **Entertainment:** total number of entertainment-related facilities (e.g., arts centres, cinemas, theatres) in the area of interest.
9. **Public Service:** total number of facilities related to public service (e.g., courthouses, fire stations, post offices) in the area of interest.
10. **Worship:** total number of worship facilities (e.g., churches, mosques, synagogues) in the area of interest.

11. **Transportation:** total number of transportation-related facilities (e.g., bus stations, parkings, taxis) in the area of interest.
12. **Shops (excluded Food):** total number of shops, food excluded, (e.g., clothing, hardware, stationery) in the area of interest.

3.1 Computation of the Weights

Let us now discuss the computation of the weights w_i that represent the key ingredient of the proposed holistic indicator to characterize the likelihood that a zone is residential. Specifically, we interviewed six decision-makers, i.e., experts from both the industry and academia with experience in the analysis or management of critical infrastructures. With the aim to construct the matrices $\mathcal{A}^{(u)}$ collecting the opinion of each decision maker, we asked the experts to fill the pictorial questionnaire reported in Fig. 1. Specifically, a questionnaire was presented to the experts where the different metrics were arranged as text boxes, and the decision makers were asked to express their preferences on pairs of alternatives by drawing arrows (the tail box is considered more important than the box at the head of the arrow) and by associating a symbol in the set $\{=, >, >>, >>>, >>>>\}$ which has been translated to a numerical value according to Saaty's scale (Table 1).

Table 1. Saaty's Ratio Scale [22].

Symbol	Value	Definition
=	1	Equal importance
>	3	Somewhat more important
>>	5	Much more important
>>>	7	Very much more important
>>>>	9	Absolutely more important

For instance, in Fig. 1 the number of shops is considered "somewhat more important" (i.e., three times more important) than the transportations. Notably, the experts were asked to compare only pairs of alternatives they felt comfortable comparing. In the example of Fig. 1, the obtained graph is disconnected (e.g., no answer involving the places of worship is provided), and thus the information gathered is insufficient to construct a proper ranking of the cost metrics; however, by combining the opinion of multiple decision makers, we obtain a connected graph and thus a ranking.

Table 4 reports the numerical value of the weights w_i^* associated to each metric; the numerical values were computed using the approach discussed in Sect. 2.4 and were normalized to their unitary sum. According to the table, the decision makers consider the total number of transportation-related facilities as the most important factor (i.e., it contributes of about 14.19% to the holistic metric), while the least important strategy is related to the number of worship places (it contributes of about 1.78% to the holistic metric).

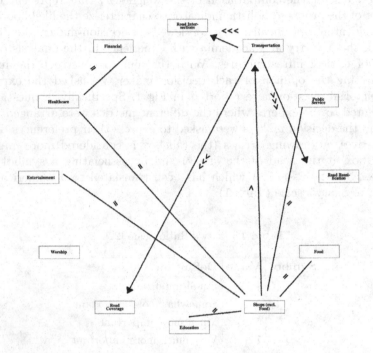

Fig. 1. Example of pictorial questionnaire filled by an expert.

Let us now assess the level of agreement of the decision makers. Figure 2 reports a matrix whose (i, j)-th entry contains the number of times the i-th metric was considered by the decision makers to be more important than the j-th one, while Fig. 3 reports a matrix whose (i, j)-th entry contains the number of times the i-th metric was considered by the decision makers to be equally as important as the j-th one. According to Fig. 2, although the decision makers agree on most of the pairwise comparisons. However, as shown in Fig. 3, in several cases the experts consider pairs of factors as equally important.

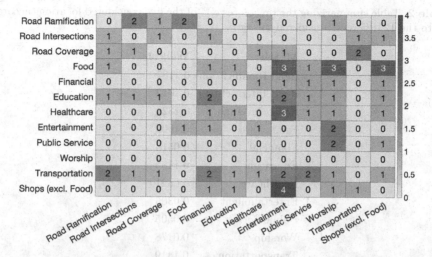

Fig. 2. Number of times the metric on the row was considered by the decision makers to be more important than the one on the column.

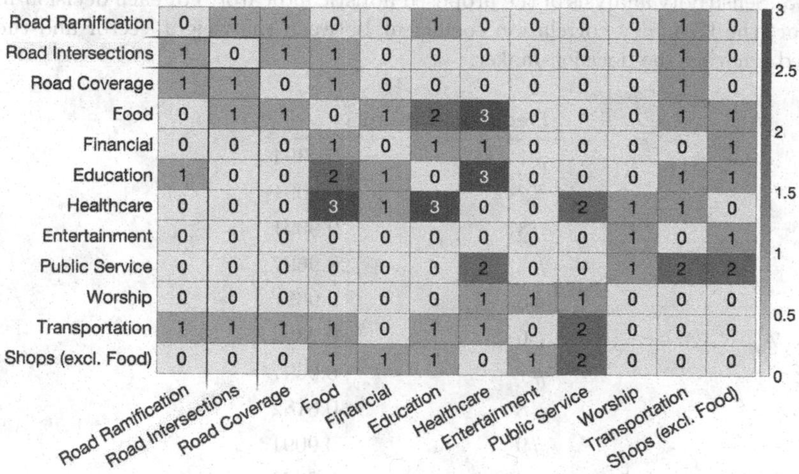

Fig. 3. Number of times the metric on the row was considered by the decision makers to be equally as important as the one on the column.

Table 2. Table summarizing the raw scores c_{ij}^{raw} of the five considered locations according to the 12 different considered metrics.

Metric	Weight
Road Ramification	0.1187
Road Intersections	0.1012
Road Coverage	0.1322
Food	0.1005
Financial	0.0516
Education	0.1135
Healthcare	0.0821
Entertainment	0.0305
Public Service	0.0505
Worship	0.0178
Transportation	0.1419
Shops	0.0596

Table 3. Sensitivity analysis of the proposed holistic indicator. For each decision-maker we report the Kendall's correlation coefficient between the weight vector and the one obtained ignoring the decision-maker.

Decision-Maker	τ
#1	0.9394
#2	0.9091
#3	0.9091
#4	0.9697
#5	0.9697
#6	0.9394
#7	0.9697
#8	0.8182
#9	0.9091
#10	0.6970
average	0.9030
st.dev	0.0855

Let us conclude the section by conducting a sensitivity analysis. Specifically, Table 1 reports, for each decision-maker, the Kendall's correlation coefficient between the weight vector and the one obtained ignoring the decision-maker. According to the table, the average correlation coefficient is 0.9030 with standard deviation 0.0855 and the coefficient for nine out of ten decision-makers is above 0.90, while only for two decision-makers the correlation coefficient is smaller, although being above 0.69. Overall, the results suggest that the decision-makers are quite in accordance in their judgements.

4 Case Study

In this section we demonstrate the effectiveness of the proposed framework by considering a case study set in Nicosia, Cyprus. In particular, we consider five locations, reported as stars over the satellite image of the area (Fig. 4). In particular, Table 4 reports the latitude, longitude and the raw scores c_{ij}^{raw} of the five considered location with respect to the 12 considered metrics. Moreover, Table 5 reports the results of the normalization. Finally, Table 6 shows the holistic indicator that is the result of the proposed Multi-Criteria decision model for the five considered locations.

In particular, according to the proposed holistic index, Location #4 is considered as the most important, while Location #3 is the least important. These result are reasonable, since Location #4 coincides with the city center, while Location #3 is in the zone of Strovolos, next to a highway. Moreover, we observe that Location #1, although being not far from the center of the city, is adjacent to the Alsos Forest and thus has smaller scores than Location #2 (which is also in a central zone) in terms of Food, Healthcare, Transportations and Shops. Finally, we observe that Location #5 is in a zone with ministries and offices and thus exhibits a small value of the holistic indicator. Therefore, overall, the considered case study suggests that the proposed holistic index can be an effective choice to discriminate between densely and sparsely populated zones.

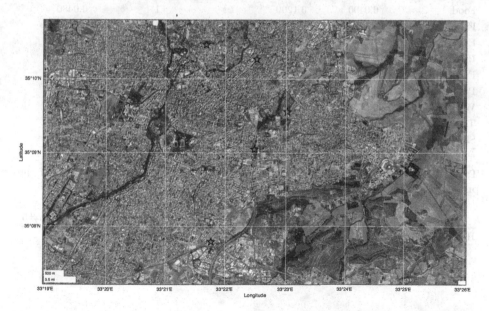

Fig. 4. Satellite map of the city of Nicosia, Cyprus, showing the five considered locations (magenta stars).

Table 4. Table summarizing the latitude, longitude and raw scores c_{ij}^{raw} of the five considered locations.

	Location#1	Location#2	Location#3	Location#4	Location#5
Latitude	35.159259	35.171152	35.129852	35.174397	35.15075
Longitude	33.383624	33.375084	33.362853	33.361405	33.374417
Road Ramification	2830	2219	1426	6799	1597
Road Intersections	2802	2136	1414	6471	1550
Road Coverage	6.6276×10^4	6.1285×10^4	4.9524×10^4	1.9280×10^4	5.0558×10^4
Food	6	16	1	126	7
Financial	2	2	0	20	4
Education	11	3	2	4	6
Healthcare	1	15	2	3	2
Entertainment	2	3	0	5	1
Public Service	0	0	0	9	0
Worship	1	1	1	13	0
Transportation	5	19	4	37	6
Shops	1	30	8	49	14

Table 5. Table summarizing the normalized scores c_{ij} of the five considered locations according to the 12 different considered metrics.

	Location#1	Location#2	Location#3	Location#4	Location#5
Road Ramification	0.2613	0.1476	0	1	0.0318
Road Intersections	0.2745	0.1428	0	1	0.0269
Road Coverage	0.1169	0.0821	0	1	0.0072
Food	0.0400	0.1200	0	1	0.0480
Financial	0.1000	0.1000	0	1	0.2000
Education	1	0.1111	0	0.2222	0.4444
Healthcare	0	1	0.0714	0.1429	0.0714
Entertainment	0.4000	0.6000	0	1	0.2000
Public Service	0	0	0	1	0
Worship	0.0769	0.0769	0.0769	1	0
Transportation	0.0303	0.4545	0	1	0.0606
Shops	0	0.6042	0.1458	1	0.2708

Table 6. Holistic index obtained for the five considered locations as a result of the proposed Multi-Criteria Decision Model.

	Location#1	Location#2	Location#3	Location#4	Location#5
Holistic Index	0.2147	0.2749	0.0159	**0.8414**	0.1097

5   Conclusions

In this paper, we have developed a holistic indicator to quantify the likelihood that a zone is residential, based on open source intelligence and multi-criteria decision-making. Moreover, we have shown the effectiveness of the proposed approach via a case study set in Nicosia, Cyprus. The proposed index can be the basis in order to orient the optimization of the distribution of resources such as power, gas or water.

Future work will be devoted to enrich the model by considering additional features (e.g., the fact roads are one-way or two-ways, etc.), possibly including features related to other typologies of infrastructures (e.g., base stations and power cabins in a zone). Moreover, we will consider the possibility to assess the likelihood that a zone is residential based on areas of different dimensions and we will inspect the possibility to tune this parameter in an automatic way, based on the characteristics of the particular city being considered.

Acknowledgement. This work was supported by the European Commission under the EXCELLENT SCIENCE - Marie Skłodowska-Curie Action: "Development of Utilities Management Platform for the case of Quarantine and Lockdown" (EUMAP), grant n. 101007641.

References

1. Arampatzis, G., Kiranoudis, C.T., Scaloubacas, P., Assimacopoulos, D.: A GIS-based decision support system for planning urban transportation policies. Eur. J. Oper. Res. **152**(2), 465–475 (2004)
2. Bozóki, S., Tsyganok, V.: The (logarithmic) least squares optimality of the arithmetic (geometric) mean of weight vectors calculated from all spanning trees for incomplete additive (multiplicative) pairwise comparison matrices. Int. J. Gen Syst **48**(4), 362–381 (2019)
3. Bozóki, S., Fülöp, J., Rónyai, L.: On optimal completion of incomplete pairwise comparison matrices. Math. Comput. Model. **52**(1–2), 318–333 (2010)
4. Carlucci, R., et al.: Architecture definition for a multi-utility management platform. In: 2021 International Symposium on Networks, Computers and Communications (ISNCC), pp. 1–6. IEEE (2021)
5. Eckle, M., et al.: Leveraging openstreetmap to support flood risk management in municipalities: a prototype decision support system. In: ISCRAM (2016)
6. Galbusera, L., Giannopoulos, G.: Exploiting web ontologies for automated critical infrastructure data retrieval. In: ICCIP 2017. IAICT, vol. 512, pp. 119–136. Springer, Cham (2017). https://doi.org/10.1007/978-3-319-70395-4_7
7. Gitau, M., Bailey, N.: Multi-layer assessment of land use and related changes for decision support in a coastal zone watershed. Land **1**(1), 5–31 (2012)
8. Godsil, C., Royle, G.: Algebraic graph theory. Graduate text in mathematics, Springer, New York (2001). https://doi.org/10.1007/978-1-4613-0163-9
9. Goetz, M.: Towards generating highly detailed 3d cityGML models from openStreetMap. Int. J. Geogr. Inf. Sci. **27**(5), 845–865 (2013)
10. Grippa, T., et al.: Mapping urban land use at street block level using openstreetMap, remote sensing data, and spatial metrics. ISPRS Int. J. Geo Inf. **7**(7), 246 (2018)

11. Herfort, B., Eckle, M., de Albuquerque, J.P., Zipf, A.: Towards assessing the quality of volunteered geographic information from openStreetMap for identifying critical infrastructures. In: ISCRAM. CiteSeer (2015)
12. Kendall, M.G.: A new measure of rank correlation. Biometrika **30**(1/2), 81–93 (1938)
13. The Mathworks Inc, Natick, Massachusetts: MATLAB version 9.9.0.1495850 (R2020b) (2020)
14. Modica, G., et al.: Land suitability evaluation for agro-forestry: definition of a web-based multi-criteria spatial decision support system (mc-sdss): preliminary results. In: Gervasi, O., et al. (eds.) ICCSA 2016. LNCS, vol. 9788, pp. 399–413. Springer, Cham (2016). https://doi.org/10.1007/978-3-319-42111-7_31
15. Modica, G., Pollino, M., La Porta, L., Di Fazio, S.: Proposal of a web-based multi-criteria spatial decision support system (mc-sdss) for agriculture. In: Coppola, A., Di Renzo, G.C., Altieri, G., D'Antonio, P. (eds.) MID-TERM AIIA 2019. LNCE, vol. 67, pp. 333–341. Springer, Cham (2020). https://doi.org/10.1007/978-3-030-39299-4_38
16. Neis, P., Goetz, M., Zipf, A.: Towards automatic vandalism detection in openStreetMap. ISPRS Int. J. Geo Inf. **1**(3), 315–332 (2012)
17. Olbricht, R.M.: Data retrieval for small spatial regions in OpenStreetMap. In: Jokar Arsanjani, J., Zipf, A., Mooney, P., Helbich, M. (eds.) OpenStreetMap in GIScience. LNGC, pp. 101–122. Springer, Cham (2015). https://doi.org/10.1007/978-3-319-14280-7_6
18. Oliva, G., Scala, A., Setola, R., Dell'Olmo, P.: Opinion-based optimal group formation. Omega **89**, 164–176 (2019)
19. Oliva, G., Setola, R., Scala, A.: Sparse and distributed analytic hierarchy process. Automatica **85**, 211–220 (2017)
20. OpenStreetMap contributors: Planet dump (2017). https://planet.osm.org. https://www.openstreetmap.org
21. Patro, S., Sahu, K.K.: Normalization: a preprocessing stage. arXiv preprint arXiv:1503.06462 (2015)
22. Saaty, T.L.: How to make a decision: the analytic hierarchy process. Eur. J. Oper. Res. **48**(1), 9–26 (1990)
23. Trovato, M.G., Ali, D., Nicolas, J., El Halabi, A., Meouche, S.: Landscape risk assessment model and decision support system for the protection of the natural and cultural heritage in the eastern Mediterranean area. Land **6**(4), 76 (2017)

Security Awareness and Crisis Management for C(I)IP

Modeling the Hierarchical Structure of Effective Communication Factors for Cyberattack Responses

Hiroka Kato[✉], Tomomi Aoyama, and Kenji Watanabe

Nagoya Institute of Technology, Gokiso, Showa-ku, Nagoya 466-8555, Aichi, Japan
h.kato.432@stn.nitech.ac.jp
http://shakai.web.nitech.ac.jp/eng/index.html

Abstract. Cyberattacks have recently been on the rise. The increasing sophistication and complexity of cyberattacks has made it difficult to prevent such attacks from occurring. Therefore, it must be important to formulate appropriate incident responses to cyberattacks limit their damage. As seen in the case of the Japan Pension Service, where damage is increased due to a lack of communication during the response to cyber incidents, good internal communication practices is essential to ensure an appropriate incident response. To minimize the impact of cyberattacks, this study constructs a hierarchical structure model using interpretive structural modeling. The results reveal that the degree of dependency that the variables have over each another according to the cross-impact matrix multiplication applied to classification analysis regarding effective intraorganizational communications during a cyberattack response. In addition, based on these results, a use case of the results will be proposed to design more effective intraorganizational communications when responding to a cyberattack.

Keywords: Incident response · Communication · Interpretive Structural Modeling

1 Background and Objectives

There are two major approaches to address cyberattacks–"to prevent attacks from occurring" and "to minimize the damage caused by attacks." Many companies and other organizations have taken various security measures to prevent cyberattacks by focusing on preventing computer security incidents. However, the increasing sophistication and complexity of cyberattacks makes it difficult to prevent them. In addition, since personal and business data are frequently compromised by such attacks, it has become imperative to control any secondary damage and respond to incidents such as cyberattacks.

In May 2015, a large-scale information leakage due to a cyberattack occurred at the Japan Pension Service [1]. Although a targeted e-mail had been opened by a staff member, no information was shared about the source address in the e-mail subject, the body of the e-mail, or other detailed information, which is

B. Hämmerli et al. (Eds.): CRITIS 2022, LNCS 13723, pp. 197–211, 2023.
https://doi.org/10.1007/978-3-031-35190-7_14

why the damage was so widespread. A sense of urgency about the cyberattack, which was felt by those with security knowledge, was not communicated to all employees and staff members, so they opened the targeted e-mail, which caused escalating damage. This case illustrates the importance of an appropriate incident response and clear communication within an organization between the department in charge of security, other departments, and management at the time of the incident.

With the objective of minimizing the damage caused by cyberattacks, a hierarchical structure model will be constructed using interpretive structural modeling (ISM) and reveal the variables' degree of dependency on one another by using cross-impact matrix multiplication applied to classification (MICMAC) analysis to examine the factors of effective intraorganizational communication during a cyberattack response. A use case of the results to design more effective intraorganizational communications when responding to a cyberattack will be then proposed.

2   Literature Review

2.1   Incident Response

It has become very difficult to prevent cyberattacks due to their increasing sophistication and complexity. According to the National Institute of Standards and Technology [2], an appropriate incident response provides the following benefits.

- Supports a systematic response to incidents (i.e., following a consistent methodology for handling incidents), so that the appropriate actions are taken.
- Helps personnel to minimize the loss or theft of information and the disruption of services as a result of an incident.
- Uses information gained during an incident to better prepare for future incidents and to provide better protection for systems and data.
- Helps with a proper response to legal issues that may arise during an incident.

The importance of an organization's incident response can be understood in terms of the aforementioned methodology. In recent years, there has been an increasing demand for an intraorganizational body such as the Computer Security Incident Response Team (CSIRT) that will enable organizations to promptly conduct an appropriate and efficient incident response. In the incident handling materials published by the Japan Computer Emergency Response Team Coordination Center (JPCERT/CC) [3], the incident response method, which centers on an in-house CSIRT, is described as follows.

1. For the incidents that the CSIRT determines should be immediately handled as a result of triage, it must first analyze the event. Not only decide whether the CSIRT should handle the incident, but also determine whether a technical response is possible.

2. If it determined that the incident should not be handled, it will report the basis for that determination in as much detail as possible in light of our organization's information security policy.'

3. When it is technically difficult for an organization to respond to an incident (e.g., a problem that can only be handled by an outsourcing company), it will formulate and implement a response plan in cooperation with management. During the process, information sharing and cooperation with information technology (IT)-related departments are conducted as necessary.

4. If the organization is able to implement technical measures independently, it will formulate and implement a response plan in cooperation with the IT and IT-related departments. Of course, information will be shared with management in the process.

5. Regardless of whether a technical response is possible, when formulating and implementing the response plan, it will request assistance and necessary information from external specialized organizations and sites (i.e., related par-ties) that may be involved in the incident as necessary.

6. After the response plan has been implemented, it will check to see if the problem has been resolved. If it has not been resolved, the event will be analyzed again, a new response plan formulated, and the plan implemented.

7. When the problem has finally been resolved, a detailed explanation of what happened is reported to the extent possible in light of the organization's information security policy.

From incident response manuals, it can be seen that communication with internal stakeholders, including responses to reporters in (2) and cooperation with management in (3) and (4), is necessary. In addition to communicating within the organization, communication with external stakeholders may also be necessary in cases such as (5). If communication with external parties is required, it is also necessary to communicate with the department in charge of cooperation with external parties.

It is clear that communication with management and other departments (i.e., so-called "internal stakeholders") is essential in an incident response methodology based on the CSIRT.

2.2 Interpretive Structural Modeling (ISM)

ISM is a technique developed to model the structure of social systems in which numerous elements are intricately interrelated [4]. ISM visualizes the invisible factor relationships that exist in a hierarchical structure.

Communication during a cyberattack response can be regarded as a system in which many effective communication factors, such as the position of the department in charge of security in the organization and communication means and channels, are intricately interrelated. ISM is used in many fields to address social issues and in literature related to the communication [5] and cybersecurity [6] fields. However, existing ISM studies have not yet examined intraorganizational communication in response to cyberattacks.

Therefore, ISM is used in this study to analyze and determine the structure of effective communication factors in an organization during a cyberattack response.

3   Procedures and Analytical Methods Used in This Study

Using ISM and MICMAC analysis, it is possible to visualize the relationship between effective intraorganizational communication factors during a cyberattack response and to understand their importance. The results of this analysis support the establishment of an intraorganizational cyberattack response communication system and contribute to the realization of a more rapid cyberattack response. This will reduce the damage resulting from cyberattacks, which is the ultimate purpose of this research. This study visualizes the structure of effective communication factors during incident responses using the ISM method based on the following procedure. MICMAC analysis is also used to analyze the "driving power" and "dependence power" of each factor and reveal the degree of interdependency between the variables.

1. **Extracting factors:** Extract factors for effective organizational communication in response to cyberattack from literature review and interview of experts.
2. **Linking factors:** Finding relationships between factors based on expert interviews.
3. **Building a hierarchical structure model:** Based on the interview results, a factor structure model is built according to the procedure of the ISM method.
4. **Discussion:** The results regarding effective intraorganizational communication determined based on the hierarchical structure model and the degree of influence and dependence of each factor established by MICMAC analysis are discussed.

3.1   ISM Method

In this study, a structural analysis of effective factors was conducted. For this purpose, Chowdhury et al. [7] will be followed, who analyzed effective factors in a different field, which established the following analytical procedure for ISM.

Figure 1 depicts a flow diagram for the development of an ISM framework. The various steps of the ISM technique are as follows.

Step 1: The key factors of the problem being considered are identified in brainstorming sessions with experienced industrialists and academicians and with the help of a literature review.

Step 2: The contextual relationships between the attributes that were determined in Step 1 are established by a continuous assessment of the experts. This relationship is represented by a matrix called a structural self-interaction matrix (SSIM). The symbols used to develop the SSIM are as follows:

V: If factor i affects factor j, but not in the other direction;

A: If factor j affects factor i, but not in the other direction;

X: If factor i and factor j affect each other; and

O: If factor i does not affect factor j and vice versa.

Step 3: After determining the SSIM, it is transformed into another matrix by replacing the relationships represented by V, A, X, and O with 0 and 1. This binary matrix is called the initial reachability matrix. The rules for substitution are as follows:

- If the value of the (i, j) cell in the SSIM matrix is V, then the value of the corresponding (i, j) cell becomes 1 and the (j, i) cell becomes 0.
- If the value of (i, j) cell in the SSIM matrix is A, then the value of corresponding (i, j) cell becomes 0 and (j, i) cell becomes 1.
- If the value of (i, j) cell in the SSIM matrix is X, then the value of corresponding (i, j) cell and (j, i) cell both become 1.
- If the value of (i, j) cell in the SSIM matrix is O, then the value of corresponding (i, j) cell and (j, i) cell both become 0.

This initial reachability matrix is then checked for contextual relationship transitivity, which is a basic assumption of ISM. According to the transitivity rule, if attribute i is related to j and j is related to k, then i is necessarily related to k. Therefore, if an (i, k) entry fulfills this criteria, then the value of (i, k) becomes 1. After checking all the entries of the initial reachability matrix and making the necessary modifications, the initial reachability matrix is converted to a final reachability matrix. The reachability matrix also reveals the driving and dependence power of the variables. The driving power of a particular factor is achieved by aggregating all of the numbers of factors that it may impact and the dependence power of a particular factor is achieved by aggregating all of the numbers of factors by which it is influenced.

Step 4: The final reachability matrix (obtained in Step 3) is used to perform level partitioning of the variables, which is done by determining the reachability and antecedent sets that are determined through the reachability matrix. The reachability set of a particular variable consists of the variables that it may influence, including itself. Conversely, the antecedent set of a particular variable comprises the variable itself and all of the variables that may influence it. Another set, called the intersections set, is then constructed from the reachability and antecedent sets. The intersection set contains the elements that follow overlapping criteria-in other words, elements common to both the reachability set and the antecedent set. An attribute that has a similar reachability and intersection set is labeled a "top level attribute." After identifying the top level factor, it is removed from the reachability, antecedent, and intersection sets. The same procedure is repeated until all of the levels of variables are identified. This iterative level partitioning is associated with the building of a hierarchical ISM model.

Step 5: This step involves developing a reachability matrix considering the levels of all of the elements. This helps organize the variables according to their driving and dependence power. This is called a conical matrix.

Step 6: In this final step, the ISM model is constructed according to the levels and reachability matrix without considering transitivity.

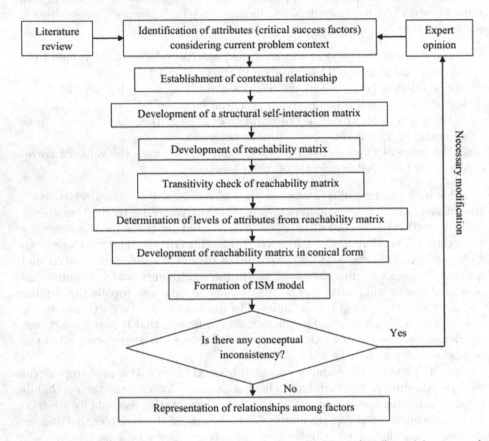

Fig. 1. Flow diagram for the interpretive structural modeling (ISM) model excerpted from [7].

3.2   Cross-Impact Matrix Multiplication Applied to Classification (MICMAC) Analysis

ISM only helps visualize the hierarchical relationships between the factors. However, MICMAC analysis assists in understanding the degree of dependency that the variables have on one another. It enables us to realize which attributes to focus on based on their driving and dependence power [7].

The factors are plotted on a graph with "driving power" on the horizontal axis and "dependence power" on the vertical axis. The factors are classified as Autonomous, Independent, Linkage, and Dependent Factors [7].

- **Autonomous factors** are critical variables that have low driving power and low dependence power. Having low driving and dependence power indicates that the factors in this category are not related to other factors. If so, it must be focused on these attributes separately and carefully.
- **Independent factors** have high driving power and low dependence power. In other words, they have a strong influence over the other success factors. Therefore, it should pay careful attention to them.
- **Linkage factors** have both high driving power and dependence power. However, they are unstable in nature, which means that if they are not improved, they will affect the other factors in the system.
- **Dependent factors** have high dependence power and low driving power and are dependent mostly on linkage or independent factors. Therefore, there should be focused on these attributes.

Chowdhury et al. [7] used ISM and MICMAC analysis together to interpret the relationship between the factors in a hierarchical model.

4   Experts Interview

Two online interviews were conducted with subject-matter experts at the Japan CSIRT Council. The Japan CSIRT Council is an organization that was established to provide a forum for solving common problems while aiming to achieve a high level of collaboration so that single CSIRT do not have to work alone [8].

In the first interview, a preliminary questionnaire asked experts to define effective intraorganizational communication during cyberattack response and the characteristics of organizations with effective intraorganizational communication, and discussed effective communication factors during cyberattack response. In response to the points raised in the first interview regarding assumptions such as company size and assumed attacks, the following assumptions were made. First, large and medium-sized companies that have a cybersecurity department (e.g., a CSIRT) received a targeted attack on a specific organization. Second, their cybersecurity department (e.g., a CSIRT) takes the lead in the response.

In the second interview, the one-to-one relationships between each factor were discussed based on the results of the first interview.

Based on the interview results, a hierarchical structure model of effective intraorganizational communication factors for a cyberattack response was developed.

5   Analysis

5.1   Extraction of Factors

A survey of the literature on organizational communication was conducted to identify factors to be used in the ISM method. In addition to the literature that studied organizational communication in the cybersecurity field [9], the search was broadened and referred to studies in the field of intraorganizational communication theory in peacetime [10–12], which are more general and in which the commonality between issues is recognized. The extracted factors of communication were converted into more specific communication factors related to organizational security, especially CSIRT, which is the target of this study. The factors are used to determine effective communication in organizations during cyberattack responses. Table 1 lists the factor number, the factor name, the effective intraorganizational communication factors during a cyberattack response, and references extracted from the literature.

According to Ikeda Miho et al. [9], cyberattack risk perception has a significant impact on communication during a cyberattack response, especially by CSIRT. It is also stated that these gaps in risk perception prevent the smooth progress of incident response. Consequently, *Risk perception* (F11) and *Incident management process* (F14) were extracted. *Alignment of interests between the security department and internal stakeholders* (F8) was extracted in reference to the opinion expressed during the first interview. Sometimes an incident response does not proceed smoothly due to a conflict of interest between the department in charge of security and other departments. The other factors were extracted from papers on effective intraorganizational communication by Blazenaite et al. [10], Chmielecki et al. [11], and Bavunoglu et al. [12] and converted into effective intraorganizational communication factors during a cyberattack response (see Table 1).

Table 1. Effective organizational communication factors during a cyberattack response.

No.	Factors extracted from the literature	Effective organizational communication factors during cyberattack response	Reference
1	Real-time communication	Promptness and timing of communication between the security department and internal stakeholders	[10]
2	Communication means	Means of communication from the security department to internal stakeholders	[10]
3	Communication network	Information communication channels from the security department to internal stakeholders	[10]
4	Information sharing in normal times	Information sharing during normal times from the security department to internal stakeholders	[10,11]
5	Volume of information	Volume and accuracy of information from the security department to internal stakeholders	[10,11]
6	Organizational structure	Positioning of the security department	[10]
7	Vertical communication	Cooperation between management and the security department	[10–12]
8	(Identified in the experts interview)	Alignment of interests between the security department and internal stakeholders	Identified in the experts interview
9	Leadership style	Leadership style of the responsible person for security (Chief Information Security Officer(CISO), etc.)	[10,12]
10	Coordination between internal and external communication sub-system	Gathering security information and know-how from outside the organization	[10]
11	Risk perception	Risk perception for security incidents	[9]
12	Organizational culture	Organizational security culture	[10]
13	Organizational objectives	Objectives of the organization's security activities	[10,12]
14	Incident management process	Management processes suitable for security incidents	[9]
15	Training and development	Ongoing security incident response training	[10]

5.2   Identifying the Relationships Between Factors

Based on the extracted factors, the second interview was conducted with security experts from the Japan CSIRT Council. The results present a discussion of the one-to-one relationships between each factor and the associations among the factors according to ISM procedures. The SSIM was then created (see Table 2).

Table 2. The structural self-interaction matrix (SSIM)

No.	Effective organizational communication factors during cyberattack response	15	14	13	12	11	10	9	8	7	6	5	4	3	2	1
1	Promptness and timing of communication between the security department and internal stakeholders	A	A	A	A	A	A	X	A	A	A	A	A	A	A	
2	Means of communication from the security department to internal stakeholders	V	A	A	A	O	A	A	O	A	A	V	A	A		
3	Information communication channels from the security department to internal stakeholders	V	A	A	A	O	A	A	O	A	A	V	V			
4	Information sharing during normal times from the security department to internal stakeholders	V	A	A	A	V	A	A	A	A	A	V				
5	Volume and accuracy of information from the security department to internal stakeholders	V	A	A	A	V	A	A	A	A	A					
6	Positioning of the security department	V	A	A	A	V	V	A	O	A						
7	Cooperation between management and the security department	V	V	A	A	X	V	A	A							
8	Alignment of interests between the security department and internal stakeholders	V	O	A	A	O	V	O								
9	Leadership style of the responsible person for security (CISO, etc.)	V	V	V	V	V	V									
10	Gathering security information and know-how from outside the organization	X	X	A	A	V										
11	Risk perception for security incidents	X	A	A	A											
12	Organizational security culture	V	V	V												
13	Objectives of the organization's security activities	V	V													
14	Management processes suitable for security incidents	V														
15	Ongoing security incident response training															

5.3   Building a Hierarchical Structure Model

The hierarchical structure model was constructed following ISM procedures based on the SSIM results (see Fig. 2). At the same time, MICMAC analysis was conducted based on the results of ISM to analyze the degree of influence and dependence of the factors (see Fig. 3).

5.4   Consideration

In the ISM model (see Fig. 2), factors on higher levels are influenced more by other factors than those on lower levels, making them difficult to manage. Therefore, there must be focused on the factors of the lowest level (Level 8) to fundamentally improve the system because they affect many other factors. Therefore, to achieve effective communication within an organization during a cyberattack response, it is most important to focus on a firm's *Organizational security culture* (F12).

According to ISM, it should start by improving and considering the *Organizational security culture* (F12), *Objectives of the organization's security activities* (F13), and *Alignment of interests between the security department and internal stakeholders* (F8) in this order.

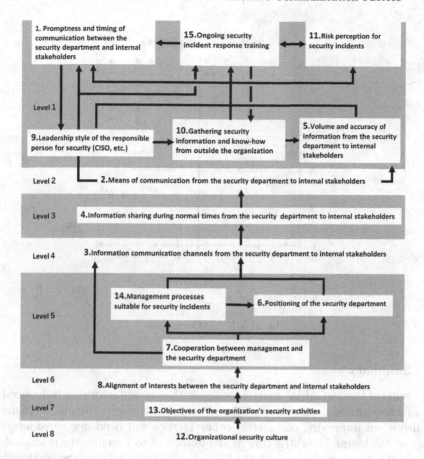

Fig. 2. ISM model

The second interview revealed that F12, which belongs to Level 8, is affected by *Leadership style of the responsible person for security (CISO, etc.)* (F9), although it is not shown in the hierarchical structure model. Therefore, it may be necessary to change a deep-rooted organizational culture by bringing in external security personnel to improve F12.

The MICMAC analysis revealed that two factors-*Means of communication from the security department to internal stakeholders* (F2) and the *Volume and accuracy of information from the security department to internal stakeholders* (F5)-are classified as Dependent Factors that are heavily influenced by other factors. However, their influence on other factors is negligible, so improving or considering these factors should be a lower priority.

The remaining 10 factors are classified as Linkage factors and are unstable due to their high degree of influence and dependence. For this reason, they should be carefully considered and improved with reference to the factor relationships in the ISM model.

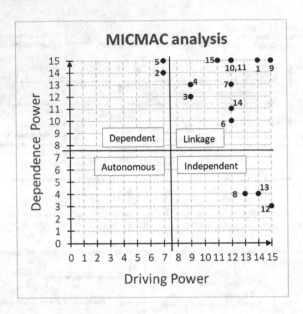

Fig. 3. MICMAC analysis

5.5 Summary

The results of the MICMAC analysis indicate that most factors are influenced by many factors and also affect many other factors. This is very difficult to manage, because when improving one factor, other factors will need due consideration. However, the hierarchical structure model helped us to visualize the relationships that should be prioritized among the factors. It is believed that the combination of the hierarchical structure model and the MICMAC analysis may be used to support the establishment of better intraorganizational communication during a cyberattack response.

6   Suggested Use Cases for Analysis Results

The results of ISM and MICMAC analysis is believed that it can assist in building more effective intraorganizational communication during a cyberattack response. Figure 4 illustrates the classifications of each factor following MICMAC analysis. The significance of the framing is as follows.

- **Critical (No framing)**: Factors that should be noted because they have a high degree of both influence and dependence.
- **Influential (Bold framing)**: Factors that should be prioritized for improvement because they have a high degree of influence but a low degree of dependence.
- **Dependent (Dotted line)**: Factors with a high degree of dependence but a low degree of impact, which can be put off until other factors are considered.

The two specific use cases featured in Fig. 4 are listed below. In each case, it is advisable to consider the level and frame of the factors.

The first case is to fundamentally improve or build effective communication within an organization to respond to cyberattacks. In this case, it is sufficient to consider each factor in order starting with Level 8 factors, considering the relationship among factors.

The second is when problems or areas for improvement are found in effective communication within the organization for responding to cyberattack. In such cases, it is necessary not only to try to improve the factors where problems or areas for improvement were found, but also to consider the influence of other factors.

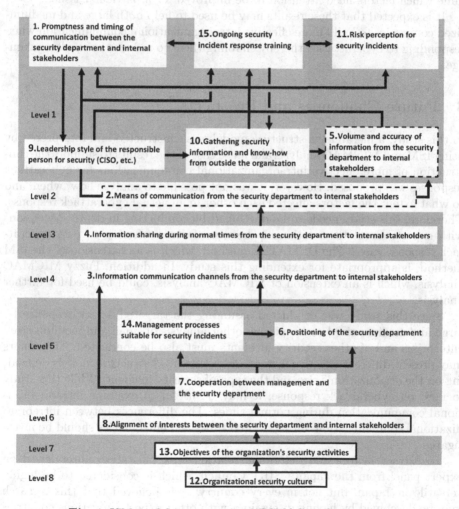

Fig. 4. ISM model incorporating MICMAC analysis results

7   Summary of This Study

This study examined effective communication within organizations when responding to cyberattacks. Effective factors during cyberattack response were extracted from a survey of the literature and interviews with subject-matter experts. A hierarchical structure model of the factors was constructed using ISM and was interpreted using MICMAC analysis. Based on these results, a use case of the results was proposed to support the construction of more effective intraorganizational communications during cyberattack response. Finding the relationships among the factors and clarifying their structure facilitated the visualization of which factors required improvement. In addition, it can determine which factors need attention to be improved for a particular issue.

It is expected that these results may be used to help both large and medium-sized companies to build more effective intraorganizational communication when responding to cyberattacks, thereby enabling them to reduce the resulting damage.

8   Future Challenges and Prospects

In this study, a hierarchical structure model was constructed and interpreted by using ISM and MICMAC analysis and a use case of the results to support the construction of more effective intraorganizational communications for cyberattack responses was proposed. However, it was not possible to analyze how, when, and to what extent the factors affected each other in an actual cyberattack response. Therefore, this study needs to be developed by conducting in-depth discussions with experts about the relationship between factors referring to past cyberattack response cases. The DEMATEL method, which is an extension of the ISM method, is appropriate for extending this study. In addition, Fuzzy MICMAC analysis, which is an extension of MICMAC analysis, could be used for further analysis.

Since this study was conducted assuming the targeted attack response by large and medium-sized companies, another analysis of small and medium-sized enterprises and of other security incidents must also be conducted. The results may present different effective factors and hierarchical structure models depending on the organization's size and the type of security incident. While this study focused on cyberattack response, it may be useful to examine intraorganizational communication during normal times. The differences between intraorganizational communication during normal times and emergencies should be investigated.

To extract factors and determine relationships, this study interviewed an expert panel from the Japan CSIRT Council, which is considered to be highly versatile in Japan, but not in every country. It is believed that this research may be developed by having discussions with other experts in various countries around the world.

Acknowledgement. This research is partially supported by the Industrial Cyber Security Center of Excellence (ICSCoE) under the Information-technology Promotion Agency, Japan. However, all remaining errors are attributable to the authors.

References

1. Japan Pension Service, Verification Report of the Verification Committee for the Incident of Information Leakage by Unauthorized Viewing at Japan Pension Service. https://www.mhlw.go.jp/kinkyu/dl/houdouhappyou_150821-02.pdf
2. Cichonski, P., Millar, T., Grance, T., Scarfone, K.: Computer Security Incident Handling Guide, vol. 800, no. 61, pp. 1–147. NIST Special Publication (2012)
3. Japan Computer Emergency Response Team Coordination Center (JPCERT/CC), Incident Handling Manual. https://www.jpcert.or.jp/csirt_material/files/manual_ver1.0_20211130.pdf
4. Sato, T.: Determination of the hierarchical structure of learning elements using the ISM method. Jpn J. Educ. Technol. 4(1), 9–16 (1979)
5. Jain, S., Ajmera, P., Jain, V.: Modelling and analysis of the classroom communication barriers using ISM: an Indian teacher's perspective. Int. J. Knowl. Learn. 15(3), 253–273 (2022)
6. Etemadi, N., Gelder, P.V., Strozzi, F.: An ISM modeling of barriers for blockchain/distributed ledger technology adoption in supply chains towards cybersecurity. Sustainability 13(9), 4672 (2021)
7. Chowdhury, N.A., Ali, S.M., Paul, S.K., Mahtab, Z., Kabir, G.: A hierarchical model for critical success factors in apparel supply chain. Bus. Process Manage. J. 26, 1761–1788 (2020)
8. NCA homepage. https://www.nca.gr.jp/outline/index.html. Accessed 29 Apr 2022
9. Ikeda, M., Takahashi, S., Uekawa, H., Kura, T., Kokogawa, T., Kishi, K.: Study of supporting risk perception and communication in cybersecurity incident response. SPT 23(2019), 1–8 (2019)
10. Blazenaite, A.: Effective organizational communication: in search of a system. Soc. Sci. 74(4), 84–101 (2012)
11. Chmielecki, M.: Factors influencing effectiveness of internal communication. Manage. Bus. Adm. Central Europe 2, 24–38 (2015)
12. Bavunoglu, Z., Gunaydin, H.M.: A model for the communication maturity levels of construction companies. Int. J. Sci. Technol. Res. 1, 53–64 (2015)

Energy Security in the Context of Hybrid Threats: The Case of the European Natural Gas Network

Peter Burgherr[1]([✉]) [iD], Eleftherios Siskos[1] [iD], Matteo Spada[2] [iD],
Peter Lustenberger[3] [iD], and Arnold C. Dupuy[4]

[1] Laboratory for Energy Systems Analysis, Paul Scherrer Institute (PSI), 5232 Villigen PSI,
Switzerland
`peter.burgherr@psi.ch`
[2] Institute of Sustainable Development, Zurich University of Applied Sciences, Winterthur,
Switzerland
[3] Global Accumulation Management, Zurich Insurance Company Ltd., Zurich, Switzerland
[4] Department of Political Science, Virginia Tech, Virginia, USA

Abstract. Energy security is a multi-faceted and trans-disciplinary concept, which has significantly broadened over time beyond its original focus on security of supply. Diversity and geopolitical aspects have been a major concern for a long time, but consideration of hybrid threats only came into public focus with the annexation of Crimea in 2014 and especially the ongoing war in Ukraine. This research presents a preliminary analysis for the European natural gas network. It complements an indicator-based approach with a synergy of Multi-Criteria Decision Analysis (MCDA) methods to assess energy security performance at the country level. A unique feature is that it applies a transparent and comprehensive methodological approach, including an interactive and iterative exchange between the analyst and decision maker (DM). The main objectives include elicitation of preferences from different DMs, identification of potential changes in preferences due to recent geopolitical events, and a comparison of countries' performance, including an assessment of the robustness of their ranking. Ultimately, this facilitates the incorporation of diverse preferences and perceptions that may have important bearing on the results, and influence collaborative strategy and policy development.

Keywords: Hybrid Threats · Energy Security · Natural Gas Network ·
Multi-Criteria Decision Analysis

1 Introduction

Energy security has many diversified dimensions, and, being at the nexus of energy, economy, society and geopolitics, is often voiced as an umbrella term [1, 2]. More recently, trade-offs and synergies with sustainability, as well as its role for a resilient, future energy system have been broadly discussed. Examples include the framing of sustainability and

B. Hämmerli et al. (Eds.): CRITIS 2022, LNCS 13723, pp. 212–221, 2023.
https://doi.org/10.1007/978-3-031-35190-7_15

resilience in terms of similarities and differences [3], energy security and its geopolitical role [4], and the relationship of resilience with security as well as its dependence on policy making [4]. Generally, energy security and sustainability are increasingly connected, linking to the security-development nexus [5], whereas resilience provides the connecting element between them [6].

Energy security has been a key factor of both governments' energy policies and military strategy since the start of the 20th century [7]. In contrast, the vulnerability of critical energy infrastructures to hybrid threats is a topic that has not received much attention outside the defense and military sector, until the 2014 annexation of Crimea [8]. Both reached a top priority status in political agendas, media and the public with the Russian invasion in Ukraine, in February 2022 [9]. The dependencies on fossil fuel imports and particularly supply chain risks have been since then in the spotlight [10]. Furthermore, the Ukraine war has also highlighted the potential collateral damage of cyberwar activities on energy infrastructure (e.g., disruption of communication services for monitoring and controlling) in the short-term [11], while its long-term and far-reaching impacts are uncontested, but associated with high uncertainties and great risks [12]. Articles published since the beginning of the war highlight aspects such as a common external energy security policy [13], the choice between two contrary strategies of national energy security vs. acceleration of energy transition [14] and the threat to European biodiversity due to policy responses focusing on food and energy security [15], among others.

Developing and implementing effective polices for complex and multidimensional problems poses a difficult and cognitively challenging task to decision makers. An established approach is the use of so-called composite indicators or indices [16], which is also widely used for assessing energy security performance across countries [17]. A literature survey using Google Scholar Advanced Search yielded the following results for the topic of this study. Although there are 17100 publications on hybrid threats or warfare since 2014 (Russian annexation of Crimea), only 1900 of them address the context of energy security. A further refinement of the search on natural gas disruptions, and subsequently on multi or multiple criteria decision-making led to 492 and only 3 publications, respectively. The latter focus on natural gas business risks and offshore wind energy development in the Baltic States [18, 19], and Russian influence in the Romanian and Greek energy sector [20].

Furthermore, the literature review also demonstrated that there is no commonly accepted definition of the term hybrid threat. However, there are several key characteristics described and used by the European Commission's Joint Research Centre (JRC) and the European Centre of Excellence for Countering Hybrid Threats (Hybrid CoE). Accordingly, a hybrid threat refers to an action carried out by state or non-state actors, which uses conventional and non-conventional methods to undermine or damage a target (e.g. infrastructure), while it exploits the thresholds of detection and attribution [21]. Similarly, there is no universal definition of energy security, but a number of key themes or dimensions can be identified, aiming to ensure a stable and abundant supply of energy to citizens and the economy [1]. Based on these premises, it is important to incorporate energy inter-dependencies into hybrid threat, risk, and resilience assessments, and subsequent strategy design [22].

With energy security being currently in the spotlight, this research provides a timely contribution for its evaluation in the context of hybrid threats. Specifically, it combines an indicator-based approach with a suite of Multi-Criteria Decision Analysis (MCDA) methods, which is then used to assess the resilience performance of the European Natural Gas network at the country level. The analysis builds upon a previously proposed framework [23], but includes several extensions and novel elements to account for the current geopolitical developments. The following methodological developments were considered and implemented, compared to the previous assessment. First, the criteria and indicator system is critically reviewed and updated. Second, preference information is elicited from a more diverse range of decision makers to account for their viewpoints. Third, a comparison of changes in preferences before and after the invasion in Ukraine is carried out. Fourth, the robustness of the country rankings is evaluated.

The remainder of this paper is organized as follows. Section 2 describes the methodological framework, selected results are presented in Sect. 3, and Sect. 4 provides conclusions and an outlook.

2   Methodological Framework

2.1   MCDA Evaluation Process

Figure 1 shows the general methodological framework used in this study[1]. It highlights that the actual MCDA calculation needs to be embedded into a comprehensive and transparent process, allowing for an interactive and iterative stakeholder exchange. Furthermore, it fosters understanding and acceptance of the results, which is a key prerequisite that science can provide unbiased, facts-based inputs to complex policy making.

In the first phase, the analyst defines and sets up the evaluation system, which starts with defining the elements of the decision making process. Then, the most suitable MCDA method for this problem was determined, using the MCDA Methods Selection Software (MCDA-MSS) [24], based on which the PROMETHEE II (Preference Ranking Organization METHod for Enrichment of Evaluations References) was chosen [25]. It is a so-called outranking method, i.e. the evaluation of one alternative depends on other alternatives (pairwise comparisons). PROMETHEE II provides a complete ranking of alternatives, based on the net outranking flow, which is the balance between the positive and negative outranking flows (Eq. 1):

$$\Phi(a) = \Phi^+(a) - \Phi^-(a) \tag{1}$$

The analyst establishes a comprehensive set of criteria/indicators that is subsequently quantified for all alternatives (i.e., countries) under evaluation. The direction (polarity) specifies if a high (low) indicator value indicates a better (worse) performance, i.e. if an indicator is maximized (max) or minimized (min).

In the second phase of the process, the decision maker gives feedback on the criteria and indicator system before endorsing it. Afterwards, specific preference information

---

[1] The novel elements incorporated compared to the initial framework [23] are detailed at the end of the introduction chapter, while the specific modifications to the indicator set are explained in Sect. 2.2.

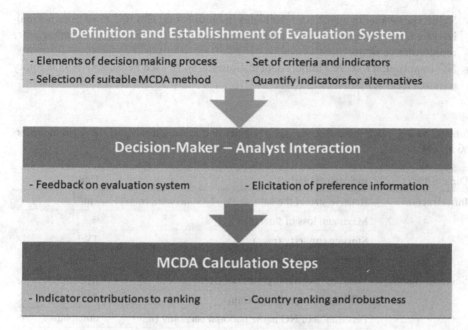

Fig. 1. Steps of proposed methodological framework.

is required. He/she provides a weight for each indicator, which represents its relative importance, with the use of the methods of the cards [26]. Furthermore, for each indicator a preference function is assigned as well as its associated thresholds that determines how pairwise evaluation differences are translated into degrees of preference.

The actual MCDA calculations are carried out in the third phase. For this study, the VISUAL PROMETHEE software was used because it offers a simple Graphical User Interface (GUI) combined with state-of-the-art method implementations and visualization of results [27].

2.2 Criteria and Indicator System

The indicators have been assigned to four dimensions that represent the major aspects of the decision problem and facilitate comprehensibility for the decision makers. Infrastructure refers to the physical pipeline network and associated elements. The socio-economic and political dimensions concern societal and economic, as well as governance aspects. External factors address geopolitical, cyber and R&D aspects. A summary of the indicator system is given in Table 1, since it has been previously described in detail [23]. However, three indicators have been modified, and the changes are explained in the following.

- Storage capacity: Data from Gas Infrastructure Europe (GIE) were used instead of S&P Platts. On the one hand, this data is publicly available (https://agsi.gie.eu/), and on the other hand, it allows considering both underground storage facilities and Liquefied Natural Gas (LNG) storage inventories.

- Skilled personnel in workforce: graduates in engineering and ICT have been normalized by total graduates in tertiary education instead of population to ensure a more representative share.
- NG importation risk: NG import data of Eurostat were used because OECD iLibrary requires a subscription.

Table 1. Overview of indicators, including polarity and measurement units. Updated indicators are in bold.

Dimension	Indicator (Polarity)	Unit
Infrastructure	Relative size of the natural gas (NG) network (max)	km^{-1}
	Maximum loss of flow (min)	%
	Storage capacity (max)	TWh
	Pipeline connections (max)	Number
Socio-Economic	Volatility of natural gas prices (min)	EUR /kWh
	NG Import Dependence (min)	%
	Penetration of NG in the national economy (min)	cf/capita
	Natural gas accident rate (min)	accident/km
	Skilled personnel in workforce (max)	%
Political	Government effectiveness (max)	percentile rank
	Ease of doing business (EODB) (max)	index
	Average number of terrorist attacks (min)	attacks/yr
External Factors	**NG importation risk** (min)	0–1 scale
	National cyber security index (NCSI) (max)	index
	Investment in emerging technologies (max)	% GDP
	NG transit blockade (max)	million USD

The present comparison of energy security performance in the context of hybrid threats considered 35 countries. This includes all countries of the European Network of Transmission System Operators for Gas (ENTSOG)[2], one Associated Partner country, six observer countries, as well as Belarus, Serbia and Turkey.

---

[2] Note that the UK left ENTSOG due to BREXIT, but a special cooperation framework has been established with UK Transmission System Operators (TSO) since 2022.

3   Results and Discussion

At the time of writing this short paper, information for three decision makers (DM)[3] from Switzerland (CHE), Greece (GRC) and USA was available (all collected after February 2022), while for several others additional consultation is needed to elicit all required preference inputs. Therefore, the results reported in the following should be considered preliminary.

3.1   Preference Information of the Decision Makers

Delving into the indicators with the highest importance, *NG Import Dependence* and *NG Importation Risk* were in the top five for all three DMs. *Pipeline Connections* and *Penetration of NG in the National Economy* were selected by the DMs from GRC and USA, whereas there was a match for *Storage Capacity* between the DMs from CHE and GRC. *Maximum Loss of Flow* and *NG Transit Blockade* were ranked high only by the DM from CHE.

Concerning the indicators with lowest importance, four out of five were the same for the DMs from CHE and GRC, namely *Volatility of NG Prices*, *Skilled Personnel in the Economy* (also chosen by the DM from USA), *Government Effectiveness* and *Ease of Doing Business*. *NG Accident Rate* was given low importance by the DM from USA and GRC. Interestingly, the DM from USA assigned *Storage Capacity* to the low importance group, while it was of high importance for the DMs from CHE and GRC.

Overall, the weights (importance) assigned to indicators were more similar between the DMs from CHE and GRC, whereas the DM from USA exhibited higher deviations and particularly for the low importance indicators. The difference in importance for *Storage Capacity* between the DMs from Europe and USA may be caused because USA clearly dominates global underground storage capacity. Furthermore, USA has a highly developed LNG market with imports mostly from Trinidad and Tobago, while its exports to South Korea, China, Japan, Brazil and Spain account for about half of all exports [28].

A comparison of indicators' importance is possible for the DM from CHE, for which preference information is also available from 2021, i.e. before the Russian invasion in Ukraine. In summary, one change each occurred in the top and bottom five indicators, respectively. For the former, the *National Cyber Security Index* was replaced with *Storage Capacity*, and for the latter *Pipeline Connections* with *Volatility in NG Prices*. This indicates that security of supply concerns have become even more important [13], while recent experience from Ukraine shows that the strategic value of cyber operations in a hybrid conflict may be limited due to the operational trilemma of its speed, intensity and control [29].

3.2   Country Ranking and Robustness

First, separate PROMETHEE II rankings were calculated for the preference profiles of the three DMs (CHE, GRC, USA) and a neutral profile (all indicators equally important),

---

[3] The term decision maker in the context of this publication refers to individuals involved in the Systems Analysis and Studies-163 (SAS-163) on "Energy Security in the Era of Hybrid Warfare" of the NATO Science & Technology Organization (STO).

which is commonly used to test the sensitivity of results [30]. Nine out of the top 10 performing countries were the same for the DM and neutral profiles, except for Finland that ranked 8th in the neutral case, but only 14th and 15th in the DM profiles. The ranking of the ten countries with the lowest performance is similarly stable, except for Ukraine that substantially decreased in the neutral case (31st), compared to the DM profiles (24th and 25th).

Second, a consensus ranking for all four profiles was produced, based on multi-scenario preference flows computed as the weighted sum (i.e., all scenarios equally weighted) of the single scenario flows. Figure 2 shows the combined performance for the 35 countries analyzed. Denmark, Netherlands and Germany hold the top positions, followed by Norway, Belgium and Switzerland. These countries also have a strong performance for ten to twelve indicators. In contrast, countries with negative Phi values perform weakly on seven (Portugal) up to 13 (Bosnia and Herzegovina, North Macedonia and Turkey) indicators.

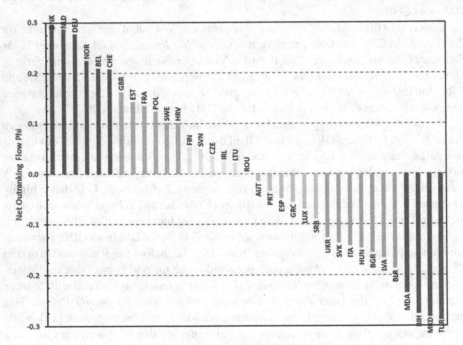

Fig. 2. Consensus country ranking for the DM (CHE, GRC, USA) and neutral profiles.

4   Final Remarks and Outlook

The preliminary results reported here, indicate that the consideration of different DMs, together with their specific viewpoints and preferences, is essential. This provides additional insights and allows evaluating trade-offs and synergies between indicators as well as robustness of the ranking, which would not be possible if only a neutral or a single personalized preference profile is used.

However, the completion of the analysis and generation of a more comprehensive set of results requires several additional steps. First, several indicators need to be updated as soon as new data become available. For example, the calculation of the *NG Importation Risk* indicator includes a political risk index for the exporting countries, which is expected to change for certain countries due to the current geopolitical situation, which in turn affects countries that have large import shares there. Second, an extended preference elicitation from DMs with different nationalities and profiles is planned. Third, a systematic robustness assessment will be carried out to identify conflicts and synergies between the DMs (i.e., multi-scenario analysis), which can arise from different preferences (e.g., importance of indicators, preference functions) or perceptions on specific indicators or alternatives (i.e., country).

The contribution of this study is twofold. On the one hand, it offers a transparent and consistent methodological framework that facilitates interaction between analyst and decision maker, and it provides a tool to account for energy security in a hybrid threat context in all its facets and complexity. On the other hand, this approach can help to increase understanding and trust among diverse stakeholders, including industry, authorities, political decision makers as well as the public.

Acknowledgements. P. Burgherr and A.C. Dupuy acknowledge support from the Systems Analysis and Studies-163 (SAS-163) on "Energy Security in the Era of Hybrid Warfare".

References

1. Ang, B.W., Choong, W.L., Ng, T.S.: Energy security: Definitions, dimensions and indexes. Renew. Sustain. Energy Rev. 42, 1077–1093 (2015). https://doi.org/10.1016/j.rser.2014.10.064
2. Winzer, C.: Conceptualizing energy security. Energy Policy. 46, 36–48 (2012). https://doi.org/10.1016/j.enpol.2012.02.067
3. Marchese, D., Reynolds, E., Bates, M.E., Morgan, H., Clark, S.S., Linkov, I.: Resilience and sustainability: Similarities and differences in environmental management applications. Sci. Total Environ. **613–614**, 1275–1283 (2018). https://doi.org/10.1016/j.scitotenv.2017.09.086
4. Paravantis, J.A., Kontoulis, N., Ballis, A., Tsirigotis, D., Dourmas, V.: A geopolitical review of definitions, dimensions and indicators of energy security. In: 2018 9th Int. Conf. Information, Intell. Syst. Appl. IISA 2018. (2019). https://doi.org/10.1109/IISA.2018.8633676
5. Gatto, A., Drago, C.: A taxonomy of energy resilience. Energy Policy. 136, (2020). https://doi.org/10.1016/j.enpol.2019.111007
6. Stern, M., Öjendal, J.: Mapping the Security-Development Nexus: Conflict, Complexity, Cacophony, Convergence? Secur. Dialogue. **41**, 5–29 (2022). https://doi.org/10.1177/0967010609357041
7. Keskinen, M., Sojamo, S., Varis, O.: Enhancing Security, Sustainability and Resilience in Energy. Food Water. Sustain. **11**, 7244 (2019). https://doi.org/10.3390/su11247244
8. Yergin, D.: Ensuring Energy Security. Foreign Aff. **85**, 69–82 (2006). https://doi.org/10.2307/20031912
9. Dupuy, A.C., Nussbaum, D., Butrimas, V., Granitsas, A.: Energy security in the era of hybrid warfare. NATO Rev. 1–5 (2021)
10. Apostol, A.C., Cristache, N., Nastase, M.: Societal resilience, a key factor in combating hybrid threats. Int. Conf. Knowl.-Based Organ. **28**, 107–115 (2022). https://doi.org/10.2478/kbo-2022-0057

11. Axon, C.J., Darton, R.C.: Sustainability and risk – a review of energy security. Sustain. Prod. Consum. **27**, 1195–1204 (2021). https://doi.org/10.1016/j.spc.2021.01.018
12. Willhuhn, M.: Satellite cyber attack paralyzes 11 GW of German wind turbines. pv Mag. Int. 7 (2022)
13. Benton, T.G., et al.: The Ukraine war and threats to food and energy security. Cascading risks from prices and supply disruptions. Chatham House, London, UK (2022)
14. Misik, M.: The EU needs to improve its external energy security. Energy Policy. 165, 112930 (2022). https://doi.org/10.1016/j.enpol.2022.112930
15. Żuk, P., Żuk, P.: National energy security or acceleration of transition? Energy policy after the war in Ukraine. Joule. **6**, 709–712 (2022). https://doi.org/10.1016/j.joule.2022.03.009
16. Strange, N., Geldmann, J., Burgess, N.D., Bull, J.W.: Policy responses to the Ukraine crisis threaten European biodiversity. Nat. Ecol. Evol. (2022). https://doi.org/10.1038/s41559-022-01786-z
17. Nardo, M., Saisana, M., Saltelli, A., Tarantola, S., Giovannini, E.: Handbook on Constructing Composite Indicators: Methodology and User Guide. OECD Publishing, Paris, France (2008)
18. Gasser, P.: A review on energy security indices to compare country performances. Energy Policy **139**, 111339 (2020). https://doi.org/10.1016/j.enpol.2020.111339
19. Morkunas, M., Cernius, G., Giriuniene, G.: Assessing Business Risks of Natural Gas Trading Companies : Evidence from GET Baltic. Energies. 12, 2647 (2019). https://doi.org/10.3390/en12142647
20. Proninska, K., Ksiezopolski, K.: Baltic Offshore Wind Energy Development — Poland ' s Public Policy Tools Analysis and the Geostrategic Implications. Energies. 14, 1–17 (2021). https://doi.org/10.3390/en14164883
21. Malutan, D.S., Korakis, I.: Russian potential for influence in the Romanian and Greek energy sector. Naval Postgraduate School, Monterey, California (2018)
22. Giannopoulos, G., Smith, H., Theocharidou, M.: The Landscape of Hybrid Threats: a Conceptual Model Public Version. European Commission (EC), Joint Research Centre (JRC), Ispra, Italy (2020)
23. Verner, D., Grigas, A., Petit, F.: Assessing Energy Dependency in the Age of Hybrid Threats. The European Centre of Excellence for Countering Hybrid Threats (Hybrid CoE), Helsinki, Finland (2019)
24. Burgherr, P., Siskos, E., Spada, M., Lustenberger, P., Dupuy, A.C.: Resilience of the European Natural Gas Network to Hybrid Threats. In: Castanier, B., Cepin, M., Bigaud, D., and Berenguer, C. (eds.) Proceedings of the 31st European Safety and Reliability Conference (ESREL 2021). pp. 3238–3244. Resarch Publishing, Singapore, SG (2021). https://doi.org/10.3850/978-981-18-2016-8_628-cd
25. Cinelli, M., Kadziński, M., Miebs, G., Gonzalez, M., Słowiński, R.: Recommending Multiple Criteria Decision Analysis Methods with A New Taxonomy-based Decision Support System. (2022). https://doi.org/10.48550/arXiv.2106.07378
26. Brans, J.-P., De Smet, Y.: PROMETHEE Methods. In: Greco, S., Ehrgott, M., Figueira, J.R. (eds.) Multiple Criteria Decision Analysis. ISORMS, vol. 233, pp. 187–219. Springer, New York (2016). https://doi.org/10.1007/978-1-4939-3094-4_6
27. Siskos, E., Tsotsolas, N.: Elicitation of criteria importance weights through the Simos method: A robustness concern. Eur. J. Oper. Res. **246**, 543–553 (2015). https://doi.org/10.1016/j.ejor.2015.04.037
28. VP Solutions: Visual Promethee 1.4 Manual. VP Solutions, Brussels, Belgium (2013)
29. US EIA: Annual Energy Outlook 2021. US Energy Information Administration (EIA), US Department of Energy (DoE), Washington DC, USA (2021)

30. Maschmeyer, L., Cavelty, M.D.: Goodbye Cyberwar: Ukraine as Reality Check. Policy Perspectives Vol. 10/3. Center for Security Studies (CSS), ETH Zurich, Zurich, Switzerland (2022)
31. Kokaraki, N., Hopfe, C.J., Robinson, E., Nikolaidou, E.: Testing the reliability of deterministic multi-criteria decision-making methods using building performance simulation. Renew. Sustain. Energy Rev. **112**, 991–1007 (2019). https://doi.org/10.1016/j.rser.2019.06.018

Cybersecurity in the German Railway Sector

Dietmar Möller[1], Lukas Iffländer[2]([⊠]) [iD], Michael Nord[3] [iD], Bernd Leppla[3],
Patrik Krause[4], Peter Czerkewski[5], Nikolai Lenski[6], and Kristin Mühl[2] [iD]

[1] Clausthal University of Technology, Institute for Mathematics, Erzstr. 1,
38678 Clausthal-Zellerfeld, Germany
dietmar.moeller@tu-clausthal.de

[2] German Centre for Rail Traffic Research, August-Bebel-Straße 10, 01069 Dresden,
Germany
{IfflaenderL,MuehlK}@dzsf.bund.de

[3] IABG mbH, Einsteinstr. 20, 85521 Ottobrunn, Germany
{nord,leppla}@iabg.de.de

[4] 3DSE Management Consultants GmbH, Seidelstr. 18a, 80335München, Germany
p.krause@3dse.de

[5] Institute of Railway Technology GmbH, Carnotstr. 6, 10587 Berlin-Charlottenburg,
Germany
pc@bahntechnik.de

[6] Fraunhofer AISEC, Breite Str. 12, 14199 Berlin, Germany
nikolai.lenski@aisec-fraunhofer.de

Abstract. Cybersecurity breaches are on the rise. Due to increased
network interconnection, industrial systems are becoming more attractive targets for such attacks. Therefore, various industries must acquire
knowledge and experience regarding cybersecurity for their IT and OT
systems. One such sector is the safety-critical railway and public transport sector. Technological leaps like digital interlocking, fifth-generation
networking, and the move from proprietary field busses to IP networking
are driving the sector into an inter-connected age. This work scrutinizes
the sector's cybersecurity awareness, knowledge, and preparedness. To
this end, we created a two-stage study comprising a quantitative online
survey to gain comprehensive insight and qualitative interviews to deepen
selected issues in a SWOT analysis. The results show that the sector still
has a long way to go regarding cybersecurity, with the average company
not meeting basic implementation levels. Furthermore, we identified multiple factors contributing to this result. Key issues are a lack of staff and
management sensitivity to cybersecurity and support from authorities.

1 Introduction

Over the last years, cyberattacks that exploit vulnerabilities of safety-critical
industrial infrastructure networks and business models negatively affected business performance. At the current stage, this trend seems to be here to stay.
This development requires increased cybersecurity awareness, knowledge, and

B. Hämmerli et al. (Eds.): CRITIS 2022, LNCS 13723, pp. 222–240, 2023.
https://doi.org/10.1007/978-3-031-35190-7_16

preparedness. Enterprises must identify and evaluate their attack surfaces and the impact of potentially successful attacks to defend their assets. In this context, cyberattacks are an unwanted reality due to the digital transformation in today's industrial sectors [7]. The railway and public transportation sector is an industrial sector that undergoes a significant transformation through digitizing information systems, operational systems, infrastructure, and the automation of the railway system processes. For example, up to now, interlocking systems were either still using mechanical, electro-mechanical, and relais technology or industrial computers interconnected by dedicated network lines. Railway infrastructure managers are currently beginning to replace these legacy systems with newer interlocking architectures that rely on custom-of-the-shelf hardware and are interconnected using Internet Protocol (IP) networks. Furthermore, the sector is a desirable target due to the possibility of inflicting extensive damage. The worst-case scenario here would be manipulating a railway switch on a high-speed line leading to a collision of two trains with up to over one thousand passengers each.

This development and the potential damage scale require cybersecurity concepts that comprise technologies, procedures, and practices designed to protect data in vulnerable systems from attacks, damage, or unauthorized access. Because of the introduction, as mentioned earlier, of ubiquitous accessibility and connectivity, railway and public transportation systems and infrastructure are becoming vulnerable to remote attacks. Remote attacks are malicious actions aimed at unauthorized entry into vulnerable railway systems and infrastructure locations without requiring physical proximity to the target. The main reasons for remote attacks are illegally stealing data, introducing malicious software. In this regard, cybersecurity teams must analyze weaknesses to gain knowledge and estimate cybersecurity risks through an efficient cyberthreat analysis to attain cybersecurity awareness. However, little reliable information exists about cybersecurity awareness in the railway and public transport sector and infrastructure. International studies explore the topic but are rather superficial [5] or broadly designed and, therefore, insufficient to gain detailed insight into these sectors.

This work provides a two-stage study to gain this insight. We first designed a questionnaire and then performed and evaluated an online survey to gain a comprehensive picture of the sector's maturity level regarding cybersecurity. To this end, we used the National Institute of Standards and Technology (NIST) framework [3] comprising the five disciplines of Identify, Protect, Detect, Respond and Recover and map our questions and the responses to these disciplines resulting in a maturity level between 0 and 5, where 3 is the desired base-level for the implementation of cybersecurity measures. We invited the entire railway and transport sectors comprising railway and public transport operators, infrastructure managers, energy suppliers, and manufacturers. Next, we interviewed selected participants from the survey to deepen our understanding of the reasons for the participants' results and to enquire about their wishes for legislative and executive support. We performed a Strengths, Weaknesses, Opportunities and Threats analysis (SWOT analysis) based on these interviews.

Parallel to inquiring the state of cybersecurity in the railway and public transport sector, we also performed similar steps to inquire the sectors readiness to adopt emerging technologies. We published this work in [6].

The remainder of this work first comprises a more detailed discussion of maturity models and the SWOT analysis in Sect. 2. Next, we describe the design and execution of both parts of this study in Sect. 3 and analyze the results in Sect. 4. Lastly, we conclude the paper in Sect. 5.

2 Maturity and SWOT Model

Data sets are essential in all industrial sectors to investigate business and economic assets [7]. Therefore, data analytics in cybersecurity is crucial to deepening knowledge of vital and critical business assets and process vulnerabilities. The information presented in this section provides the basis for a maturity and SWOT analysis model to evaluate the existence, effectiveness, and efficiency of cybersecurity awareness and cybersecurity strategies in railways and public transportation sectors.

2.1 Maturity Model

The term maturity refers to the state of being complete, comprehensive, ready, or perfect. Therefore, a maturity assessment measures the current maturity level of a particular aspect of an organization in a meaningful way, enabling stakeholders to identify strengths and improvement points and prioritize measures to reach higher maturity levels accordingly. Over 70 different maturity models are available, from domains within the spectrum of business information systems, computer science, and others, showing the great variety of widespread maturity models [7]. In this regard, maturity models propose maturity levels that give a global vision of company performance, a gap analysis of current capabilities, and an indication for measures to meet strategic objectives. Prominent information security models are listed in Table 1 [7].

As shown in Table 1 most maturity models use a five or six level maturity scale that can range, e.g., from zero (lowest assessment level) to five (highest assessment level), as presented in Table 2 [2]. Table 2 also shows that with each level, the maturity increases. In this context, the maturity model shows if objectives attain a sufficient level or require action.

This assessment reveals the main obstacles to efficient and effective cybersecurity method application. The maturity model creates additional value from data records obtained in a self-assessment. As part of the self-assessment, in addition to pseudonymized personal information about the representative of the partaking company (e.g., role in the company, area of responsibility, and others), we collected information about the company (e.g., industrial sector, workforce size, market share, sales, and others). The queried data indicates whether a roadmap in the context of cybersecurity strategy and awareness (partially) exists. Such a roadmap ultimately results in strategic activities and responsibilities to increase the current maturity levels.

Table 1. Maturity Models: Level Context and Specific Focus [7].

Maturity Model	Level Context	Specific Focus
catch Maturity Index	1. Computerization 2. Connectivity 3. Visibility 4. Transparency 5. Predictive Capacity 6. Adaptability	Specific to production, logistics, sales, marketing, services, and research and development activities.
COBIT Model	0. Non-existent 1. Initial/ad hoc 2. Repeatable but intuitive 3. Defined process 4. Managed and measurable 5. Optimize	Framework by information system audit and control association, or for information technology (IT) management mechanism
NIST CSF Model	1. Policy 2. Procedure 3. Implementation 4. Testing 5. Integration	Tracking progress implementing information security maturity levels from the current state to the defined target state, using clear structured documentation.
NIST PRISMA Model	1. Policy 2. Procedure 3. Implementation 4. Test 5. Integration	Improve information security programs, support critical infrastructure protection planning, and facilitate the exchange of effective security practices in organizations' communities.
SSE-CMM Model	1. Conducted informal design 2. Planned and tracked 3. Well defined 4. Quantitatively controlled 5. Continuous improvement	Provides the industry with a safety standard of the design engineering software with best practices but is no specific guidance on how to achieve security solutions.

Table 2. Assessment Criteria for Maturity Level.

Maturity Level	Assessment Criteria for Cybersecurity
0	No activities
1	Concepts but no concrete implementation yet
2	Concepts partially implemented
3	Full implementation and thorough documentation
4	A continuous state-of-the-art and efficient monitoring
5	Subject to a continuous improvement process

In connection with the study's objective of evaluating cybersecurity in the railway and public transport sector, the technological dimension considers the company's current technical environment (actual state) under investigation. Another dimension used in the model is the organization, focusing on the organizational framework, e.g., integrating cybersecurity guidelines to prevent cyberattacks. This dimension also includes issues associated with critical development paths for the company and employees with the necessary know-how and the essential and approved budget. Other dimensions are Information Technology (IT) infrastructure, Operation Technology (OT) infrastructure, continuous improvement process, and others.

A radar chart—the graphical representation of multivariate data in a two-dimensional plot with multiple variables—shows the assignments of the evaluation criteria using the scale given in Table 2. Figure 1 shows an example of a fictitious category of a radar chart referring to the NIST cybersecurity framework. NIST describes cybersecurity outcomes organized in a hierarchy of functions [3]. These functions are:

Identify (ID): Supports understanding and managing cybersecurity risks;
Protect (PR): Supports the ability to limit the impact of a potential cybersecurity event;
Detect (DE): Enables timely discovery of cybersecurity events;
Respond (RS): Includes appropriate activities taking action regarding cybersecurity incidents;
Recover (RC): Supports timely recovery to normal operation to minimize the impact of a cybersecurity incident.

2.2 SWOT Analysis Model

A SWOT is a pragmatic approach to assessing a company's current economic and technological situation realistically and reliably in specific subject areas [4]. It gives insight into existing omissions, e.g., insufficient cybersecurity strategy in the IT or OT area, delayed implementation of technological innovations, no sustainable use of new technologies, and others. We execute a SWOT analysis by examining the company's internal and external environment. However, the SWOT analysis itself is not a strategic plan. It only describes existing states or shows which developments or events are possible momentarily. For this purpose, we define the company's internal and external environment as follows:

- The internal environment describes the company's current state comprising individual strengths and weaknesses.
  - Key strengths include innovation, know-how, customer benefits, patents, qualified employees, and technology leadership.
  - Weaknesses include low employee qualification levels, insufficient innovation levels, no skimming pioneer behavior, or no agile behavior to respond to customer requirements.

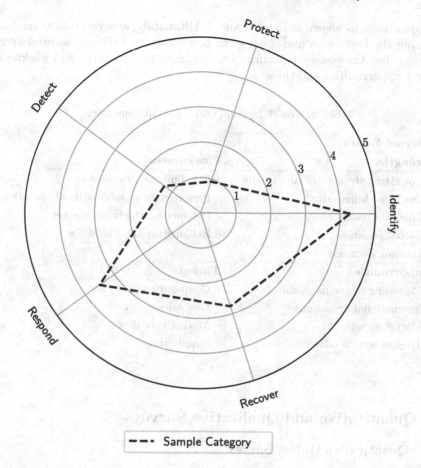

Fig. 1. Sample Radar Chart with Five Axes (dimensions) of the NIST Framework and Six Maturity Levels shows an Example Comparison of the Maturity Levels of Different Companies.

- The external environment, on the other hand, describes individual influencing factors of the company's opportunities and risks.
  - These factors include, e.g., the development of the industry structure, trends in technological change (such as digitization, emerging new technologies, like the Internet of Things (IOT)), assigned to the potential opportunities.
  - However, in the context of risks, these factors can also show a negative tendency, e.g., no strategy to deal with the increase in cyber threat attacks or exchange rate fluctuations due to the company's one-sided export orientation.

Table 3 [4] shows the generic SWOT analysis dimensions expanded by depicting the underlying intrinsic core questions in the respective dimension. In practice, the SWOT analysis analysis requires data sets usually extracted from core questions, as shown in Sects. 3 and 4. Ultimately, analysis results facilitate selecting the key topics and areas of responsibility and derive essential activities regarding the core cybersecurity issues comparing strengths and weaknesses against opportunities and threats.

Table 3. SWOT Internal and External Dimensions.

Internal Factors	
Strengths	**Weaknesses**
– Consistent strength of core products	– Low build-out expansion
– Disciplined innovator	– Performance of international operations
– Financial resources	– Reliance on the home market
– Global presence	– Reliance on old innovation
External Factors	
Opportunities	**Threats**
– Clustering of company units	– Competition
– International operations	– Low sales
– Market growth	– Market volatility
– Trusted service offers	– Supply risks

3 Quantitative and Qualitative Surveys

3.1 Quantitative Online Survey

We conducted an online survey as part of a two-stage process to collect the required data for the maturity model and SWOT analysis. The maturity levels result from the answers. Thus obtained data allows for an initial assessment of the status quo. A disadvantage of closed online surveys is the missing possibility for participants to contribute specific comments. We compensate for this within the two-stage process by the subsequent expert interviews.

The first part of the online survey consisted of ten queried items about observed cyberattacks, attack types, damage levels, and obstacles preventing a successful implementation. The second block of the online survey queried the five NIST core functions (see Sect. 2.1). The questions correspond to the maturity model reflecting the individual levels for each core function. The question wording assures unambiguous assignment answers. In addition to the five NIST core functions, we also covered the topics of organization, IT systems, OT Systems, and IT and OT infrastructure. For example, gathering information about the organization and the NIST core function PR, the question arises, "Does your company ensure to train all employees in cybersecurity?". With 51 questions, this is the most extensive part of the survey. Appendix A shows sample questions from the online questionnaire for clarification.

Finally, we recorded demographic data on the company, such as employees and turnover. In addition, the companies were assigned to respective subsectors of the railway industry: We considered the following seven subsectors: (1) railway operators, (2) railway infrastructure managers, (3) railway energy suppliers, (4) railway vehicle manufacturers and maintenance workshops, (5) Railway infrastructure suppliers, (6) Transit authorities and public transport operators, and (7) distributors.

Since the questions were in closed form, the participating company had no opportunity to comment. However, the representative of a participating company could voluntarily submit personal contact information for a subsequent interview at the end of the questionnaire.

We chose the arithmetic mean for the evaluation. The mean refers to the total number of responses in the respective category. A category is, for example, a NIST core function or the intersection of a NIST core function and the number of employees.

We chose LimeSurvey for the online survey based on availability, acceptance, ease of use, and compliance with data protection requirements.

3.2   Qualitative Interview Survey

Interviews represent the second part of the two-stage process of gaining data required for the maturity model and SWOT analysis. They build upon the online survey results and offer the opportunity to delve deeper into selected topics with open questions. For this reason, we chose the form of semi-structured interviews [1].

Essentially, the interviews pursued four core objectives. On the one hand, they aimed at clarifying contradictions, conspicuous values, or outliers from the online questionnaire. For this purpose, we readdressed the affected topics without directly addressing their need for clarification but instead by openly discussing these topics. On the other hand, we posed detailed questions regarding the degree of maturity. One such example was the question about the cybersecurity officer in the company. While the online questionnaire only asked about such a role, the interviews also addressed the quality of this role. The quality includes the responsibility scope, time availability, and whether the position is dedicated or shared with another responsibility. In this context, we also surveyed the company-wide cybersecurity strategy. Appendix B shows sample questions from the interview questionnaire for clarification.

The third core objective was data collection for the SWOT analysis. A self-assessment of existing obstacles explored weaknesses (in the case of internal factors) and threats (in the case of external factors). At the same time, the interviews explored measures and necessary assistance to overcome these obstacles. In addition, the interviewers queried the strengths and opportunities. Companies with a high cybersecurity maturity knowledge allow us to derive recommendations to improve for less well-positioned companies.

We adapted the interview questions to each interview partner to achieve these goals. For this, we defined specific criteria based on their answers in the online questionnaire, determining relevant topics concerning the objectives mentioned earlier to deepen further.

We chose the interviewees based on various criteria gained from the outcome of the online survey. The goal was to find a representative group for the targeted sectors. To this end, we ensured to cover all sectors and adjusted the number of interviews per sector to its relative size. In addition, we chose interviewees that cover the entire maturity and company size spectrum. The participants will receive their anonymized results and individual maturity level as an expense allowance.

4   Results

While the online survey reflects all answers about cybersecurity in the railway sector, the interview survey results reflect representative participants and substantiate the online survey results.

Using a representative survey, we performed an empirical study to survey the cybersecurity status quo in the railway and public transport sectors. We assessed the degree of maturity using the NIST framework core functions (see Sect. 2.1.

We identified, segmented, and categorized 711 companies from the railway and local public transportation sector. The goal was to provide a corresponding dimension for each subsector for the evaluation. We carried out a mailing campaign personalized to the companies to achieve the highest possible number of participants and ensure their willingness to participate in the online survey.

The cover letter made the companies aware of the research project and asked for their participation in the online survey. Therefore, the letters emphasized the study's importance for future planning (who is using the survey) and the need for broad participation. Parallel to the mailing campaign, we enabled access to the online survey. To increase participation, we advertised the survey at professional conferences and with lobby organizations for various subgroups.

4.1   Online Survey

As described in Sect. 3.1, the online survey aims to provide a comprehensive overview of cyberattacks on past and future use of cybersecurity tools. Based on the NIST core functions, the degree of maturity of the participating companies results from an extensive questionnaire.

Table 4 shows the online survey results regarding the percentage of participants per sector in the online survey and the interview. Furthermore, it shows the NIST maturity level from the online survey in the individual focal points and the overall maturity level across the sectors. Online survey participants comprised, e.g., Chief Information Security Officers(CISOs) or IT department heads. In addition to the contacted 711 companies, four companies actively applied and signed up to participate, leading to a sample of 715 companies. In total, 60 companies completed the online survey.

Table 4. Results for Sample, Participants, and NIST Maturity Level per Sub-sector of Online Survey.

Sectors	Survey Partici-pants						NIST Maturity Level (based on Online Survey)					
	Sample		Online*		Interview		ID	PR	DE	RS	RC	Total
	Number	Share	Number	Share	Number	Share						
Railway Operators	420	59	23	38	2	17	1.98 ± 0.72	2.15 ± 0.71	1.96 ± 0.74	1.76 ± 0.73	2.55 ± 0.73	2.10 ± 0.74
Infrastructure Managers	116	16	11	18	1	8	1.01 ± 0.81	1.24 ± 0.76	1.03 ± 0.83	0.69 ± 0.61	1.63 ± 0.96	1.15 ± 0.83
Public Transport Authorities	106	15	12	20	4	33	1.79 ± 0.75	2.15 ± 0.79	1.55 ± 0.91	1.73 ± 0.80	2.57 ± 0.88	1.99 ± 0.86
Rolling Stock Suppliers	38	5	8	13	4	33	2.31 ± 1.04	2.36 ± 1.15	1.87 ± 1.09	1.93 ± 1.12	2.49 ± 1.06	2.24 ± 1.10
Infrastructure Suppliers	27	4	2	3			2.15 ± 2.26	2.43 ± 0.91	1.94 ± 2.05	1.58 ± 1.55	2.06 ± 1.99	2.12 ± 1.94
Energy Suppliers	1	0	3	5			2.77 ± 2.06	2.49 ± 0.97	1.63 ± 1.76	1.56 ± 1.37	2.30 ± 1.56	2.28 ± 1.75
Others	7	1	1	2	1	8	data not displayed for anonymization					
Overall	715	100	60	100	12	100	1.89 ± 0.42	2.07 ± 0.40	1.69 ± 0.43	1.58 ± 0.40	2.36 ± 0.43	1.96 ± 0.42

* Participants self-selected the sector they would assign themselves during the survey.

Depending on the sectors, we received replies from between 5.48% (23 out of 420 railway operators) and total coverage (for the energy supplier sector). Note that we only contacted a single energy supplier in our categorization, but a total of three companies assigned themselves as energy suppliers.

In the following section, we go into more detail about the online survey results using various analyses.

Maturity Level Regarding Company Size Based on Employee Numbers We wanted to verify a common assumption that companies with a higher number of employees attain a higher level of maturity. The results regarding the overall maturity level in Fig. 2 show a moderate positive correlation between the number of employees and the maturity level with a Spearman Coefficient of $r = .42$.

Small companies below ten employees never achieve a maturity level of 2 or higher. In contrast, the second quantile for companies up to 10,000 employees cap below a maturity level of 3. However, for these companies, we found outliers that exceed the median by a fair number in the first quantile. In comparison, for companies between 250 and 10,000 employees, we saw these outliers in the opposite direction in the fourth quantile. Large companies with 10,000 employees show a significantly higher maturity level than all other categories and are the only category where the first quantile reaches a level of 5. Enormous and tiny companies have considerably smaller outliers. Figure 2 also clearly indicates that the underlying evaluation method selection was sufficient concerning the result since we detected a relevant correlation.

In Fig. 3, we compared the five NIST maturity subcategories. The figure shows the results for small (1-49 employees), medium (50-999 employees), and large (1,000 or more employees) companies as well as the overall average. It becomes apparent that medium companies match the average well. Furthermore, the figure shows that the increase in average maturity level between the company sizes occurs for every NIST criteria. On the one hand, minor differences occur for RC and DE. RC is already at a higher level for small companies than other objectives. On the other hand, ID and RS significantly improve with company size. PR improves at an intermediary level. Furthermore, the radar chart shows

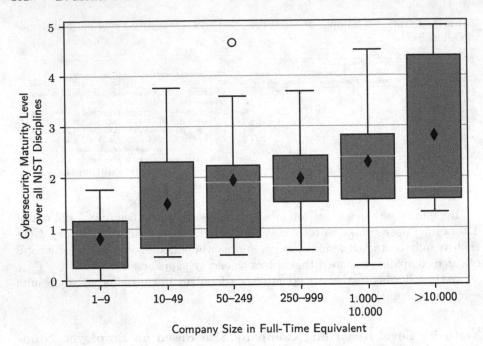

Average shown as diamond in the box plot. Horizontal line inside the box shows the median. The upper and lower bound of the box represent the 25 % and 75 % quantile. Circles are outliers.

Fig. 2. Maturity Levels by Number of Employees.

that even larger companies have significant shortcomings for the RS and DE objectives.

Large companies stick to processes, specifications, guidelines, or instructions. They have a clear structure and clearly define roles and responsibilities. With this assumption, we expected higher cybersecurity maturity levels for larger companies. Conversely, smaller companies probably lack effective strategies for consistent cybersecurity. Although the potential dangers emanating from current cyber risks became public over the last years, many smaller companies are unaware of the security gaps in their own company and how to arm themselves in the long term. However, a low budget or the lack of filling the corresponding position could also be a reason.

Maturity Level Comparison Between Railway Sectors. Figure 4 shows the maturity level analysis by sector. Individual maturity levels among the railway operators, vehicle manufacturers, and public transport authorities are very diverse. Especially the railway operators cover the entire spectrum between 0 and 5. Notably, the number of companies in the respective sectors varies greatly. For this reason, it is impossible to conclude that there is a dependency on the degree of maturity in the individual sector without further in-depth analysis.

The railway infrastructure managers are significant outliersana regarding the median and all quantiles. While the median for all other sectors is around a value of 2, the infrastructure managers only reach a level of 1. Only a single outlier reaches a level of almost 3. Here, it is noteworthy that the critical infrastructure regulations in Germany (KRITIS regulation) primarily affect infrastructure managers.

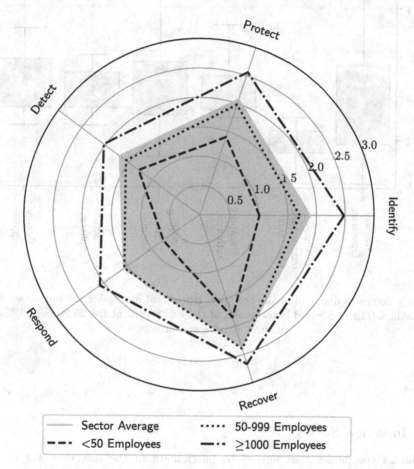

Theta axis is limited to 3.0 for better viewability since no category exceeds this level.

Fig. 3. NIST Framework Maturity Level Relative to Company Sizes.

Figure 5 gives a more detailed account of the average sectorwise performance in the different NIST categories. Notably, in the first group, all sectors tend to be stronger in the *Recover* discipline than in the others. Railway operators and transport authorities show virtually equal performance for the *Protect*, *Respond* and *Recover* categories while transport authorities are stronger for the *Identify* and *Detect* metrics. In the second group, the results are relatively similar, with the rolling stock suppliers performing stronger in the *Respond* and *Recover* metrics. The energy suppliers are an outlier due to their comparatively strong *Identify* result.

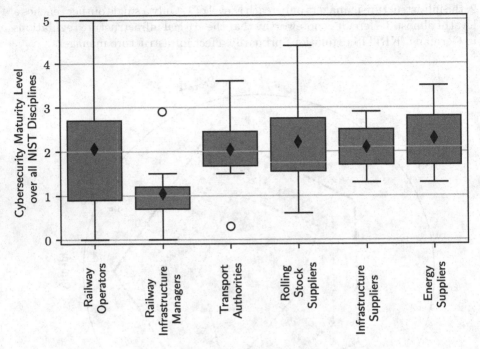

Average shown as diamond in the box plot. Horizontal line inside the box shows the median. The upper and lower bound of the box represent the 25 % and 75 % quantile. Circles are outliers.

Fig. 4. Maturity Levels by Sector.

4.2 Interview Survey

Of the 24 companies that agreed to participate in the interview survey, we selected twelve companies for an in-depth discussion, paying attention to a representative selection. For each of the interviewed companies, we created an individual questionnaire consisting of an initial question about the motivation to participate, and six to ten key questions, depending on the company, to deepen the answers from the online survey. Finally, we posed an open question regarding further suggestions and wishes regarding legislative and executive actions and how to help the company improve its cybersecurity issues. We replaced companies that signed up for the follow-up but did not respond with suitable replacement candidates.

The interviews lasted between one and two hours. The interviewers took minutes in the form of bullet points. According to their information, the interview participants were CISOs or IT department heads. Table 5 shows a SWOT example resulting from the interview part. In the following, we will combine the interview survey results with the online survey results.

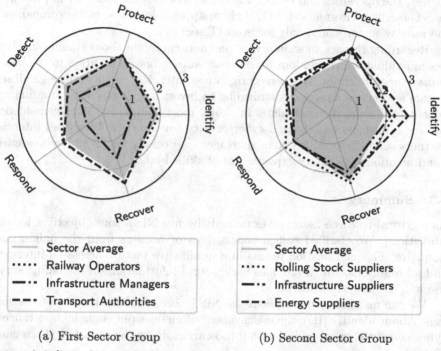

(a) First Sector Group   (b) Second Sector Group

Theta axis is limited to 3.0 for better viewability since no category exceeds this level. Sectors split for better viewability.

Fig. 5. Maturity Levels in NIST Framework for Different Company Sizes.

Throughout all interviews, the German railway sector shows high robustness to external influences as its strengths. Every interview partner mentioned at least one of the three factors, long-proven technology, independent communication networks, or well-rehearsed procedures.

Weaknesses depend on the subsector. While operators and transportation authorities see themselves as highly dependent on manufacturers and the technology they offer, the whole railway sector lacks support from public authorities and politics regarding cybersecurity and lacks management attention to cybersecurity.

In total, all interview partners see the potential for adopting regulations. Here, they mentioned conflicts between German federal and European law and

KRITIS. In addition, all companies see a lack of realization friendliness of upcoming regulations. All interview partners would appreciate at least one of the following: As early as possible pre-information, implementation support, and sector-specific regulations. One interview partner had the idea that external service providers could cover cybersecurity tasks for the railway sector as—according to that interview partner—many companies would struggle to get that job done. At last, the operators and transportation authorities see room for improvement in cybersecurity awareness for OT (where applicable); most of the companies in the railway sector would only focus on IT security.

Regarding threats, most interview partners complain about standardized and less individualized regulations for different subsectors. In addition to the lack of management attention to cybersecurity, most interview partners through all subsectors see their management struggling to invest in cybersecurity as a financial benefit that is hard to calculate. In short, most companies' management does not see a business case behind cybersecurity investments. Lastly, all interview partners suffer from skilled labor shortages - especially for IT and cybersecurity - and mention high salary expectations of skilled labor.

4.3 Summary

As a critical research issue, we examined the five NIST core objectives for contradictions. We clarified conspicuous values or outliers from the online questionnaire. This clarification results in a qualitative picture across all interviews and all questions, which provides background information on the online survey results., as shown in Table 5.

We can make statements about the NIST core functions based on these findings. About Identify (ID), the management often does put enough importance on cybersecurity, employees deal with it too carelessly, or the role of a cybersecurity officer is vacant.

In many companies, the NIST core function Protect (PR) is more pronounced about cybersecurity awareness by employing information security or data protection officers and having appropriate security systems in operation or operating their own decoupled networks.

Concerning the NIST core function Detect (DE), findings show that railway companies are aware of this topic to varying degrees. For example, some companies actively or automatically search for anomalies in their systems, e.g., log files or research publicly known incidents, and then compare their circumstances with their systems.

According to the online survey, the NIST core function Respond (RS) has the lowest established level of maturity in the railway and transportation sector. The interview findings identified that the main drivers are the low importance of cybersecurity within companies, the lack of accountability, and the lack of standards. There is often a lack of experience in dealing with the relevant processes.

Regarding the NIST core function Recover (RC), answers such as outdated backup systems, obstructive specifications from the manufacturers, regulatory authorities, and institutions for data recovery provide an initial justification for the current maturity level.

4.4   Limitations

The main limitation of our study is the under-participation in some sub-sectors, which challenges its representativeness. Cybersecurity is a sensitive topic that many companies do not want to discuss, fearing to reveal significant weaknesses. A more representative result would therefore require obligatory participation. For example, regular security audits by the European or federal railway agencies could comprise a section on security in the future.

Table 5. SWOT Analysis Based on the Interviews.

Strengths	Weaknesses
– Reliable hardware and physical structures in the area of IT and OT	– High dependence on suppliers regarding technical standards for the procured hardware and software (the offered standard is not always the current standard)
– Physically decoupled communication channels	– Limited support from authorities and politics regarding the adoption of measures to increase cybersecurity
– Increased awareness of issues relating to current developments in information and cybersecurity within the IT department	– Lack of cybersecurity awareness among management and employees
– Well-established organizational structure and working processes	– Dependence on suppliers to set up IT, including in some cases for back-up recovery
– Usually very motivated and committed IT departments with an interest in cybersecurity	– Discontinuation of support and updates of older products by the manufacturer
Opportunities	**Threats**
– Use of external service providers to take over cybersecurity tasks	– Generalized regulations for different subsectors and use cases hinder companies through lack of individuality, practicability, and failure to address needs
– Increasing the awareness of cybersecurity in the OT area	– Financial benefits of investments in cybersecurity are underestimated
– Continuous creation of positions to ensure the "cybersecurity" function (currently often only secondary)	– IT skill shortage coupled with high salary expectations
– Adjustment of KRITIS regulations in the direction of "ease of implementation" and a higher degree of individualization per user	– Increasing risk of vulnerability due to increasing digitization and thus increasing potential entry points
– In-house policies to increase cybersecurity (e.g., password rules)	– Widening of the technological gap due to a lack of funding opportunities
– In-house training or webinars on the topic of cybersecurity or data protection	
– Exchange platforms within the industry on the topic of cybersecurity	
– Consistent creation of back-ups for IT and OT	
– Open and transparent communication on the actual threat situation	

5 Conclusion

Industrial sectors that go through digitization face many challenges that confront each other. Against this background, cybersecurity is a challenge, as "corporate values" must be protected here. In this process, all parties must attain a certain level of cybersecurity awareness to create resilient cybersecurity concepts comprising technologies, processes, and training. The German railway sector is currently undergoing this transformation, and, in this work, we took a closer look at the attained cybersecurity awareness levels. To this end, we performed a two-stage process comprising an online survey and phone interviews based on which we created a maturity model and conducted a SWOT analysis analysis. We designed a questionnaire to cover the five NIST criteria, *Identify*, *Detect*, *Protect*, *Respond*, and *Recover*, with general questions for all sectors discriminating between OT and IT. The interview survey followed up on inconsistencies between answers and deepened our understanding of the causes of the obtained maturity levels.

Thus, we obtained and discussed quantitative and qualitative results. Our approach shows that the size of an enterprise in the railway sector directly correlates with its maturity level: the more employees the company has, the higher the cybersecurity level. We also found that, e.g., infrastructure managers generally attain a relatively low maturity level. Railway operators are very diverse, and their maturity levels disperse across the entire spectrum. Through the phone survey, we achieved a deepened understanding of strengths (e.g., a reliable hardware structure), weaknesses (e.g., a lack of management understanding of cybersecurity), opportunities (e.g., an increase of cybersecurity awareness for operational technology), and threats (e.g., the shortage of skilled labor).

We have shown that our approach yields an extensive dataset and insights into the railway sector's cybersecurity awareness. We intend to deepen our understanding based on the existing data in future work and integrate our results with our European partners. Furthermore, in parallel, we performed a similar study regarding the current and planned application of and knowledge about new technologies [6]. In future work, we will combine the two studies to give common findings and suggestions for legislative and executive actions.

Acknowledgments. This research paper originates from the German Centre for Rail Traffic Research (DZSF) project "Study Security & New Technologies". We will publish the full report soon [8].

A Sample Questions from the Online Questionnaire

1. What cybersecurity measures is your company pursuing?
2. What percentage of your company's revenue do you plan to spend on cybersecurity over the next 3 years?
3. What percentage of your company's staff are full-time equivalents dedicated to cybersecurity?

4. What forms of cyberattacks have occurred in your company in the last 3 years?
5. How many of the cyberattacks mentioned in the previous question have occurred as a total in your company in the last 3 years?
6. How do you assess the current cyber security risk considering current technologies in your company?
7. What benefits does your company see for implementing cybersecurity?
8. What obstacles may be standing in the way of your company's cybersecurity goal?
9. What was the average loss you incurred from cyberattacks in the last 3 years, as a percentage of your company's revenue?
10. Which statement(s) best describes the cybersecurity strategy in place at your company?
11. Does your company have a cybersecurity officer role?
12. Does your company have a strategy in place to sustainably counter attacks?
13. Does your company ensure that all employees are trained in cybersecurity?
14. Has your company implemented a monitoring process to assess cybersecurity awareness?
15. Are employees in your company able to identify and report cybersecurity anomalies?
16. Does your company have established processes for dealing with acute cybersecurity attacks?
25. Has your company defined measures for dealing with an acute cybersecurity attack?
40. Have you identified assets and their potential protection needs of the IT infrastructure used in your company?
41. Have you conducted a vulnerability assessment of the IT infrastructure deployed in your organization?
42. Have you conducted a threat analysis of the IT infrastructure used in your company?
57. Do you have measures in place to ensure cybersecurity in the supply chain at your company?

B   Interview Questions Adapted to Each Interview Partner

– *If, in the online questionnaire, the company stated to have a strategy for a certain NIST function, but we calculated a low degree of maturity for that function:*
  • You stated that your cybersecurity strategy includes measures to ensure *[description of the function in question]*. Please explain how these are implemented in your company.
– *For each criterion mentioned in the online questionnaire to impede the improvement of cybersecurity within the company:*

- You stated that *[description of the criterion]* might be impeding the improvement of cybersecurity within your company. We would like to elaborate on that. Why is the *[description of the criterion]* missing, in your opinion?
- *The question depends on whether or not the company stated to provide cybersecurity training to their employees.*
  - *If they do not:* You stated that employees do not receive cybersecurity training. Why was a decision against such training made?
  - *If they do:* You stated to provide training for cybersecurity to your employees. Please provide further detail for this training.[If they were not addressed in the answer, the following details would be inquired individually: frequency of training, obligation to complete training, the scope of the training, and review of understanding after the training]
- *For new technologies that the company stated to be using and highly knowledgeable about:*
  - You stated to be using *[description of the new technology]* or to at least be conducting a pilot run with it. What are currently, or have been in the past, the biggest impediments in the use of this technology?

References

1. Adams, W.C.: Conducting semi-structured interviews. In: Handbook of Practical Program Evaluation, pp. 492–505. John Wiley & Sons, Inc. (2015). https://doi.org/10.1002/9781119171386.ch19
2. Becker, J., Knackstedt, R., Pöppelbuß, J.: Developing maturity models for IT management. Bus. Inf. Syst. Eng. **1**(3), 213–222 (2009). https://doi.org/10.1007/s12599-009-0044-5
3. Framework for improving critical infrastructure cybersecurity, version 1.1. Technical report, National Institute of Standards and Technology (2017)
4. Leigh, D.: SWOT analysis. In: Handbook of Improving Performance in the Workplace: vol. 1–3, pp. 115–140 (2019). John Wiley & Sons, Inc. https://doi.org/10.1002/9780470592663.ch24
5. Liveri, D., Theocharidou, M., Naydenov, R.: Railway cybersecurity. Technical report, European Union Agency for Cybersecurity, ENISA (2021). https://www.enisa.europa.eu/publications/railway-cybersecurity/@@download/fullReport
6. Möller, D., et al.: Emerging technologies in the era of digital transformation: state of the art in the railway sector. In: Proceedings of the 19th International Conference on Informatics in Control, Automation and Robotics - ICINCO, pp. 721–728. INSTICC, SciTePress (2022)
7. Möller, D.P.F.: Cybersecurity in Digital Transformation. SCSSN, Springer, Cham (2020). https://doi.org/10.1007/978-3-030-60570-4
8. Nord, M., Leppla, B., Möller, D., Krause, P., Lenski, N., Czerkewski, P.: Studie Security und geplanter Technologieeinsatz. Technical report, Deutsches Zentrum für Schienenverkehrsforschung beim Eisenbahn-Bundesamt (2022). https://doi.org/10.48755/dzsf.220011.01

The Understanding of Vulnerability of Critical Infrastructure

Amelia Tomalska(✉) [iD]

University of Warsaw, Krakowskie Przedmieście 26/28, 00-927 Warsaw, Poland
aj.tomalska@uw.edu.pl

Abstract. The aim of this paper is to present a problem of insufficient understanding of vulnerability of critical infrastructure. The paper looks at this issue with regard to the definition of vulnerability of critical infrastructure, its content as well as the limitations of current approaches to critical infrastructure protection. The recent events linked to the Covid-19 crisis showed the necessity to shift current approach to critical infrastructure protection from prevention-oriented to resilient-based. The implemented in this research methodology is based on a critical analysis of the existing literature.

Specifically, this paper emphasizes the need to understand the concept of vulnerability of critical infrastructure in terms of attributes of the system rather than flaws. It also highlights the marginalization of identification of vulnerability of critical infrastructure only to pre-event actions and its limited applicability solely to physical domain. Due to inability to foresee and prevent all threats from occurring, the approach to critical infrastructure protection requires adaptation of a new strategy based on identification of root causes of vulnerability related to capacity, competence and performance of critical infrastructure.

Keywords: critical infrastructure · vulnerability identification · resilience · protection

1 Introduction

Critical infrastructure is a broad term that still evolves. Generally speaking critical infrastructure provides the most important services to society such as water, food, financial, ICT, energy, transportation and health services. Any dysfunction of critical infrastructure poses a threat to continuity of functioning of the country and the well-being of citizens [1]. Therefore, effective protection of critical infrastructure is crucial, but it also poses a great challenge, what exemplify recent events. Namely, the Covid-19 pandemic proved that the security of critical infrastructure for a long time has been taken for granted. The pandemic caused the change in demands for critical services, what found many critical infrastructure operators unprepared to respond effectively [2]. It also revealed the importance of vulnerability identification that has been marginalized or not included in risk assessment methodologies [3]. In case of future unexpected or difficult to estimate threats, the identification of root causes of vulnerability of critical infrastructure plays a

B. Hämmerli et al. (Eds.): CRITIS 2022, LNCS 13723, pp. 241–248, 2023.
https://doi.org/10.1007/978-3-031-35190-7_17

vital role. However, to comprehend the applicability of the concept of vulnerability of critical infrastructure, it is necessary to first understand the meaning of this term. This would contribute to enhancing the resilience of critical infrastructure by eliminating or reducing the vulnerabilities of critical infrastructure that might contribute to crisis situation or any kind of the incapacitation. The situation caused by Covid-19 can be used as a lesson learnt which might in future contribute to more effective protection of critical infrastructure based on resilience with identification of vulnerabilities and application of appropriate countermeasures.

2 Limitations of the Current Understanding of Vulnerability of Critical Infrastructure

The concept of vulnerability of critical infrastructure is relatively new and it still evolves [4]. Broadly speaking, vulnerability of critical infrastructure is a term which does not have one, common definition. It can be defined as a flaw or weakness in the design, implementation, operation or management of the critical infrastructure which makes it more susceptible to incapacitation when exposed to a threat [5]. ISO 27001 describes vulnerability as "a weakness of an asset or control that could potentially be exploited by one or more threats." [6]. The perception of vulnerability in this case is evaluative, identifying vulnerability with some kind of an error made at different stages. This however is not always the case. According to other definitions, vulnerability of critical infrastructure can be described as an operational attribute, physical feature that makes critical infrastructure more susceptible to exploitation by a threat, or as a system property focusing on degree of consequences in relation to the impact of a threat, degree of exposure to the threats and degree of resilience [5, 7]. These definitions do not indicate the necessary negative aspect of vulnerability, but rather define it as a feature of the system. This approach seems to be more accurate, especially in case of vulnerabilities resulting from interdependencies between different critical infrastructures or environmental contexts within which the system is embedded [8]. In that event vulnerability should not be understood as a flaw, but rather as an attribute of the system.

It should also be noted that presented definitions suggest the dual nature of vulnerability, namely its physical, technical dimension relating to the vulnerabilities of the hard-components and its operational, social character referring to established procedures and management capabilities. However, due to adopted in many European Union countries understanding of critical infrastructure in terms of assets or hard technologies, the physical as well as operational dimension of vulnerability would relate to vulnerabilities affecting only those critical objects, facilities [9, 10]. Recent events linked to Covid-19 pandemic proved that critical infrastructure has grown in scope to include the network of people who are essential in terms of operating of critical infrastructure, but also in scale. Namely, the crisis spawned by the outbreak of Covid-19 exposed the importance of frontline health care workers as well as the healthcare system dependency on other systems, including transport of necessary equipment such as personal protective equipment or ventilators to hospitals [11]. It demonstrates that critical infrastructure should rather be perceived as an interconnected process, aiming to deliver essential service, which involves various stakeholders. Such understanding of critical infrastructure is in line with the recently proposed European Union Directive on the resilience of critical entities, which defines critical infrastructure as critical entities providing essential services [12]. This shift in defining critical infrastructure as a complex system composed of technological and social components implies the necessity to rethink the notion of vulnerability, which should also be more elaborate and applicable to other domains [10, 13].

Moreover, it should be emphasized that the previously mentioned definitions of vulnerability have one crucial aspect in common, namely the threat-centric perception of vulnerability. Meaning that the vulnerability identification is driven by the set of identified threats to critical infrastructure. The spectrum of threats that could affect critical infrastructure is usually broad, including physical, cyber-attacks, natural disasters or accidents occurring on daily basis [14]. They are however mostly physically, cyber-oriented what also results from aforementioned understanding of critical infrastructure through the prism of objects, assets. Accordingly, the risk management methods focus mostly on asset hardening, physical resistance of critical infrastructure to endure the identified threats and to prevent critical infrastructure from failure [15]. Due to fast changing threat landscape, including the unpredictability of future impacts of climate change on critical infrastructure, state-sponsored hybrid actions, biological threats or new technologies, traditional approach to protection of critical infrastructure based on prevention seems to be ineffective. In case of black swan events, such as the Covid-19 pandemic, difficult to foresee, precisely estimate and prepare for, the overreliance on prepared in advance protection plans with risk assessment based on identification of vulnerabilities to selected threats might endanger the undisturbed continuity of functioning of critical infrastructure [16–18].

In addition, due to concentration on identification and assessment of threats, the risk management cycle refers to the vulnerability only in the context of pre-event actions such as prevention, protection and pre-event mitigation. This implies that the drivers of vulnerability would be considered only before the occurrence of the threat and the damage. The vulnerability then would be identified solely in terms of capabilities to detect the possible threats and to determine the scale of potential consequences. This means that the vulnerabilities relating to post-event actions such as mitigation, response and recovery would not be considered [19, 20]. It should be emphasized that the reduction of vulnerabilities before they occur as failures is crucial. Nevertheless, due to increasing level of interdependencies and interconnectivity of critical infrastructure, the capability of critical infrastructure operator to react to and respond to future unanticipated threats as well as adapt to changes rather than only overcome them is becoming more and more important [21]. Furthermore, the growing complexity of critical infrastructure creates additional vulnerabilities to the system which might as well result in indirect, cascading consequences not limited to one domain. Therefore, it is becoming very difficult to precisely analyze all of the components of critical infrastructure and estimate their vulnerabilities prior the adverse event [15]. This suggests the need to focus on vulnerabilities that might negatively influence the response actions and degree of loss after the adverse event [19]. It requires taking into consideration not only current vulnerabilities to specific, identified threats, but also system's potential vulnerabilities to the future, unknown events, combined with expectation of inability to prevent all threats from occurring and capability to respond to them [8].

3 The Multidimensional Nature of Vulnerability of Critical Infrastructure

To make critical infrastructure more secure, especially in case of future unknown unknowns, the designed and applied countermeasures should focus on enhancing critical infrastructure resilience. The term resilience can be understood as "the ability of an infrastructure to prepare to cope with changing conditions and adapt to them, and to resist and recover rapidly from disruption, including deliberate attacks, accidents or natural events" [22]. The level of resilience of critical infrastructure is largely determined by the process of identification of vulnerabilities. However, the implementation of resilient approach to critical infrastructure protection requires a paradigm shift from the focus on threats towards identification, assessment and management of vulnerabilities [21]. The identification of root causes of vulnerability should consider broader scope of critical infrastructure domains where vulnerabilities might be embedded at different stages of operating, namely before as well as after the occurrence of the adverse event.

Considering critical infrastructure as a complex system, composed of various, interacting components, the root causes of vulnerability can be divided into following factors:

• capacity, which would include mission identification, supporting system identification, dependencies and interdependencies, system reconstitution and related to them infrastructure, equipment and staff;

• competence relating to knowledge and skills of personnel including operation and management attributes such as responsibilities, communication, organization, logistics, knowledge about the environment in which critical infrastructure operates and critical infrastructure endurability;

• performance understood as capability of critical infrastructure to function under all circumstances and public-private cooperation in protection of critical infrastructure [4, 14].

The first factor, referring to capacity of critical infrastructure, aims to identify vulnerabilities related to identification of the critical infrastructure most important functions to fulfil the mission of the delivery of essential service. It requires thorough analysis of the processes, sub-processes and supporting them key assets, systems, networks, hardware, software and also essential staff. This also involves identification of internal and external dependencies and interdependencies between infrastructures. As a result of in-depth analysis of the system, through conduct of the Business Process Analysis (BPA) and Business Impact Analysis (BIA), critical infrastructure operator will be able to identify existing vulnerabilities and apply proper countermeasures or prepare for potential vulnerabilities resulting from identified relationships between infrastructures as cascading failures [23, 24]. The conduct of BIA, defined as: "a process of analyzing operational functions and the effect that a disruption might have upon them" would also enable to gather required information to prepare business continuity plan [25, 26]. The analysis of capacity of critical infrastructure would also involve understanding and estimation of reconstitution time in case of occurrence of the adverse event including acceptable time delays, repair parts requisitions and fix implementation. Moreover, this would enable to prioritize the most important parts of critical infrastructure system, crucial for the delivery of essential services to the country and society under all circumstances. It should also be noted that the critical infrastructure as an entity is not static and therefore requires constant technology upgrades. The recognition of critical infrastructure capacity is crucial not only in order to understand the system better and eliminate the vulnerabilities, but also to be able to react more effectively in case of crisis caused by impossible to mitigate vulnerabilities [14].

The second factor, namely the competence, relates to the importance of organizational resilience. According to ISO 22301 competence is described as an "ability to apply knowledge and skills to achieve intended results" [25]. It involves issues such as internal organization of critical infrastructure, the management skills of the personnel and knowledge about internal and external factors, which might affect critical infrastructure operations. The PESTLE framework can be used to monitor and analyze the environment within which critical infrastructure functions, and notice any changing conditions. The PESTLE acronym stands for Political, Economic, Social, Technological, Legal and Environmental factors which might create vulnerabilities that can affect critical infrastructure [27]. The clear division of roles and responsibilities, as well as implementation of the procedures and policies are crucial, however they should not be overestimated. The competence is directly linked to ability to adapt to unexpected crisis situation for which procedures, rules have not been prepared. To mitigate the possible vulnerabilities caused by this factor, the trainings, exercises are required to test the existing strategies, communication within organization and with other stakeholders as well as the ability of the staff to be creative and innovative when faced with unanticipated problems. These exogenous and endogenous factors need to be addressed in order to facilitate adaptation of critical infrastructure to changing conditions. Moreover, in case of endurability the development and constant update of prepared contingency plans, back-up systems, spares are necessary in order to reduce the effects of adverse events and to maintain the critical functions of critical infrastructure [8, 27].

The performance factor relates to capabilities of critical infrastructure and public-private partnership. The term capability refers to a capacity combined with competence. It relates to comprehensive implementation and management of all resources required for critical infrastructure to operate. It highlights the need of holistic approach to identification of vulnerabilities at different stages, namely before, during and after the adverse event. It directly relates to the required capabilities of critical infrastructure to anticipate, absorb, adapt to and recover from a disruptive event. It includes the onsite and offsite capabilities relating to crisis management. The onside capabilities include measures undertaken by critical infrastructure operator aiming to implement following properties which characterize the resilient system, namely: robustness, redundancy, resourcefulness and rapidity [17, 28]. The offside capabilities involve the interactions, information exchange between critical infrastructure operator and public sector such as law enforcement, emergency medical response, fire response or intelligence services. These actions would help to raise awareness of the complexity of the system, including dependencies and interdependencies between critical infrastructures and thereby prepare suitable strategies, protection plans and programs [29]. The effective cooperation between emergency responders and critical infrastructure operator, based on agreed procedures, joint exercises, trainings would help to eliminate the vulnerabilities which might hinder the coordination and response actions to all disruptive events [20]. In addition, the cross-sectoral partnerships between critical infrastructure operators involving civil society should be established in the process of building resilient critical infrastructure [30].

4   Conclusions

For a long time the identification of vulnerability of critical infrastructure has been under-estimated and mostly referred to physical flaws of critical infrastructure. Due to fast changing threat landscape, growing complexity and interconnectedness between critical infrastructures, the protection of critical infrastructure requires a shift from prevention-based approach to resilience-based [9]. It should be highlighted that the resilience of critical infrastructure is largely determined by the process of identification of vulnera-bilities. In this case, the vulnerability should rather be understood in terms of features or attributes of the system. The identification of root causes of vulnerability of critical infrastructure should include the wider scope of domains where vulnerabilities might be embedded, taking also into account the post-event stage. This would require the analy-sis of the following factors, namely the capacity, competence and performance. These factors reflect the complex nature of critical infrastructure, which consists of various, interacting technical and social components, which to manage require adequate skills and knowledge as well as onside and offside capabilities to identify vulnerabilities which might hamper crisis management actions, and also well-functioning public-private coop-eration [4, 14]. The proper identification of vulnerabilities would enable to understand the system better and notice any warning signs which might result in crisis situation. Consequently, these actions would contribute greatly to more secure and resilient critical infrastructure.

References

1. Klaver, M., Luiijf, H., Nieuwenhuijsen, A.: RECIPE : good practices manual for Cip policies, for policy makers in Europe (2011)
2. Carvalhaes, T., Markolf, S., Helmrich, A., Kim, Y., Li, R., Natarajan, M., et al.: COVID-19 as a Harbinger of Transforming Infrastructure Resilience. Frontiers in Built Environ. 6(148), 1–8 (2020). https://doi.org/10.3389/fbuil.2020.00148
3. Theocharidou, M., Giannopoulos, G.: Risk Assessment Methodologies for Critical Infras-tructure Protection. Part II: a New Approach, Joint Research Centre, European Commission, Luxembourg (2015). https://doi.org/10.2788/621843
4. Zio, E.: Challenges in the vulnerability and risk analysis of critical infrastructures. Reliab. Eng. Syst. Saf. 152, 137–150 (2016). https://doi.org/10.1016/j.ress.2016.02.009
5. Kröger, W., Zio, E.: Vulnerable Systems. Springer (2011). https://doi.org/10.1007/978-0-85729-655-9
6. ISO, BS: 27001: 2013. Information technology – Security techniques – Information security management systems - Requirements. BSI (2013)
7. Department of Homeland Security, DHS Risk Lexicon- 2010 edition, Washington, DC (2010). 21 Apr 2022 https://www.dhs.gov/xlibrary/assets/dhs-risk-lexicon-2010.pdf
8. Brooks, N.: Vulnerability, risk and adaptation: A conceptual framework. Tyndall Centre Working Papers, 38, (2003)

9. Tomalska, A.: Preparing critical infrastructure for the future: Lessons learnt from the Covid-19 pandemic. Secur. Defence Q. (2022). https://doi.org/10.35467/sdq/146603

10. Egan, M.: Anticipating future vulnerability: defining characteristics of increasingly critical infrastructure-like systems. J. Contingencies Crisis Manage. **15**, 4–17 (2007). https://doi.org/10.1111/j.1468-5973.2007.00500.x

11. Ranney, M., Griffeth, V., Jha, A.: Critical Supply Shortages - The Need for Ventilators and Personal Protective Equipment during the Covid-19 Pandemic. N. Engl. J. Med. **382**(18), e41 (2020). https://doi.org/10.1056/NEJMp2006141

12. European Commission: Proposal for a Directive of the European Parliament and of the Council on the resilience of critical entities. COM (2020) 829 final. European Commission, Brussels (2020)

13. Galbusera, L., Cardarilli, M., Giannopoulos, G.: The ERNCIP Survey on COVID-19: Emergency & business continuity for fostering resilience in critical infrastructures. Saf. Sci. **105161**, 139 (2021). https://doi.org/10.1016/j.ssci.2021.105161

14. Baker, G.: A Vulnerability Assessment Methodology for Critical Infrastructure Sites. In DHS Symposium: Rand D Partnerships in Department of Homeland Security, Boston, Massachusetts (2005)

15. Linkov, I., Bridges, T., Creutzig, F., Decker, J., Fox-Lent, C., Kröger, W., et al.: Changing the resilience paradigm. Nat. Clim. Chang. **4**(6), 407–409 (2014). https://doi.org/10.1038/nclimate2227

16. Mishra, P.: COVID-19, Black Swan events and the future of disaster risk management in India. Progress in Disaster Science, 8 (2020). https://doi.org/10.1016/j.pdisas.2020.100137

17. Longstaff, P.: Security, resilience, and communication in unpredictable environments such as terrorism, natural disasters, and complex technology. Harvard University, Cambridge, Massachusetts, Center for Information Policy Research (2005)

18. Schmid, B., Raju, E., Jensen, P.: COVID-19 and business continuity – Learning from the private sector and humanitarian actors in Kenya. Prog. Disaster Sci. **11**, 1–8 (2021). https://doi.org/10.1016/j.pdisas.2021.100181

19. McGill, W., Ayyub, B.: The meaning of vulnerability in the context of critical infrastructure protection, in Critical infrastructure protection: Elements of risk, pp.25–48, George Mason University, Fairfax (2007)

20. Petit, F., Bassett, G., Black, R., Buehring, W., Collins, M., Dickinson, D., et al.: Resilience measurement index: An indicator of critical infrastructure resilience, Office of Scientific and Technical Information (OSTI), Argonne National Laboratory (2013)

21. Cardona, O., Van Aalst, M., Birkmann, J., Fordham, M., McGregor, G., Rosa, P., et al.: Determinants of risk: Exposure and vulnerability. In: Managing the Risks of Extreme Events and Disasters to Advance Climate Change Adaptation: Special Report of the Intergovernmental Panel on Climate Change. Cambridge University Press, pp. 65–108 (2012).https://doi.org/10.1017/CBO9781139177245.005

22. Presidential Policy Directive – PPD21: Critical Infrastructure Security and Resilience (2013). Available at: https://obamawhitehouse.archives.gov/the-press-office/2013/02/12/presidential-policy-directive-critical-infrastructure-security-and-resil, last accessed: 2022/03/24

23. Federal Emergency Management Agency: Business Process Analysis and Business Impact Analysis User Guide, DC: Department of Homeland Security (2019)

24. Cybersecurity & Infrastructure Security Agency: National Critical Functions Status Update to the Critical Infrastructure Community, U.S. Department of Homeland Security (2020)

25. ISO, BS: 22301: 2012. Societal security. Business continuity management systems. Requirements. BSI (2012)

26. Torabi, S.A., Rezaei Soufi, H., Sahebjamnia, N.: A new framework for business impact analysis in business continuity management (with a case study). Saf. Sci. **68**, 309–323 (2014). https://doi.org/10.1016/j.ssci.2014.04.017

27. Anwar, M., Gill, A., Fitzgibbon, A., Gull, I.: PESTLE+ risk analysis model to assess pandemic preparedness of digital ecosystems. Secur. Priv. **5**(1), e187 (2022). https://doi.org/10.1002/spy2.187
28. Bruneau, M., Chang, S., Eguchi, R., Lee, G., O'Rourke, T., Reinhorn, A., et al.: A framework to quantitatively assess and enhance seismic resilience of communities. Earthquake Spectra, (19)4, pp. 733–752, (2003). https://doi.org/10.1193/1.1623497
29. Fisher, M., Gamper, C.: Policy evaluation framework on the governance of critical infrastructure resilience. Inter-American Development Bank, Washington, D.C. (2017)
30. Monstadt, J., Schmidt, M.: Urban resilience in the making? The governance of critical infrastructures in German cities. Urban Stud. **56**(11), 2353–2371 (2019). https://doi.org/10.1177/0042098018808483

Is There a Relationship Between Grid Operators' Cybersecurity Level and Electricity Outages?

Øyvind Toftegaard[1,2]([✉]), Bernhard Hämmerli[2,3], and Jon-Martin Storm[4,5]

[1] The Norwegian Energy Regulatory Authority, Oslo, Norway
oyvintof@stud.ntnu.no
[2] Norwegian University of Science and Technology, Gjøvik, Norway
[3] Lucerne School of Computer Science and Information Technology,
Luzern, Switzerland
[4] The Norwegian Water Resources and Energy Directorate, Oslo, Norway
[5] University of Oslo, Oslo, Norway

Abstract. The main causes of electric power outages are natural calamity and various technical challenges. Technical challenges include cyber issues. We have used a correlation analysis to explore relationships between 56 Norwegian grid operators' cybersecurity levels and outages. We have collected technical risk scores through BlackKite's technical cyber rating tool and management risk scores from a survey performed by the Norwegian Water Resources and Energy Directorate. Further, we collected outage data from the Norwegian Transmission System Operator. Our results show no clear relationship between grid operators' cybersecurity level and outages. In an extension of our analysis, we found strong correlation between distribution substations and load disconnectors, and outages. Future work may therefore concentrate on cybersecurity specifically for these two grid component categories.

Keywords: Cybersecurity · Electricity · Power · Outage

1 Introduction

Electrical power was available 99.9% of the time in Norway in 2020 [6]. However, this still meant that every customer on average experienced 2 outages of more than 3 min. On average, every customer experienced 2 h and 13 min without electricity during 2020. Even shorter outages may have consequences such as a smelter facility's material will become solid, or people can't call for assistance during a medical emergency. The consequences of such outages are therefore considerable and should be avoided.

Our definition of outages is all types of unplanned electricity loss, including very short periods of electricity loss. With blackouts, we understand larger outages with many affected customers. With cascading effects, we understand an

B. Hämmerli et al. (Eds.): CRITIS 2022, LNCS 13723, pp. 249–255, 2023.
https://doi.org/10.1007/978-3-031-35190-7_18

event where a series of outages leads to a blackout. With cyber rating, we understand an objective and non-intrusive measurement of an organization's technical security performance.

In this paper, we explore the relationships between the number and duration of outages that Norwegian grid operators have reported, and the cybersecurity level of these grid operators. This paper is structured as follows: In Sect. 2, we make a short introduction to previous research on the causes of outages and how it relates to cybersecurity. In Sect. 3, we explain the methodology we apply to analyze if there are any relationships between grid operator's cybersecurity level and outages. In Sect. 4 we present the results of our analysis, which we subsequently discuss in Sect. 5.

2   Previous Research

In an analysis of the impact of cyberattacks on power system blackouts [3], the authors investigated the causes of the largest 3% of 955 blackouts in North America. The causes identified were cascade outage, earthquake, wildfire, geomagnetic storm, extreme climate, sabotage, and equipment failure. The authors pointed out the potential impact of cascading effects and that a coordinated software-based attack may have a higher impact than physical sabotage.

A large amount of research is done on the causes of electricity blackouts and measures to ensure blackouts do not occur again. According to [4], numerous factors are involved when operating a power system, making blackouts very complex to understand. The authors claim no principles have been found at the current stage of research, that define the properties of blackouts. Similar to in [3], the authors enhance the large consequences of cascading failures.

The authors in [7] have classified types of blackouts and conducted a statistical summary from 2011 to 2021. Cyber issues are one of their classes. Although, as illustrated in Table 1, cyber issues are by far the smallest class, it may be perceived as significant since the authors have chosen to give it an individual class.

Table 1. Statistics of blackouts globally (2011–2021) [7].

Blackout class	Average population affected (mill/year)	Average occurrences/year
Natural calamity	50	4.2
Transmission failure	70	1.9
Generation failure	100	1.8
Cyber issues	5	1
Human/equipment/unknown error	20	1.5

In the next section, we describe our research design for identifying relationships between outages and the cybersecurity level of Norwegian grid operators.

3 Methodology

We have used a correlation analysis to explore relationships between cybersecurity risk indicators and electricity outages from a sample of 56 Norwegian grid operators. We expect any relationship between cybersecurity level and electricity outages to be linear and therefore applied Pearson's r as correlation coefficient.

We collected technical risk indicators through a passive evaluation of grid operators during March 2022 using BlackKite's Technical Cyber Rating tool [2]. Their tool returned scores for 19 cybersecurity categories as listed in the leftmost columns of Table 2. The scores were provided as ordinal data in form of letter grades from A - F. We converted the letter grades for each technical risk indicator to value 6 to 1, where 6 represented the highest cybersecurity level.

The Norwegian Water Resources and Energy Directorate surveyed Norwegian grid operators on cybersecurity in May 2021 [5]. The survey included 20 questions about the internal organization of cybersecurity management and the implementation of security measures (see middle columns of Table 2). We utilized the raw data from that survey to indicate the grid operator's internal security management level. The raw data was provided as ordinal data with Yes/No answers or levels of fulfillment of the various categories (see middle columns of Table 2). We gave "Yes"-answer value 10 and "No" the value 0. If hours of cybersecurity education were less than 1 per week, we set the value 0, while for 1 or more hours we set the value 10. We gave the answer "Small" value 0, "Moderate" value 5, and "Large" value 10. We gave Basic ICT versions value 0 and advanced value 10. If the answer "Never" were given we set the value 0, we gave "Seldom" the value 5, and "Often" the value 10. For answers "Don't know" for any of the categories, we set the value 0.

We also collected detailed data on time, duration, number, and causes of outages for 2021 from the Norwegian Transmission System Operator's reporting system Fosweb [1] (see rightmost columns of Table 2). Our access to outage data including their causes enabled us to filter out and remove outages caused by natural calamity and attrition. This left us with technical or technically related causes for outages in our data set.

4 Results

Table 3 shows r-values for the number and duration of outages, and the 39 cybersecurity risk indicators. An r-value of 1 means perfect correlation and if r is 0 it means no correlation. If r is negative, it's an inverse relationship, indicating that a higher security level would reduce the number or duration of outages.

Table 4 lists correlation values between the number of outages and the 19 grid components. Figure 1 illustrates the relationship between the number of outages and the highest correlating two grid components. An r^2-value above 0.9 indicates the explained variance is above 90%. We have included our regression model in the figure, where y = total number of outages, x_1 = distribution substations, x_2 = load disconnectors and a,b,c = coefficients of our regression analysis.

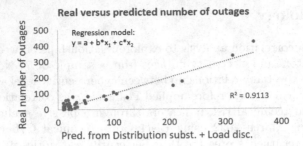

Fig. 1. Real outages vs prediction from Distribution substations + Load disconnectors.

5   Discussion

Our correlation analysis of 39 cybersecurity risk indicators as shown in Table 3 exhibited low correlation between all 39 indicators and the number and duration of outages. The correlation between the number and duration of outages in itself is high (OD in Table 3). This makes sense as the higher the number of outages the longer the duration without electricity. The low r-values for the 39 indicators, suggests there are other factors than cybersecurity that are much more heavily related to outages. Therefore, this correlation analysis supports the outcome, that the cybersecurity level is not a prominent reason for outages in Norway in 2021, as cybersecurity risk indicators do not show a correlation to the number of outages.

There may be weaknesses in our research design that resulted in the low correlation. When using ordinal data we do not know the variations between the classes. Therefore, it could have impacted the result of our analysis if either all data had been collected as continuous variables, or if we had used a rank correlation analysis such as Spearman's ρ instead of Pearson's r. Further, 56 grid operators are a low number of subjects for any correlation analysis. We also have a challenge with incongruent time as technical risk data was collected in 2022 while the remaining data was collected in 2021. Last, the Norwegian grid operators turned out to have a quite homogeneous level of cybersecurity, making correlation analysis more difficult. For technical risk indicators, 63% of all scores registered were 6, and for management risk indicators, 56% of all scores registered were 10. Despite these weaknesses, we believe the very low r-values reported in Table 3, indicate a low likelihood of finding any relationship there.

As our results indicate that cybersecurity does not lead to outages, we extended our analysis to look for prominent grid component categories related to outages. The results presented in Table 4 show high correlation, above 0.9, for two grid component categories: Distribution substations and load disconnectors. A regression analysis of these two parameters shows the good accordance with the linear model (see Fig. 1), with an r^2 value at 0.9113. Based on this result it could be interesting in the future, to assess whether the cybersecurity of distribution substations and load disconnectors can be related to outages.

Table 2. 39 cybersecurity risk indicators and 19 grid component categories.

Nr	Technical risk	Indicator	Nr	Management risk	Indicator	Nr	Grid comp
1	DNS Health	Grade (1–6)	20	ICT-strategy	Yes/No	1	Unidentified part
2	Email Security	Grade (1–6)	21	ICT security strategy	Yes/No	2	Circuit breaker
3	SSL/TLS Strength	Grade (1–6)	22	ICT security in meetings	Never/ Seldom/ Often	3	Distribution substation
4	Application Security	Grade (1–6)	23	ICT contingency in meetings	Yes/No	4	Installation (wiring)
5	DDoS Resiliency	Grade (1–6)	24	ICT or SCADA security exercise last 12 months	Yes/No	5	Wiring cabinet
6	Network Security	Grade (1–6)	25	ICT security audits in management meeting last 12 months	Yes/No	6	Power cable
7	Fraudulent Domains	Grade (1–6)	26	Incidents reported in management meeting last 12 months	Yes/No	7	Power line
8	Fraudulent Apps	Grade (1–6)	27	ICT versions procured	Basic/ Advanced	8	Load disconnector
9	Credential Management	Grade (1–6)	28	Home office risk discussed by management last 2 years	Yes/No	9	Substation
10	IP Reputation	Grade (1–6)	29	Digitalisation risk discussed by management	Yes/No	10	Busbar
11	Hacktivist Shares	Grade (1–6)	30	Information security certification (e.g. ISO27001)	Yes/No	11	Signal transmission
12	Social Network	Grade (1–6)	31	Hours a week per employee for cybersecurity education	Hours	12	Fuse
13	Attack Surface	Grade (1–6)	32	Security accounted for in pilot projects	Small/Mod./ Large	13	Fuse switch disconnector
14	Brand Monitoring	Grade (1–6)	33	Management's security culture	Small/Mod./ Large	14	Disconnector switch
15	Patch Management	Grade (1–6)	34	Management's threat awareness	Small/Mod./ Large	15	Voltage transformer
16	Web Ranking	Grade (1–6)	35	Cybersecurity education of managers (legal requirements)	Small/Mod./ Large	16	Power station supply
17	Information Disclosure	Grade (1–6)	36	Cybersecurity education of managers (risk management)	Small/Mod./ Large	17	Current transformer
18	CDN Security	Grade (1–6)	37	Use of annual sectorial threat report	Yes/No	18	System failure
19	Website Security	Grade (1–6)	38	Management knowledge of cybersecurity procurement rules	Yes/No	19	Protective relay
			39	Fulfillment of cybersecurity procurement rules	Small/Mod./ Large		

Table 3. Correlation of outages, their duration, and the 39 security risk indicators. OD = Correlation between the number of outages and their duration. NA = Not applicable.

Nr	Outages (r-value)	Duration (r-value)	Nr	Outages (r-value)	Duration (r-value)	Nr	Outages (r-value)	Duration (r-value)	Nr	Outages (r-value)	Duration (r-value)
OD		0.939	10	-0.033	-0.009	20	0.096	0.097	30	NA	NA
1	-0.013	0.015	11	NA	NA	21	-0.003	-0.007	31	0.048	0.005
2	0.152	0.155	12	NA	NA	22	0.302	0.328	32	0.354	0.405
3	-0.129	-0.111	13	-0.114	-0.100	23	0.121	0.143	33	0.204	0.224
4	-0.398	-0.370	14	0.419	0.380	24	0.206	0.194	34	0.155	0.153
5	-0.023	-0.062	15	-0.066	-0.105	25	0.069	0.155	35	0.041	0.119
6	0.068	0.084	16	0.219	0.254	26	-0.082	-0.003	36	0.114	0.165
7	0.063	-0.004	17	-0.058	-0.022	27	NA	NA	37	0.157	0.143
8	NA	NA	18	-0.106	-0.106	28	-0.151	-0.214	38	-0.010	0.003
9	-0.281	-0.295	19	0.338	0.341	29	0.069	0.105	39	0.259	0.296

Table 4. Correlation of outages and the 19 grid component categories.

Nr	Outages (r-value)	Nr	Outages (r-value)	Nr	Outages (r-value)	Nr	Outages (r-value)	Nr	Outages (r-value)
1	0.832	5	0.331	9	0.465	13	0.175	17	0.605
2	0.654	6	0.860	10	0.668	14	0.764	18	0.059
3	0.933	7	0.793	11	0.614	15	0.568	19	0.748
4	0.788	8	0.950	12	0.724	16	-0.048		

6   Conclusion

We did not identify any clear relationship between the cybersecurity level of Norwegian grid operators and electric power outages. Our results demonstrate there are other factors than cybersecurity that are much more heavily related to outages. While continuing to care for natural calamity risk, grid operators should maintain a high level of cybersecurity to avoid other cyber-related consequences.

In the future, outages may be connected statistically with the grid operator's cybersecurity level. Therefore, government bodies may continuously perform a similar analysis to what we have presented in this paper, and if such monitoring shows a clear relationship between cybersecurity level and outages, cybersecurity focus and investments should be prioritized accordingly in the sector.

Future research may focus on whether the cybersecurity of distribution substations and load disconnectors can be related to outages. If so, securing these components with for example monitoring and redundancy mechanisms could reduce the number and duration of outages.

Acknowledgments. We would like to thank Dr. Susanne Nikolic at Lucerne School of Computer Science and Information Technology for providing recommendations on the methodology for our correlation analysis.

References

1. Fosweb. Accessed 15 Aug 2022 https://www.statnett.no/for-aktorer-i-kraftbransje
   n/systemansvaret/fosweb/
2. Technical Cyber Rating. Accessed 15 Aug 2022. https://blackkite.com/technical-
   grade/
3. Sheng, S., Yingkun, W., Yuyi, L., Yong, L., Yu, J.: Cyber attack impact on power
   system blackout. IET Conference publications, pp. 1–5 (2011)
4. Gou, B., Zheng, H., Wu, W., Yu, X.: The Statistical Law of Power System Blackouts.
   In: 38th North American Power Symposium, pp. 495–501. IEEE, USA (2006)
5. Tøien, F., Fagermyr, J., Treider, G., Remvang, H.: IKT-sikkerhetstilstanden i kraft-
   forsyningen 2021. Norwegian Water Resources and Energy Directorate, Oslo (2021)
6. Avbruddsstatistikk. Accessed 15 Aug 2022. https://www.nve.no/reguleringsmyn
   digheten/publikasjoner-og-data/statistikk/avbruddsstatistikk/
7. Sharma, N., Acharya, A., Jacob, I., Yamujala, S., Gupta, V., Bhakar, R.: Major
   Blackouts of the Decade. 9th International Conference on Power Systems, pp. 1–6.
   IEEE, India (2021)

Emerging Importance of Cybersecurity in Electric Power Sector as a Hub of Interoperable Critical Infrastructure Protection in the Greater Metropolitan Areas in Japan

Kenji Watanabe(✉)

Graduate School of Engineering, Nagoya Institute of Technology, Aichi, Japan
watanabe.kenji@nitech.ac.jp

Abstract. Electric power sector as a key component of critical infrastructures (CIs) which are essential for our modern socio-economic activities, are considered particularly important as stipulated in the Cybersecurity Basic Act in Japan. The trend of increasing cybersecurity risks in the electric power sector is accelerating, and at the same time, changes in industrial structure and the introduction of various new technologies related to automation and remote control will make it difficult to ensure the effectiveness of cybersecurity in the sector. As potential risks in the greater metropolitan areas in Japan with rapid increase in power failure sensitivity are emerging, the stakeholders of the electric power sector should establish a cross-sector incident response framework and regional interoperable collaboration scheme among CI providers in the areas such as Tokyo, Osaka, Nagoya supported by the government and its agencies.

Keywords: Cyber-physical security framework · power failure sensitivity · cross-sector incident response · regional interoperability · BCP

1 Introduction

Electric power sector as a key component of critical infrastructures (CIs) which are considered particularly important to our modern socioeconomic activities and defined as one of the national critical infrastructure providers stipulated in the Cyber Security Basic Act in Japan. As of 2021, 14 sectors have been specifically designated: information and communications, finance, aviation, airports, railroads, electricity, gas, government and administrative services, healthcare, water supply (drinking water), logistics, chemicals, credit, and petroleum [1] (Fig. 1).

B. Hämmerli et al. (Eds.): CRITIS 2022, LNCS 13723, pp. 256–264, 2023.
https://doi.org/10.1007/978-3-031-35190-7_19

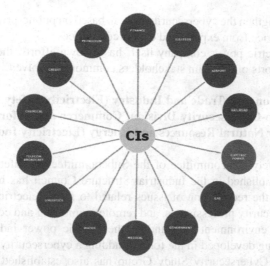

Fig. 1. Electric power sector in the 14 critical infrastructure sectors in Japan

These are the critical infrastructures that form the basis of people's daily lives and economic activities, and are expected to cause particularly great disruption if their functions are disrupted or degraded. Based on the recognition of the vulnerability, the Japanese government is working to improve the level of cybersecurity with stakeholders in each sector by the responsible ministries and its agencies.

Each of the critical infrastructure sectors does not exist independently, but rather provides services while interdependent on each other, and the electric power sector is the hub of the interdependence among these critical infrastructures. The electric power sector is in a position to demand a more resilient cybersecurity system because the social and business impacts of service outages and functional degradation in the sector would be significant, making it an ideal target for cyberattacks that could cause social disorder or demand a ransom.

In the electric power sector, the changes in the industrial structure associated with the deregulation of, and the introduction of new technologies and platforms to, power generation, transmission, distribution, and control have brought about a phase that can no longer be managed within the existing framework for information security alone, including in terms of professional resources.

2 Electric Power Sector Initiatives Spanning the Public and Private Sectors

In response to these dynamic changes in the business environment and cybersecurity-related exposure of the electric power sector, electric power companies (existing and new entrants), competent ministries (Ministry of Economy, Trade and Industry and Agency for Natural Resources and Energy), industry associations (Federation of Electric Power Companies of Japan, etc.), and electric power ISAC (Information Sharing and Analysis Center), which are the main stakeholders in the cybersecurity of the electric power sector, are working to strengthen the cybersecurity system based on public-private partnerships, while obtaining advice from experts and expert committees.

While each electric power company itself has its own efforts, the following is an overview of the efforts of the main stakeholders commonly involved.

(1) Ministry of Economy, Trade and Industry (Electricity Safety Division, Industrial Safety Group-Cybersecurity Division, Commerce and Information Bureau, etc.) & Agency for Natural Resources and Energy (Electricity Industry and Market Office)
The Electricity Safety Subcommittee of the Subcommittee on Safety and Consumer Product Safety established in the Industrial Structure Council has been holding discussions based on the recognition of issues related to future electric security regulations, training of security professionals, and remote monitoring and control in response to changes in the environment surrounding the electric power industry. Resilience discussions are being developed in the form of adding a cybersecurity perspective [2].

The Industrial Cybersecurity Study Group has also established several working groups (WGs) to discuss the direction of cybersecurity policy, of which the Electricity Sub-Working Group (SWG) was established under WG1 (Institution, Technology, and Standardization) to analyze the current situation surrounding cybersecurity in the electric power sector and the status of cybersecurity overseas. The SWG is discussing issues and directions that should be addressed by the public and private sectors.

In the process, the SWG has been discussing cybersecurity measures of major electric power companies, measures of new entrants to the industry, and measures to deal with supply chain risks, while keeping in mind the framework of the Cyber Physical Security Framework (CPSF) (Fig. 2), which is currently being standardized internationally based on a Japanese proposal, and addressing supply chain risks, among others [3].

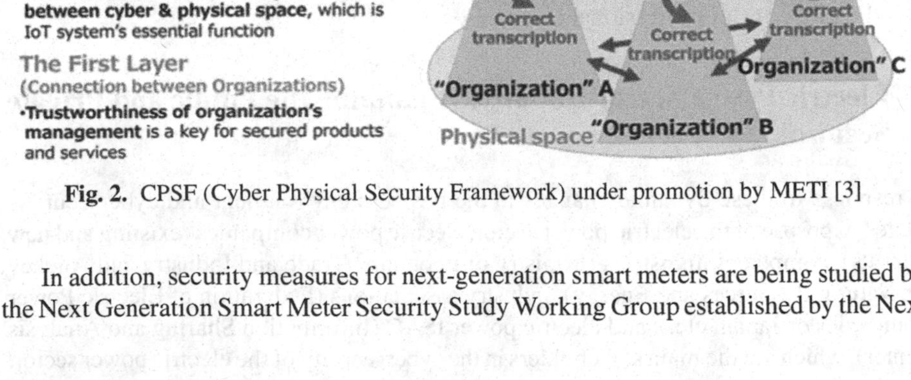
The Third Layer
(Connections in Cyberspace)
•Trustworthiness of data is a key for secured products and services
The Second Layer
(Connections between Cyber & Physical space)
•Trustworthiness of "transcription function" between cyber & physical space, which is IoT system's essential function
The First Layer
(Connection between Organizations)
•Trustworthiness of organization's management is a key for secured products and services
Cyberspace
Data
Correct transcription
"Organization" A
"Organization" B
"Organization" C
Physical space

Fig. 2. CPSF (Cyber Physical Security Framework) under promotion by METI [3]

In addition, security measures for next-generation smart meters are being studied by the Next Generation Smart Meter Security Study Working Group established by the Next

Generation Smart Meter System Study Group, considering changes in specifications and the future vision of business beyond the industry [4].

(2) Federation of Electric Power Companies of Japan (DENJIREN)
The major 10 electric power companies (Tokyo, Kansai, Chubu, Tohoku, Kyushu, Chugoku, Shikoku, Hokkaido, Hokuriku, and Okinawa), which have been the core members of the Federation of Electric Power Companies of Japan (DENJIREN), an industry organization of electric utilities, have recognized that the new entrants to the electric power industry, who will be interconnected through the deregulation of the power supply network, do not necessarily have the same level of cybersecurity measures as the traditional major electric power companies. Recognizing this, they are promoting the enhancement of measures for the entire electric power industry, including small electric power companies, in parallel with efforts to strengthen their systems as major electric power companies.

In addition, the Japan Electrical Engineering Standards Committee (JESC) has published the Electric Power Control System Security Guidelines (2019) and Smart Meter System Security Guidelines (2019) as Japan Electrical Engineering Standards Committee (JESC) standards, and major electric utility providers are working on strengthening the security of electric power control systems and smart meter systems while aiming for compliance with these standards.

(3) Electric Power ISAC (Information Sharing and Analysis Center)
The Electric Power ISAC was established in 2017 to promote cybersecurity initiatives through collaboration between general transmission and distribution companies that are responsible for power system operations and businesses linked to the power system, such as power generation companies, etc. It collects, analyzes and shares cybersecurity-related information among member companies. It also serves as the secretariat of the Capacity for Engineering of Protection, Technical Operation, Analysis and Response (CEPTOR), an organization related to the NISC (National center for Incident readiness and Strategy for Cybersecurity) that shares information between the public and private sectors. The ISAC is also a member of the committees operated by NISC. It also conducts cybersecurity exercises with the participation of 10 major electric power companies, J-Power, JERA, and new electric power companies, with the aim of improving cybersecurity incident response capabilities through cooperation within the industry. In the most recent exercise, even under the situation where the CIVID-19 was spreading, efforts were being made to confirm the ability to respond to incidents using a complex exercise scenario in which a power outage is caused by two factors: a natural disaster and malware infection.

3   Challenges and Requirements in the Electric Power Sector

As described above, the trend of increasing cybersecurity risks and exposures in the electric power sector is now accelerating, and at the same time, changes in industrial structure and the introduction of various new technologies related to automation and remote control will make it difficult to ensure the effectiveness of cybersecurity in the electric power sector. In order to ensure the effectiveness of cybersecurity in the electric power sector, there will be many situations where it will not be possible to compete only with stand-alone organizations on the power supply side or in cooperation with industry associations and competent ministries and agencies. Therefore, the electric power sector should expand its scope of the fields they make efforts in and invest resources (human, hardware/software, fund) in.

3.1 Cross-Disciplinary Efforts Across the Electricity Supply Chain

It is impossible to perfectly ensure stable availability on the power supply side, but the ultimate goal of cybersecurity is to ensure that end-users or consumers are able to secure necessary power when they need it. From this perspective, it is necessary to strengthen the resilience, both cyber and physical, of not only the conventional power sector but also the individual organizations and processes that make up the power supply chain, including fuel procurement, power generation, transmission and distribution, wholesale and retail sales, and storage and consumption.

3.2 Strengthening Self-Help Systems on the Demand and Consumption Sides

In relation to the above, focusing on the two aspects of electricity demand and supply, it is essential to not only make efforts on the power supply side but also to encourage the demand or consumption side through efficient and effective risk communication. Specifically, even in the event of some failure on the supply side, demand side and consumption side organizations should shift operations and services that must be continued or restored as soon as possible to alternative means or operations based on their business continuity plan (BCP) [5, 6].

3.3 Enhancement of Cybersecurity Incident Response Capabilities

Electric power companies, although they are critical infrastructure providers, cannot continue to invest a large amount of management resources in cybersecurity because they are private enterprises and are always required to make economic rationality from the viewpoint of stakeholders and financial institutions. The limitations of the private sector should be covered by mutual aid within the industry and public-private mutual aid (not public aid), while aiming to strengthen the cybersecurity response capability of the entire electric power sector.

In addition, as a system within the organization of electric power companies, the information system related departments and cybersecurity departments should not be left alone to handle cybersecurity issues, but rather, top management should be involved at an early stage to make management decisions on issues that may result in suspension or reduction of power supply, even if the trigger event is a cyber incident. And electric power companies are required to establish a system that involves top management at an early stage to communicate with external stakeholders in a timely manner while making management decisions, and to continue to ensure the feasibility of the system through regular drills and exercises assuming the situation that they may be required to make management decisions to proactively shut down power supply [7] (Fig. 3).

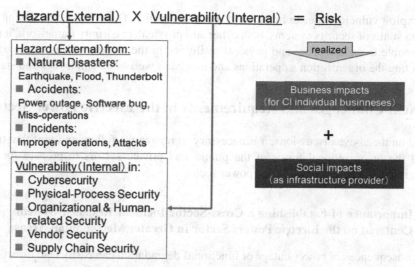

$$\underline{\text{Hazard (External)}} \times \underline{\text{Vulnerability (Internal)}} = \underline{\text{Risk}}$$

Hazard (External) from:
- ■ Natural Disasters:
  Earthquake, Flood, Thunderbolt
- ■ Accidents:
  Power outage, Software bug, Miss-operations
- ■ Incidents:
  Improper operations, Attacks

Vulnerability (Internal) in:
- ■ Cybersecurity
- ■ Physical-Process Security
- ■ Organizational & Human-related Security
- ■ Vendor Security
- ■ Supply Chain Security

realized

Business impacts
(for CI individual businnesses)

+

Social impacts
(as infrastructure provider)

Fig. 3. Impact analysis based on hazard and vulnerability assessment

3.4 Establishment of a Dynamic Security Management System

The "system" subject to cybersecurity is a mechanism that cannot function only with ICT and systems without the involvement of humans and processes, the final provision of services and execution of various operations would not be possible. Considering this "trinity" structure (Fig. 4), it is not possible to ultimately protect "systems" simply by taking measures and actions only for the elements of ICT and systems just because they are cybersecurity-related issues [8].

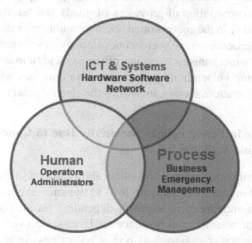

ICT & Systems
Hardware Software
Network

Human
Operators
Administrators

Process
Business
Emergency
Management

Fig. 4. Trinity framework of the Dynamic Security Management System

Cyberattacks are only one of the means for attackers targeting critical infrastructures, and they will try to efficiently achieve their objectives through combined attacks that exploit vulnerabilities in human and process systems. Therefore, by reviewing the current status of security systems, both cyber and physical, in a trinity framework, it will be possible to ensure cyber and physical resilience in the electric power sector while protecting the organization's operations and assets, as well as its employees and staffs.

4   Next Challenges and Requirements in the Electric Power Sector

Based on the above discussions, it is necessary to realize the following items that transcend the organizational forms of the public and private sectors to prepare for the emerging cyber risks in the electric power sector.

4.1   Importance of Establishing a Cross-Sector Incident Response System Centered on the Electric Powers Sector in Greater Metropolitan Areas

The consequences of power outage or functional degradation can easily lead directly to the cessation or stagnation of socioeconomic activities and social disruption, and examples of the consequences have already been seen in natural disasters such as earthquakes, typhoon, flood, and snow damage, rather than cybersecurity-related incidents. This indicates that cybersecurity incidents also cause physical damages that have been already recognized in natural disasters which Japan has experienced many, and as mentioned in the CPSF concept in 2-(1), it is essential to operate security management with both cyber and physical aspects in mind.

Especially in greater metropolitan areas centering on Tokyo, Osaka, and Nagoya, the continuous concentration of human, logistics, money, and information flows and the dynamic changes in inflows and outflows have been intensifying. This situation has been driven by the horizontal division of labor through supply chains and networks and the geographic concentration of providers of goods and services in the pursuit of efficiency and rationality in the concentrated socioeconomic activities. This has also led to a surge in interdependence among socioeconomic activities via people, goods, money, and information. Such mechanisms to ensure efficiency and rationality in normal times have ironically become vulnerability to various chain damages when service failures occur in critical infrastructure sectors, including the electric power sector.

4.2   Rapid Increase in Power Failure Sensitivity Due to Concentration of Socioeconomic Activities

This rapid increase in interdependence and vulnerability among socioeconomic activities in greater metropolitan areas in Japan can lead to dynamic expansion of damage that could not have been anticipated in advance, depending on the context (time of day, day of week, season, weather, and presence of large-scale events) of power-related disturbances such as power outages and power reductions. In particular, the drastic inflow and outflow of people during the daytime due to commuting to and from work and school in metropolitan areas can be seen, for example, in the extremely high gap between the daytime and nighttime population in central Tokyo, and the simultaneous dysfunction of urban functions through dependency among critical infrastructure due to power failure is likely to lead to dangerous situations involving social disorder and "nth-order" disasters (chain of secondary disasters and beyond) that require an immediate evaluation or sheltering of the affected or isolated people.

Given this situation, the sensitivity of greater metropolitan areas to electric power disruptions is increasing rapidly, and as a result, the increase in cyber risk and its impact on socioeconomic activities in the areas is also accelerating. In addition, failures occurring in critical infrastructures such as transportation, finance, logistics, municipal administration, medical care, and broadcasting, which are linked to functional failures in the supply side critical infrastructure sectors such as electricity, gas, water, and telecommunications, directly lead to the disruption of urban functions and the degradation of service levels, and have a significant impact on all socioeconomic activities in the area and the damage to critical infrastructures can be substantial. This can be an incentive for attackers to target critical infrastructure in the greater metropolitan areas.

4.3 Urgently Needed Regional Critical Infrastructure Provider Collaboration and Interoperability in Each Greater Metropolitan Area in Japan

National cybersecurity for critical infrastructure has been discussed by the Cabinet Expert Committee on Critical Infrastructure and its effectiveness has been continuously verified through the annual cross-sector exercise of critical infrastructure conducted by the Japanese government in collaboration with thousands of participants from private and public sectors. However, since cyber incidents that occur in critical infrastructure are likely to have physical consequences, it is necessary to ensure coordination and interoperability among critical infrastructure providers that actually operate in a particular region, especially in greater metropolitan areas [9].

The Chubu Cyber Security Community (CCSC) in the Chubu region where Nagoya, the third largest city in Japan locates, is actually implementing such efforts, promotes information sharing and the implementation of exercises under a region-specific structure, with local electric power companies as the secretariat, and critical infrastructure providers such as gas, telecommunications, railroads, airports, finance, and highways, along with prefectural police, experts, and specialists [10, 11].

In the future, it will be necessary to promote the establishment of a more effective operational system by adding a framework that not only addresses cybersecurity in the electric power sector as one of the critical infrastructure sectors, but also in the electric power supply chain and across sectors in the region. In doing so, it is important for those involved in the electric power sector to keep a bird's-eye view of the cybersecurity situation in society as a whole, and to be constantly aware that the efforts of the electric power sector should not be limited to piecemeal, individual optimization, such as "Not see the wood for the trees".

5 Conclusions

In this paper, emerging importance of cybersecurity in the electric power sector is discussed through reviewing current challenges of the stakeholders in the electric power sector and considering potential risks especially in the greater metropolitan areas in Japan with rapid increase in power failure sensitivity due to concentration of socioeconomic activities.

As a hub of interoperable critical infrastructure protection, stakeholders of the electric power sector should establish a cross-sector incident response system and regional interoperable collaboration scheme among CI providers and related entities in the greater metropolitan areas supported by the government and its agencies.

References

1. Cybersecurity Strategic Headquarters (Government of Japan): The Cybersecurity Policy for Critical Infrastructure Protection (4th Edition, Tentative Translation), 18 April 2017.https://www.nisc.go.jp/eng/pdf/cs_policy_cip_eng_v4.pdf
2. Electric Power Safety Subcommittee, Subcommittee on Safety and Consumer Product Safety, Industrial Structure Council (in Japanese). (https://www.meti.go.jp/shingikai/sankoshin/hoan_shohi/denryoku_anzen/index.html. Accessed 15 May 2022
3. Cyber Security Division, Commerce and Information Policy Bureau, Ministry of Economy, Trade and Industry, The Cyber/Physical Security Framework (CPSF), Version 1.0, 18 April 2019
4. Electric Power Sub-Working Group, Working Group 1 (Institution, Technology and Standardization),Industrial Cyber Security Study Group (in Japanese). (https://www.meti.go.jp/shingikai/mono_info_service/sangyo_cyber/wg_seido/wg_denryoku/index.html. Accessed 15 May 2022
5. ISO 22301:2012 Societal security – Business continuity management systems—Requirements, International Organization for Standardization (2012)
6. ISO/TS 22317:2015 Societal Security – Business continuity management systems – Guidelines for business impact analysis (BIA), International Organization for Standardization (2015)
7. Pöyhönen, J., et al.: Cyber situational awareness in critical infrastructure protection. Ann. Disaster Risk Sci. 3(1), (2020). Special issue on cyber-security of critical infrastructure (2020)
8. Ani, U.D., McK, J.D., Watson, J.M., et al.: A review of critical infrastructure protection approaches: improving security through responsiveness to the dynamic modelling landscape. In: IET Conference Proceedings, The Institution of Engineering & Technology, 1 May 2019
9. Pöyhönen, J., Nuojua, V., Lehto, M., Rajamäki, J.: Cyber situational awareness and information sharing in critical infrastructure organizations. Inf. Secur. 43(2), 236–256 (2019)
10. Watanabe, K., Hayashi, T.: PPP (Public-Private Partnership)-based business continuity of regional banking services for communities in wide-area disasters. In: Rome, E., Theocharidou, M., Wolthusen, S. (eds.) CRITIS 2015. LNCS, vol. 9578, pp. 67–76. Springer, Cham (2016). https://doi.org/10.1007/978-3-319-33331-1_6
11. ISO 22396:2020, Security and resilience - Community resilience - Guidelines for information exchange between organizations. International Organization for Standardization (2020)

A Water Security Plan to Enhance Resilience of Drinking Water Systems

Rui Teixeira[1], Philipp Hohenblum[2], Peter Gattinesi[3], Monica Cardarilli[4(✉)], and Rainer Jungwirth[4]

[1] Water Division and Sanitation, Municipality of Barreiro, Barreiro, Portugal
[2] Environment Agency Austria, Vienna, Austria
[3] Water Infrastructure and Security, London, UK
[4] European Commission, Joint Research Centre, Ispra, Italy
`monica.cardarilli@ec.europa.eu`

Abstract. Drinking water infrastructure represents the backbone of our modern society. Uninterrupted drinking water supply is necessary to maintain population health and for continuity of interconnected services. Therefore, drinking water systems must be appropriately protected against malicious attacks which might cause deliberate waterborne contamination, inducing service disruption with cascading effects.

The implementation of security measures to enhance resilience against hostile actions on the physical and cyber integrity of water infrastructure is essential and requires an appropriate planning process. In this regard, a Water Security Plan provides support to drinking water utilities with the information and tools they need to develop and implement in case of deliberate chemical/biological contamination to the drinking water supply system.

Keywords: Drinking water infrastructure · Security planning · Intentional contamination

1 Introduction

1.1 Drinking Water Policy Framework

Water is a lifeline sector which serves communities and businesses on a daily basis raising a number of shared challenges among water authorities, utility operators and other relevant stakeholders.

The implementation of EU water policy [1] is one of the main reasons to develop common understanding of the key issues and to agree on common solutions to ensure a harmonized implementation at EU level.

To achieve this, a Common Implementation Strategy (CIS) was established in 2001, developing several guidance documents to address topics from the identification of water bodies [2] to recommendations on monitoring [3, 4] and reporting [5, 6], up to public participation [7] and economics [8].

B. Hämmerli et al. (Eds.): CRITIS 2022, LNCS 13723, pp. 265–273, 2023.
https://doi.org/10.1007/978-3-031-35190-7_20

In particular, drinking water policy ensures that water intended for human consumption can be supplied safely on a life-long basis, and this represents a strong contribution to the broader EU water protection [9], management and treatment.

To this end, the new Drinking Water Directive [10] strengthens the core function of drinking water systems for society and the internal market, introducing new obligations for water operators and national authorities at EU level, and reinforcing the recommendations of the World Health Organisation on safety standards for drinking water from source to distribution [11].

Furthermore, water systems are among the pillars of the CER Directive [12] which designates drinking water infrastructure among the "critical entities" in the face of both physical and digital risks [13]. To that purpose, widespread recognition is given to this essential asset which must be protected better and become more resilient against several risks that might affect drinking water supply systems.

1.2 Disruption of Drinking Water Systems

The European Commission defines critical infrastructure as an asset, system or part thereof located in Member States that is essential for the maintenance of vital societal functions such as health, safety, security, economic or social well-being of people [14–16], and the disruption or destruction of which would have a significant impact on a Member State as a result of the failure to maintain those functions [17].

Specifically, drinking water systems are vulnerable to unintentional – e.g. climate change-induced [18–21] or accidental [22–24] – and intentional threats which might cause severe service disruption with cascading effects to interconnected critical services that depend on the water distribution system (e.g., hospitals, schools, industry).

Despite having low likelihood, recent news on malicious attacks [25–28] on drinking water infrastructures demonstrates that the threat is realistic and underscores the high impact malicious activities can have on such essential infrastructure.

1.3 Water Safety and Security

The infrastructure associated with the production and distribution of drinking water is potentially vulnerable to a wide range of deliberate malicious actions, which can include physical sabotaging of equipment, cyberattacks on information or operational control systems and contamination of drinking water. Such hostile attacks can jeopardize the physical integrity of water supply systems and the quality of the water supplied.

Nowadays, drinking water infrastructure is not considered a critical infrastructure in all countries [29] in Europe, however it is among the critical entities as defined in the upcoming CER directive [12]. Most national governments recognise their water supply as vital to national security. In that light, surveillance and assessment of the credibility and seriousness of threats is a task of the security intelligence services [30].

While safety and security are closely related., water safety is used to address any type of contamination threat to drinking water except intentional contamination, while water security should be framed in the context of the relevant national and European counterterrorism initiatives.

Indeed, as part of the EU's counterterrorism strategy, the European Commission maintains a chemical, biological, radiological and nuclear (CBRN) action plan to enhance preparedness against CBRN security risks. The 2017 CBRN action plan details a number of measures at national and European levels, including measures aimed at ensuring more robust preparedness for and responses to CBRN security incidents [31].

Any deliberate contamination of drinking water is likely to be perceived as an act of terrorism or as a part of a hybrid attack and it could have a severe adverse impact on public health as well as public order.

Guidelines have been prepared by the World Health Organisation (WHO) and take the form of a drinking water safety plan [32, 33]. Although water safety is already a task for water utilities and competent authorities, the security aspect of drinking water distribution systems is often neglected or underestimated.

1.4 Water Security Planning

The implementation of security measures to enhance resilience of drinking water infrastructure against malicious actions is essential and requires an appropriate planning process [34].

In this regard, water security planning can support drinking water utilities with the information and tools they need to develop and implement in case of deliberate chemical/biological (CB) contamination to the drinking water supply system.

A Water Security Plan (WSecP) has been developed within the European Reference Network for Critical Infrastructure Protection (ERNCIP) and elaborated in various documents and guidance material by the Thematic Group on "Chemical and biological risks to drinking water" [35].

To that purpose, the Water Security Plan (WSecP) aims to support prompt response and recovery from CB contaminations affecting the drinking water supply system, reducing the impact severity such as the potential escalation to service disruption and disease outbreaks which could have catastrophic consequences [36, 37].

For example, in the framework of increasing resilience and bolstering capabilities to address hybrid threats, the WSecP implementation guidance [37] has been quoted by the Joint Staff Working Document – Sixth progress Report [38]. In particular, it recognizes the added value of ensuring a coordinated approach to identify security vulnerabilities and establish security measures for water supply systems, including a communication strategy to facilitate a fast and effective response.

Where a water safety plan already exists [39], the water security planning should be integrated into the safety planning approach, since the latter does not explicitly or specifically consider intentional contamination.

2 Water Security Plan Lifecycle

The Water Security Plan is structured into four phases - to be accompanied by periodic review and continuous updating -, based on the timeline of a potential contamination emergency [40], as outlined in Fig. 1.

1. Planning and preparation;

2. Protection: event detection and confirmation;
3. Response and event management;
4. Remediation, rehabilitation and recovery.

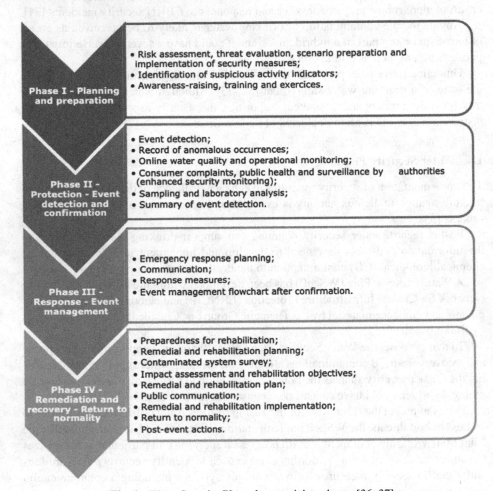

Phase I - Planning and preparation
- Risk assessment, threat evaluation, scenario preparation and implementation of security measures;
- Identification of suspicious activity indicators;
- Awareness-raising, training and exercices.

Phase II - Protection - Event detection and confirmation
- Event detection;
- Record of anomalous occurrences;
- Online water quality and operational monitoring;
- Consumer complaints, public health and surveillance by   authorities (enhanced security monitoring);
- Sampling and laboratory analysis;
- Summary of event detection.

Phase III - Response - Event management
- Emergency response planning;
- Communication;
- Response measures;
- Event management flowchart after confirmation.

Phase IV - Remediation and recovery - Return to normality
- Preparedness for rehabilitation;
- Remedial and rehabilitation planning;
- Contaminated system survey;
- Impact assessment and rehabilitation objectives;
- Remedial and rehabilitation plan;
- Public communication;
- Remedial and rehabilitation implementation;
- Return to normality;
- Post-event actions.

Fig. 1. Water Security Plan: characterizing phases [36, 37]

2.1 Planning and Preparation

Planning represents the first action to be taken by water utilities to mitigate water security incidents. The first step is team building - assigning roles and tasks at senior management level - followed by risk assessment, whereby potential threats of malicious activities are considered in conjunction with the infrastructure vulnerabilities and site-related specificities. The potential impact from an incident is assessed, in terms of casualties and numbers of people affected by loss of access to drinking water. From this, the risks to the operator and its customers, particularly hospitals, administrative buildings, hotels, and commercial centers, where contamination could have serious consequences, are assessed according to event severity through a series of guiding questions [37] being developed to support water utilities in this task.

To ensure the continuous provision of essential services, the implementation of security measures to protect drinking water infrastructure against deliberate contamination is a top priority. This requires water utilities an appropriate planning process incorporating risk assessment checklists, establishment of communication channels and screening methods. Security protocols with emergency authorities need to be established to guide what should be done when an emergency occurs, including common training and exercise activities to familiarize utility personnel and response partners with the response procedures.

2.2 Protection: Event Detection and Confirmation

The Water Security Plan should clearly link the real-time detection of events from online monitoring systems with the interfaces to the laboratory for identification and confirmation testing. Early detection sensors, parameter analyses and contamination warning systems play a key role in supporting water security through the protection of water supply systems and distribution networks, and should be integrated into normal operations. Locations of sensors need to be decided not only on security aspects but also on other operational aspects, as well as according to vulnerabilities, population at risk, etc. The water utility needs to embrace the installation of sensors and have a clear verification and maintenance process to make sure data is reliable.

In addition to technological monitoring, staff involvement for real-time detection of any suspicious activity, vandalism or sabotage, should be highly encouraged. Also important is the feedback that can be provided by consumers, health authorities and other entities, such as the regulator of water services, civil protection, local government, the environmental agency, and police authorities.

2.3 Response and Event Management

The Water Security Plan aims at minimizing response time in the event of a confirmed contamination and helps develop procedures for responding to events that affect the drinking water, including the identification of alternative water supply.

Operators should have a clear emergency communication plan for timely notification in case of contamination, as well as effective emergency response measures, including isolating the contaminated area of the system, disinfecting the system, disseminating 'boil water' advisories, and discharging contaminated water. Utilities should have the necessary basic chemicals, equipment, and procedures ready for response to an emergency.

In the event of a waterborne contamination, the water utility must provide public notice to its customers as soon as possible, in coordination with health and security authorities, as well as public water system regulatory agencies.

2.4   Remediation, Rehabilitation and Recovery

Finally, the WSecP includes elements for the preparation of a recovery plan so that the drinking water system can return to normality as soon as possible.

The remediation and rehabilitation process aims to minimize exposure to contaminated water and will be instigated when a contamination incident is confirmed. All remedial activities leading to the full return to the normal provision of uncontaminated drinking water should be identified, evaluated and implemented as soon as possible. The documentation of these activities will be the basis for determining that the remediation goals were attained. During this phase, internal communication and with the public remains essential, and only official and trustworthy communications channels should be used.

Post-remediation monitoring will provide long-term assurance that the system can maintain normal operation and business continuity. Monitoring activities may include periodic sampling, periodic inspection and maintenance of the water distribution system components and treatment equipment as well as public communication of monitoring activities and results.

Finally, appropriate protocols and procedures should be applied for the discharge of contaminated water, to be considered as integral part of the treatment process for drinking water decontamination.

2.5   Cyclical Revision, Improvement and Dissemination

Water utilities must be prepared to cope with disruptive events by providing a properly constructed and maintained Water Security Plan which will reduce the risk of a waterborne disease outbreak.

Therefore, regular updating of the WSecP forms an essential part of its lifecycle and must be thoroughly considered [37]. In particular, the WSecP should include an annual complete inspection of the water system infrastructure – i.e. to identify and immediately correct any deficiencies from the source to the last connection/fixture in the distribution network. Furthermore, backflow prevention devices should be tested as necessary, ensuring the system is receiving proper maintenance.

It is pivotal that the WSecP is constantly reviewed and improved. By doing so, the planned security and response measures, including the Emergency Response Plan, can be validated against actual events whenever possible, and the plan is kept operative and up to date.

In this regard, involvement of the public water system regulatory agency, emergency services and public health authorities is recommended for assistance with the cyclical security assessment activities and effectiveness of the security plan, as needed.

Furthermore, the inclusion of lessons learned from past damaging or other security events, including terrorist incidents is a good practice to take into account as well as the consultancy of external experts to periodically evaluating the quality and completeness of the WSecP implemented [37].

In that light, it is paramount essential to ensure information-sharing among all the parties involved, including internal collaborators and external entities. Anyway, the rational on a "need-to-know" basis must be applied, especially when disseminating sensitive information on system vulnerabilities [37].

Moreover, the WSecP should contain some criteria related to its dissemination also to new employees, for instance that new employees must be evaluated and vetted before being given access to the plan [41].

3   Conclusions

Water systems are critical to communities and businesses' daily activities. Protection of drinking water systems must be a high priority for local officials and water system owners and operators to ensure an uninterrupted water supply, which is essential for the protection of public health (safe drinking water and sanitation) and safety (firefighting), as well as for the normal functioning of societies.

In particular, drinking water utilities must be prepared for the threat of deliberate attacks, including terrorist activities as well as hybrid threats aiming to contaminate the water supply or damage the water system itself.

Therefore, it is necessary to increase the resilience of drinking water infrastructure against potential intentional disruptive events to ensure the continuous provision of the service, where protection is one element alongside prevention, preparedness, response and recovery. To achieve this, it is essential to have a thorough understanding and knowledge of the type of man-made threats that drinking water infrastructure can face.

To this purpose, each drinking water system operator should conduct security vulnerability assessment and management as part of their Emergency Response Plan to determine if there are areas needing improved security measures, according to the most critical (security) risk scenarios. In that light, the Water Security Plan is designed to provide the water operator with the basis for implementing specific measures to improve the security of the water system against malicious threats.

Therefore, the WSecP - through its lifecycle - provides a valuable support to water operators for assessing existing and potential risks, preventing intentional waterborne contamination, minimizing response time, and improving early detection capabilities, where the integration of safety and security aspects and private-public partnership should be fostered in the daily operation.

Overall, adequate security measures will help to prevent loss of service due to terrorist acts, vandalism, or accident. The appropriate level of security is best determined by the water utility operator at the local level, working together with intelligence services and any other relevant authorities for a more comprehensive design and implementation.

References

1. European Commission. Directive 2000/60/EC of the European Parliament and of the Council. Off. J. Eur. Communities (2000)
2. European Commission. Guidance document n° 2 – Identification of water bodies (2003)
3. European Commission. Monitoring under the water framework directive (2003)
4. European Commission. Common implementation strategy for the water framework directive (2000/60/EC). Guidance document n° 15, Guidance on Groundwater Monitoring, Technical Report-002–2007, May 2007

5. European Commission. Common implementation strategy for the WFD. Guidance Doc, **428**(21), May 2000
6. WFD-CIS. Guidance document n° 35: WFD reporting. Common Implement. Strateg. WFD, Guid. Doc. (35) (2016)
7. European Commission. Common implementation strategy for the water framework directive (2000/60/EC). Public Participation in relation to the Water Framework Directive (2003)
8. European Commission. Guidance document n° 1. Implementation Challenge of the Water Framework Directive (2003)
9. Quevauviller, P., Vargas, E.: Protection des eaux souterraines. Cadre technique de la législation européenne. Tech. l'ingénieur Anal. dans l'environnement eau air [P 4 220], November 2017
10. The European Parliament and the Council of the European Union. Directive (EU) 2020/2184, EU (revised) drinking water directive. Off. J. Eur. Communities, **2019**, 1–62 (2020)
11. WHO – EU. Drinking water parameter cooperation project, pp. 1–228 (2017)
12. Directive (EU) 2022/2557 of the European Parliament and of the Council of 14 December 2022 on the resilience of critical entities and repealing Council Directive 2008/114/EC
13. DIRECTIVE (EU) 2022/2555 OF THE EUROPEAN PARLIAMENT AND OF THE COUNCIL of 14 December 2022 on measures for a high common level of cybersecurity across the Union, amending Regulation (EU) No 910/2014 and Directive (EU) 2018/1972, and repealing Directive (EU) 2016/1148 (NIS 2 Directive)
14. Pant, R., Thacker, S., Hall, J.W., Alderson, D., Barr, S.: Critical infrastructure impact assessment due to flood exposure. J. Flood Risk Manag. **11**(1), 22–33 (2018)
15. Chang, S.E.: Socioeconomic impacts of infrastructure disruptions. In Oxford research encyclopedia of natural hazard science (2016)
16. De Bruijne, M., van Eeten, M.: Systems that should have failed: critical infrastructure protection in an institutionally fragmented environment. J. contingencies Cris. Manag. **15**(1), 18–29 (2007)
17. Council Directive 2008/114/EC of 8 December 2008 on the identification and designation of European critical infrastructures and the assessment of the need to improve their protection
18. Taylor, R.G., et al.: Ground water and climate change. Nat. Clim. Change, **3**(4), 322–329(2013)
19. Delpla, I., Jung, A.V., Baures, E., Clement, M., Thomas, O.: Impacts of climate change on surface water quality in relation to drinking water production. Environ. Int. **35**(8), 1225–1233 (2009)
20. DeNicola, E., Aburizaiza, O.S., Siddique, A., Khwaja, H., Carpenter, D.O.: Climate change and water scarcity: the case of Saudi Arabia. Ann. Glob. Health **81**(3), 342–353 (2015)
21. Beniston, M., Stoffel, M., Hill, M.: Impacts of climatic change on water and natural hazards in the Alps: can current water governance cope with future challenges? Examples from the European "ACQWA" project. Environ. Sci. Policy **14**(7), 734–743 (2011)
22. Kim, S., et al.: Chemical accidents in freshwater: Development of forecasting system for drinking water resources. J. Hazard. Mater. **432**, 128714 (2022)
23. Zhang, X.J., Chen, C., Lin, P.F., Hou, A.X., Niu, Z.B., Wang, J.: Emergency drinking water treatment during source water pollution accidents in China: origin analysis, framework and technologies (2011)
24. Wang, L., Zhang, L., Lv, J., Zhang, Y., Ye, B.: Public awareness of drinking water safety and contamination accidents: a case study in Hainan Province. China. Water **10**(4), 446 (2018)
25. Hassanzadeh, A., et al.: A review of cybersecurity incidents in the water sector. J. Environ. Eng. **146**(5), 3120003 (2020)
26. Barak, I.: Critical infrastructure under attack: lessons from a honeypot. Netw. Secur. **2020**(9), 16–17 (2020)

27. Kozik, R., Choras, M.: Current cyber security threats and challenges in critical infrastructures protection. In: 2013 Second International Conference on Informatics and Applications (ICIA), pp. 93–97 (2013)
28. The New Work Times. Dangerous stuff: hackers tried to poison water supply of Florida town (2021)
29. Pitchers, R.: Overview of standards/guidelines and current practices for vulnerability assessment of Drinking Water Security in Europe. EUR 27853 EN, Publications Office of the European Union, Luxemburg 2015 (2016). ISBN 978-92-79-57772-7, 10. 2788/91, JRC100531
30. Gonçalves, M.: A security intelligence approach for risk management in drinking water supply systems: the view of a national security intelligence service (2020)
31. European Commission: Action Plan to Enhance Preparedness against Chemical, Biological, Radiological and Nuclear Security Risk (2017)
32. WHO. Water safety plan manual: step-by-step risk management for drinking-water suppliers. WHO Libr. (2009)
33. WHO. Water safety plan: a field guide to improving drinking-water safety in small communities (2014)
34. Batlle Ribas, M., et al.: Water security plan - Towards a more resilient drinking water infrastructure. Techniques de l'ingenieur (2022)
35. Hohenblum, P.: Chemical and Biological Risks in the Water Sector–a Thematic Area in the European Commission's ERNCIP. In: Water Contamination Emergencies, pp. 330–333 (2013)
36. Teixeira, R., Carmi, O., Raich, J., Gattinesi, P., Hohenblum, P.: Guidance for production of a Water Security Plan in drinking water supply. In: Theocharidou, M., Giannopoulos, G. (eds.) EUR 29846 EN, Publications Office of the European Union, Luxembourg (2019), ISBN 978-92-76-10967-9, https://doi.org/10.2760/415051, JRC116548
37. Teixeira, R., Carmi, O., Gattinesi, P., Hohenblum, P.: Water security plan implementation manual for drinking water systems. In: Cardarilli, M., Giannopoulos, G. (eds.), EUR 30954 EN, Publications Office of the European Union, Luxembourg (2022), ISBN 978-92-76-46484-6, https://doi.org/10.2760/608997, JRC126684
38. Joint Staff Working Document - Sixth Progress Report on the implementation of the 2016 Joint Framework on countering hybrid threats and the 2018 Joint Communication on increasing resilience and bolstering capabilities to address hybrid threats. SWD (2022) 308 final
39. Commission Directive (EU) 2015/1787 Amending Annexes II and III to Council Directive 98/83/EC on the Quality of Water Intended for Human Consumption (2015)
40. Communication from the Commission to the European Parliament, the European Council, the Council, the European Economic and Social Committee and the Committee of the Regions, A Counter-Terrorism Agenda for the EU: Anticipate, Prevent, Protect, Respond (2020)
41. CISA, Insider Threat Mitigation Guide (2020)

Author Index

B. Hämmerli et al. (Eds.): CRITIS 2022, LNCS 13723, pp. 275–276, 2023.
https://doi.org/10.1007/978-3-031-35190-7

Printed in the United States
by Baker & Taylor Publisher Services